JOHN

416 RIDGEWAY
St. JSAPH, MI 49085
6-12-18

THE DEALS THAT MADE THE WORLD

THE
DEALS
THAT
MADE THE
WORLD

**Reckless Ambition, Backroom
Negotiations, and the Hidden
Truths of Business**

Jacques Peretti

wm

WILLIAM MORROW
An Imprint of HarperCollins*Publishers*

HarperCollins books may be purchased for educational, business, or sales promotional use. For information, please email the Special Markets Department at SPsales@harpercollins.com.

Originally published in a slightly different form under the title *Done* in the United Kingdom in 2017 by Hodder & Stoughton.

A portion of this book has appeared in a slightly different form in *The Guardian*.

FIRST EDITION

Designed by Bonni Leon-Berman

Library of Congress Cataloging-in-Publication Data has been applied for.

ISBN 978-0-06-269829-2

18 19 20 21 22 RS/LSC 10 9 8 7 6 5 4 3 2 1

To Esme and Theo

CONTENTS

INTRODUCTION

In the early 1990s, I began working as a journalist for the BBC. At that time, there was an assumption, as there still is today, that "high politics"—the practice of government in the hushed corridors of Capitol Hill, the Kremlin or Downing Street—is where real power lies. World leaders making decisions that will profoundly shape our lived experiences.

As economists and journalists, we interrogate the consequences of these decisions, analyzing every permutation of outcome in TV news reports and over acres of print. We seek to understand the characters, even the psyches, of the politicians who make these world-historic decisions, in the hopes they will shine further light on their motivations.

We imbue the tiniest actions of politicians with significance, even interpreting their body language at press conferences or global summits—an overly strong handshake or a domineering arm on the shoulder—as proof of a nuanced shift in the geopolitical power balance between two superpowers.

This divining is now the day-to-day preoccupation of every reputable news outlet on the planet. But all of this presupposes that politicians are at the true seat of power.

Much is made of a president's first hundred days in office: the time to capitalize on victory and bring about meaningful legislative change. But one K Street lobbyist told me you could knock a zero off the hundred days and be closer to the truth. The only time America came close to dynamic government during the first hundred days was under Franklin D. Roosevelt.

When Donald Trump reached his first one hundred days, the White House pointed to thirteen bills from Congress that had been signed by the new president. But these bills were not to enact new legislation but to roll back laws passed by his predecessors.

The flamboyant flourish of a fountain pen to dismantle old legislation is far easier and quicker than constructing new legislation, which takes time and agreement from multiple stakeholders. Undoing legislation becomes the rhetoric of dynamic government rather than its reality.

We still assume politicians wield power but we have come over time to believe they wield it very badly. Neither is true—neither do they truly wield the power we assume they do nor do they exercise it as badly as we imagine. Instead, the locus of power has shifted. Washington's Pew Institute has monitored public trust in government for over forty years and found that it has steadily but surely declined, mirroring a real decline in government's political power.

President Trump was elected in 2016 as a public acknowledgment of this decline of political potency and trust in the governmental machine. But his election was also the apotheosis of its failure. Many of those who voted for him did so because he seemed to be the opposite of a politician. He was in "business," though he wasn't in truth a self-made businessperson either. He was a "deal maker," though it was unclear what real deals he had ever done.

One thing we knew for sure, he was against "the swamp"— the murky world of pleading special interest groups and lobbyists working on behalf of the bête noire of the 2016 election, "global corporations," supposedly strong-arming politicians to do their will behind closed doors. In truth, the swamp—the miasma of competing interests swirling around every govern-ment since time immemorial—is simply a fact of government, and the problem with promising to drain it is that it will refill just as quickly as it has been drained.

How does this swamp work?

I experienced it for myself firsthand. Before working for the BBC, I worked as a researcher in Parliament. I saw close up how the political process works, and it was very far from what I had imagined. The majority of politicians didn't appear to do very much. They made speeches, went for lunch, got interviewed on TV (or spent a lot of time trying to be). Westminster politics was memorably described at the time by one commentator as "show business for ugly people."

When I moved from Parliament to news reporting, I dis-covered that that power hadn't simply disappeared, it had been gradually shifting toward industrialists and entrepreneurs over the course of a century and a half. During my first week in news, this shift was revealed in a single moment in the hos-pitality room. I had produced a report about an oil company alleged to be polluting a large section of the Canadian coast-line. There was a furious argument between a representative of the oil company and a member of a prominent environmental pressure group lobbying to stop the oil company. In the studio, they had practically come to blows.

In the hospitality room afterward, they were having a drink. The oil company exec turned to the environmentalist: "That was very good," he said. "You were excellent." "Thank you," the environmentalist replied. "You know," the oil exec contin-ued, "we could really do with someone like you. Give me a call." They exchanged cards, and three weeks later, the envi-ronmentalist was working for the oil company.

They had cut a deal and the bargain was this: the oil rep understood what the environmentalist could do for his company, coming under serious heat, and the environmentalist spotted an opportunity. But what kind of opportunity? To "sell out" and make money for himself? Or the chance to influence a multinational company from within, to make the kind of changes he might not have been able to action from outside?

This was real politics in operation and it was complicated. There was no easy moral position to take on that conversation between the environmentalist and the oil company exec because it was far from obvious who was outfoxing whom, or what the true motivations or strategic outcome would be for either. What was clear was that there were no politicians present.

Of course, politicians cut deals behind the scenes as well, but the macro-picture for politicians has profoundly altered in the last thirty years. Governments have become increasingly powerless since the collapse of the Bretton Woods agreement on fixed exchange rates in 1971, after which corporations began to wield ever greater transnational power without recourse to cutting a deal with government. Corporations now run the global show not so much through evil Machiavellian design but as a geopolitical inevitability.

This is evident from any cursory look at a map of the world. To a child, the world appears neatly ordered; countries have borders marked by pretty-colored lines. In one respect, the map is correct. Governments govern vertically within the narrow parameters of their borders. But because they operate nationally, they sometimes have narrower geopolitical influence than corporations, which work horizontally across the planet with scant concern for the little colored lines.

This is why the anti-globalist rhetoric of Donald Trump the

candidate disappeared when he became president. Because the reality of government means not just accepting the swamp, but accepting globalization as well.

We live in a globalized world but continue to wrongly frame our understanding of that world in a preglobalized way: with politicians and nation-states as the sole units of power.

I suggest shaking the snow globe and seeing things differently.

My years of reporting have shown me that it is not always politicians and world events that fundamentally transform our everyday lives, but often business deals. Not the sort we read about in the business pages—above-the-line takeovers, acquisitions and mergers—but deals made in secret: high up in boardrooms, on a golf course or over a drink in a bar. Just like the deal I witnessed going on in that hospitality room in my first week in news.

These deals can have ramifications far beyond business. They have changed how we spend and think about money; the way we work; how we conceptualize wealth and risk, tax and inequality. These deals invented and then taught us to embrace the concept of the consumer upgrade. These deals have even altered the shape of our bodies.

In this book, I examine ten deals that have been especially crucial in shaping modern society. Each deal I examine sprung from a single idea that would go on to change the collective mind-set, rebooting society to think in a new way: "engineering dissatisfaction" at the moment of purchase, so the consumer became enthralled to perpetual upgrade; inventing "obesity" as an insurance mechanism long before a real obesity epidemic existed; medicating modern life by expanding the definition of illness to include myriad anxieties and syndromes; harnessing technology in our pockets to roboticize our lives at the very moment automation threatens to make many of us redundant.

These deals were no shadowy conspiracy. On the contrary, they were brilliant business ideas, though often with an effect far beyond the simple business innovation intended. Very few of the people I interviewed ever imagined the potential ramifications of what they were suggesting. They all to some extent had an extraordinary eureka moment—a blinding insight into how to do business differently—but few could have predicted quite how profound that insight would be in changing how we live.

1

THE UPGRADE
Engineering Dissatisfaction

THE DEAL: General Electric, Phillips, Osram and the Phoebus cartel of lightbulb manufacturers meet to limit the life span of an average lightbulb.

AIM: To systematize planned obsolescence and invent the upgrade

WHERE: Lake Geneva, Switzerland

WHEN: 1932

Forty miles outside San Francisco is the town of Livermore. Halfway down the main street lined with cafés and antiques shops is a fire station, and high up on the back wall, away from the gleaming vintage fire truck, polished daily by retired volunteers with bushy white moustaches, is the pride and joy of Livermore. Making a low hum, flickering an eerie yellow glow, is a lightbulb. But unlike any other lightbulb on earth, this one has not burned out in 117 years.[1]

The Shelby Electrical Company made the Centennial Bulb in 1901. A hand-blown carbon filament that once emitted thirty watts, it now gives four watts, like a child's night-light, but it still works. Why, if Livermore Fire Station has a lightbulb still burning after well over a century, does the rest of the world have ones that burn out after six months?

Today, the upgrade is a way of life. We change our phones every eleven months; our partner on average every two years, nine months.[2] We belong to the global cult of what product designers call "infinite new-ism"—a distrust of anything "old," when "old" might mean we upgraded it just a couple of weeks ago. And the Shelby lightbulb is the first clue to understanding how the perpetual upgrade became central to modern consumer culture.

The second clue is 5,600 miles away, in Germany. In 1989, as communism collapsed and crowds clambered over the Berlin Wall, a historian named Helmut Herger walked unnoticed into a building in East Berlin, the headquarters of the Osram Electrical Company.

Inside, Herger found overturned filing cabinets and papers strewn across the floor. He was sifting through the administrative detritus when something caught his eye: confidential minutes from a 1932 Geneva meeting between two senior members of the Osram executive board and the five biggest electrical companies on earth. When, two decades on, I met Helmut in a Berlin café and I asked him what was so special about these papers, he opened his briefcase.

The five biggest lightbulb manufacturers on earth had gathered to create a secret cartel, known as Phoebus, with one aim: to stop anyone from creating a lightbulb that lasted more than six months.[3] The papers proved something we all vaguely believe exists when our kettle mysteriously stops working six months after we buy it and as it turns out actually does exist: planned obsolescence.

Herger showed me the signatories at Phoebus's inaugural

meeting: William Meinhardt, the CEO of Osram, and Anton Philips, the founder of the Dutch electrical giant now called Philips Electronics, who with the heads of the other biggest electrical companies on earth present, wanted to systematize obsolescence, imposing a global policy on the life span of a lightbulb and putting any company that did not follow their rules out of business.

The others included America's General Electric, AE from Britain, Compagnie des Lampes from France, GE Sociedad Anonyma of Brazil, China's biggest producer of electrical goods, Edison General, Lámparas Eléctricas from Mexico and Tokyo Electric. These companies did not simply produce lightbulbs. They provided the basic infrastructure of modern life: street lighting; copper wiring for phone lines; cabling for ships, bridges, train and tram lines. They made consumer durables such as refrigerators and ovens; provided the electrics for cars, homes and offices.

Two thousand years of ingenuity in manufacturing durable goods would stop. Henceforth, mass production would reverse engineer an object from the moment it should break, backward. Each object would have a different life span drawn up on a spreadsheet. Helmut Herger showed me the categories meticulously calibrated on a sliding scale of obsolescence, scrawled in boxes in spidery handwriting, each box stipulating life span.

Was Phoebus doing anything wrong? In 1932, the free world balanced on a knife edge between economic depression and recovery. Hitler was poised to take power in Germany. The Phoebus plan to systematize planned obsolescence did not simply sell more lightbulbs, but saved capitalism and therefore democracy when it was most perilously threatened. It kept people buying.

If Phoebus was to receive any pushback from the consumer for producing a lightbulb that suddenly stopped working, there was this bigger picture. But Phoebus didn't receive any pushback. Not yet.

The Newest New Thing

Outside the Apple Store on Regent Street, London, two thousand people wait for the new iPhone. They stand patiently, scrolling through the last iteration of Apple's flagship product, which, in ten minutes' time, will be obsolete. The police overseeing the queue scroll through their phones too. The line snakes around the building, down the next street and into an adjacent park.

Those nearest the front have been waiting nearly forty-eight hours. The man at the very front sits on a fishing chair with a roll-up mattress and plastic tarpaulin to keep off the rain. He has a small gas cooker with which he heats up soup. He began queueing on Saturday afternoon. It is now Monday morning.

"Do you mind telling me," I ask him, "what the new iPhone will do that your old phone doesn't?" He frowns, annoyed at the stupidity of the question. "What do you mean?" "Well, you've been queueing nearly forty-eight hours in the cold, so I'm just wondering what's so special about the new phone?"[4] He sighs and leans forward. "It's new."

It is four minutes to nine, and when the doors open and the whooping Apple employees in their blue T-shirts try to hold back the rushing human tide, my new friend will be, for a very short period of time, the first person in the world to own the newest iPhone. In two minutes, the first buyers will put it on eBay and then it will be old.

Obsolescence is built into newness—it is the flaw at the heart of everything we buy. Not far from the Livermore Fire Station and the oldest bulb in the world is a warehouse filled with brand-new tech goods that have never even been used: phones, tablets, laptops, printers, microwave ovens, satnavs, headphones, drones. They are all still in their boxes, unopened, donated to charity by companies that bought the products in bulk but then upgraded to another product before even opening them.

"Where's all this stuff bound for?" I ask the foreman of the warehouse. To Baltimore, Bangladesh, anywhere that people want it. The trouble is, he admits, they don't want it, because out-of-date technology is as unappealing to the poorest half of the world as it is to the richest.[5] We all want the newest new thing.

The Phoebus cartel invented planned obsolescence and the rules companies would follow: the parameters for the upgrade diktat whether it be a lightbulb or an iPhone. But to choose ourselves to upgrade a product before it has stopped working, to make the upgrade a desire on the part of the consumer, required a new idea. One rooted in psychology.

Engineering Dissatisfaction

We think patronizingly of the 1950s as a naïve time when the public could still have the wool pulled over its eyes, but nothing was further from the truth. War had politicized and educated the public. As a result of working in factories and on production lines, people knew both how things were made and what they were worth. This meant they were wise to being conned.

The 1951 Ealing Studios comedy *The Man in the White Suit*

stars Alec Guinness as a scientist who accidentally invents a miraculous new material that never wears out or gets dirty. But instead of being hailed as a genius, union leaders and industrialists gang up to destroy him. The film is a satire about planned obsolescence and the complicity of industry and unions in perpetuating it on the public. Guinness's antihero wears a symbolic white suit standing for public integrity and honesty in a world of murky collusion.

But Roger MacDougall, John Dighton, and Alexander Mackendrick's script is far from anticapitalist. It pours scorn on both workers and bosses. This was a new, potentially dangerous kind of public disillusion: the disillusion of the consumer. Disillusionment with consumerism threatened the growth of the economy at a critical moment when Western governments needed the public to buy.

In 1951, the year *The Man in the White Suit* was released, the Korean War broke out. The world faced a stark choice between two competing brands: "communism" and "capitalism." For capitalism to win, President Truman needed consumers to do their duty and begin shopping for big-ticket purchases in Britain and America, powering a consumer boom and thus economic recovery. Consumerism was not merely shopping, it was an ideological weapon for fighting the Cold War.

But there was a problem. Planned obsolescence made a mockery of the consumer doing their duty to buy. If consumers were aware that what they were buying was designed to break after a period of time, then there was a danger they might stop buying. So manufacturers wanted to reboot the credibility of consumerism in the minds of the consumer. They needed a new conjuring trick.

Alfred P. Sloan Jr., the CEO of General Motors, had steered

the company sensibly for thirty years. Though a proficient boss, Sloan had for decades operated in the shadow of a colossus, Henry Ford of rival company Ford Motors.

Ford's genius had hinged on one simple breakthrough. In the 1880s and 1890s, he had become fascinated by meat packers in Chicago. They had figured out how to pull animal carcasses apart efficiently, piece by piece along a conveyor belt. In effect, they had created the first modern production line. What, Ford thought, if you reversed the process? Instead of using a production line to deconstruct a cow, what if one used it to construct a car?

Henry Ford pioneered mass production with the assembly line that built the Model T Ford in 1908. Now, in 1956, nine years after Ford's death, Sloan had his own idea to revolutionize the car industry, and transform planned obsolescence.

At a 1954 advertising conference, Milwaukee industrial designer Brooks Stevens had addressed delegates with what he believed was the greatest challenge facing postwar industry: "instilling in the buyer the desire to own something a little newer, a little better, a little sooner than necessary."[6] Sloan saw how to make this happen. To resurrect the discredited doctrine of planned obsolescence, he would engineer a new mindset for the consumer, one in which we ourselves would choose to make a product obsolete. GM wouldn't need to mechanically engineer a vehicle to break but could rely on the customer to become unhappy with it. Sloan described the whole process in two brilliantly chilling words: "engineered dissatisfaction."

In Sloan's autobiography, *My Years with General Motors*, he outlined the theory in more detail: "The changes in the new model [of car] should be so novel and attractive as to create demand . . . and a certain amount of dissatisfaction with past models as compared to the new one."[7] At the beginning of each factory year, a car should be made available that would appeal to upwardly mobile Americans, keen to show their neighbors their incremental economic progress from last year through the cipher of a new upgraded car. Sloan had pioneered what we now call market segmentation by offering cars to everyone at every level on this economic ladder. He called it "a car for every purse and purpose." If there was a more expensive car to aspire to, then the consumer would strive to upgrade to that one. Sloan had "engineered dissatisfaction" in the consumer by inventing the rolling upgrade.

In San Francisco, I meet the man who was at the heart of Sloan's project, Tom Matano. Matano grew up in late 1940s Tokyo marveling at American design such as the Parker pen, the Coke bottle and the GE refrigerator. The first chance he got, Matano headed to the States to become an apprentice designer at General Motors.[8]

One of Tom's early assignments was to work on the first car designed to "engineer dissatisfaction": the 1956 Chevrolet Bel Air. On a beautiful spring day Tom drives me across the Golden Gate Bridge in an original model. "You see the shine on the dashboard?" Tom points to the brilliant blue sheen reflecting the sky. "That color was derived from nail varnish. The car was to be an accessory, matching your new coat or handbag."

The car came with a catalogue too, showing customers what the upgrade model would look like, available in just six months' time. The catalogue is key to understanding Sloan's thinking. The catalogue offered all the upgradable features of the forthcoming car that one's current car lacked: a slightly better radio, different upholstery patterns, a more luxurious-looking steering wheel and shift stick. The objective was that, at the very moment somebody bought a Chevrolet, they were made instantly aware there was a better one coming, which would make the new car obsolete.

How did Tom feel about working in this way? "We were fashion designers, not car designers. The vehicle under the hood, no change. But we had to work on improving the add-ons: upholstery, tail-fins, bright new colors. These were the things that drove the sale." Alfred P. Sloan had upended everything. Reliability and performance were now secondary in selling a car; what mattered most were cosmetic changes.

Tom's apprenticeship at GM put him in good stead, as he went on to become head of design at Toyota. I asked him whether he felt there was anything disingenuous about the tactic. "Not really. It was a genius idea of Sloan's, to keep the car under the bonnet virtually the same and sell it as a new car. That is brilliant."

What Sloan did was reboot obsolescence by turning it into a nagging kernel of doubt that the clock is always ticking on the new thing we have just bought. Yet there is a brief moment of pleasure to be had: the moment you hold a brand-new purchase in your hand and these doubts are banished. It is the moment my friend at the front of the Apple queue was hoping to feel briefly with his new iPhone. The newest new thing, with no taint of impending obsolescence.

The Drug and the Loop: Decision, Reward, Endorphin Rush

Gabe Zichermann lives a stone's throw from the Golden Gate Bridge. A bear of a man, with a gleaming bald head and a penchant for speaking as fast as his vocal cords will allow, he seems too big for his tiny, ultra-minimal, Asian fusion house, complete with contemplation zone and bamboo garden. Zichermann is one of the chief prophets of the neuroscience of selling, studying exactly what ignites in our brains the very moment we buy something.[9]

He talks with an intense energy about what happens at that point of sale: "Once upon a time, the narrative was brand loyalty over a lifetime to a cigarette brand or a washing powder, but now that loyalty is through the upgrade." In other words, we have so many consumer options, we won't stick with a brand simply because of the brand's reputation. It's not enough anymore. But if a brand—such as Apple or Land Rover—can build a long-term relationship over years by promising a new upgrade in a year's time, loyalty is reestablished.

"It is what keeps us with the same brand of car or phone," says Zichermann, "because we now tell ourselves that we believe it is always improving."

And this upgrade does not stop with the product. We think our lives should be pushing ever forward, with a better job, house or partner. There are upgrades to be sought in every aspect of life: a more relaxing vacation, a better body at the gym, a healthier diet.

But it is what happens at the very nanosecond of purchase that fascinates Zichermann, and has made him the go-to guy for big companies seeking to get truly inside our heads. "When we buy something new, our brain treats this decision as a reward. And a small endorphin rush is created, which we enjoy, because it's a high. A drug. So a loop is created between decision, reward, endorphin rush. And this loop becomes addictive."

A report by *Psychology Today* discovered that even the anticipation of shopping brings a release of dopamine into the brain, and this increases with online shopping.[10] Of 1,680 shoppers polled by the journal, 76 percent of Americans say they get more excited when a product arrives in the mail than when it's bought in store, and the anticipation of the package is the height of the rush. Once it has been opened, they wish to repeat the dopamine rush, so another purchase is made.

We glibly use the phrases "retail therapy" and "shopping addiction," but these are crude terms for a complex neurological process that is real. It is not the object that shoppers crave, but the endorphin rush that comes with purchasing something new. This rush dissipates so quickly, it is gone before people have even left the shop, repeated only when another purchase is made. And with no purchase is this intense relationship of endorphin rush and engineered dissatisfaction stronger than with the iPhone.

Are You Getting It?

It was 2007 and a tall man in a black turtleneck walked out into a lecture theater to complete silence. A giant silver Apple glowed in the darkness behind him. The man stopped and faced the audience. "This is a day," he said, "I have been looking forward to. Every once in a while, a revolutionary product comes along that changes everything. One is very fortunate if you get to work on one of these in your career."

There was not a sound in the auditorium. The man paused, looked around and continued.

"In 1984, Apple introduced the Macintosh. It didn't just change Apple, it changed the whole computer industry. In

2001, we introduced the first iPod. It didn't just change the way we listen to music, it changed the entire music industry." The audience started clapping quietly.

"Well, today, we're introducing three revolutionary products." He turned to the huge screen behind him and an icon appeared. "The first is a widescreen iPod with touch controls." The applause began to intensify.

"The second is a revolutionary mobile phone." A white telephone appeared magically in a green square. The crowd began to whoop and some of the audience got to their feet. "And the third is a breakthrough internet communications device." The place erupted.

"Three things. An iPod, a phone, and an internet communicator." He repeated the words slowly and deliberately, over and over like a mantra. "An iPod, a phone, and an internet communicator." The icons began to spin around and around faster and faster, becoming one. "Are you getting it? Are you getting it? These are not three separate devices. This is one device, and we are calling it iPhone."[11]

Steve Jobs turned on his heel and the world was a different place. At the time, Jobs's hailing of the iPhone as "revolutionary" may have seemed a bit of marketing hyperbole, but he had actually undersold his achievement. The iPhone was not to be part of the future, it was going to make it. The original iPhone had more computing power than Apollo 11, but its real power lay in what no one—not even Steve Jobs—could predict.

The iPhone was not going to become simply a digital tool for interacting with the physical world; it would remake the physical world to its own digital design. And all this from an object the size of the compass that Christopher Columbus used to reach America 515 years before. Like Columbus, Jobs had dared to be first to a new world of which he could scarcely imagine its true scale.

Respraying the Giraffe Versus Inventing a New One

One of the designers Steve Jobs brought in to develop the iPhone was Dan Crow. We meet in his London offices at "Silicon Roundabout" in Shoreditch. The iPhone was an extraordinary invention, but I wondered how indebted its upgrade iterations (the 5, 6, 7 plus, 10, X, etc.) had been to Alfred Sloan's theory of "engineered dissatisfaction." How conscious was the company of a debt to perpetual upgrade when developing it?

Dan sips his water and replies. "Apple had got better and better at iterating over many years, starting in the 1970s. Now partly that is driven by upgrade, right? And that is interesting. But the problem is that it's all driven by technology, and inevitably innovation with technology slows."

Steve Jobs had spotted a problem with engineering dissatisfaction. At some point, as one keeps releasing the iPhone 6, the iPhone 7, the iPhone 8, the iPhone X, the public begins to see through it. "You can put a sensor or better camera or make the phone gold or whatever, but you are inevitably going to see a natural plateauing of the product. There's a point where it gets about as good as it's ever going to get."

This inevitable slowing of innovation requires inventing something new, which is why Apple did not focus solely on computers after the success of the Macintosh in the 1970s. Jobs's genius was to create a giraffe, then throw the drawings away and create a rhino, then a lion and then a shark. He knew the public was never going to keep buying the giraffe, no matter how many times Apple resprayed it a different color.

And color, Dan Crow says, is the giveaway that something is over. When a company gets down to changing a product's color, it is scraping the upgrade barrel. Bright new colors are an unintended signal to the public that a product is done genuinely improving. It happened for the Chevrolet Bel Air and it hangs over the iPhone, which is why Apple is now focused on trying to invent the next elephant.

Steve Jobs learned from Sloan and General Motors that one can get away with the upgrade only for so long. Ultimately a new species is needed. That is what Jobs truly learned from Alfred Sloan.

What Next?

In 2009, Apple filed for a patent for in-car camera technology, one that tech analysts predicted could be used to detect hand gestures and control a car or as part of an augmented-reality experience. In 2011, Apple filed for another patent: a small but crucial modification of the iPhone allowing the user to unlock and start their car using their phone.

Apple was designing the next species—not simply getting in on driverless technology, as Tesla, Google and Uber are all jockeying to be part of, but something more spectacular. Apple CEO Tim Cook teased shareholders with a cryptic comment: "Do you remember when you were a kid, and it was Christmas Eve, and it was so exciting?" he told them. "You weren't sure what was going to be downstairs. Well, it's going to be Christmas Eve for a while."

But the clues are coming together. Unlike Google and Tesla, who have been testing their driverless cars on public roads, Apple's engineers have been using a disused World War II naval base outside San Francisco, as *The Guardian* revealed in 2015.[12] According to the base's owners, GoMentum, it is "the largest secure test facility in the world."

The *Wall Street Journal* investigated Apple's car ambitions and discovered that since February 2015, Apple has hired Doug Betts from Fiat and Paul Furgale, the Swiss researcher who led the V-Charge project to develop self-parking cars. It has also hired fifty top engineers previously at Tesla, and a clutch of battery-life tech experts from Samsung in South Korea and from electric car battery maker A123 Systems.[13]

Apple's next big project is called Project Titan and is not so much the creation of an autonomous car but of an entire transportation system, with an entire reimagining of what the vehicles in this system look, do and are for.

In August 2017, tech expert Steven Milunovich uncovered a secret Apple office in Berlin devoted, he said, to realizing this new transportation system, using the car experts hired by Apple. "Project Titan is likely to be a transportation platform—not a car," Milunovich said, "but the entire experience."

In June 2017, Tim Cook confirmed the rumors by revealing to Bloomberg that Apple is focusing on "autonomous systems . . . a core technology that we view as very important. We sort of see it as the mother of all AI projects."

If cars drive themselves, coordinating the transportation system becomes the AI challenge rather than any one car. Apple already has AI interests in health care and IT, but cracking a coordinated AI transportation system dwarfs these as a challenge.

But it doesn't end there. Cook told *Good Morning America* in September 2017 that Apple was developing augmented-reality technology because "it gives us the capability to sit and be very present, talking to each other, but also have other things— visually—for both of us to see."

By applying augmented reality to driverless cars, the inside of a car becomes an AR entertainment pod moving within a transportation system powered by AI, and Apple will run both under the umbrella of Project Titan. Augmented reality alone is predicted to be worth $165 billion as a market by 2024, and the autonomous car is predicted to be on the market by 2021.

If Apple pulls it off, it will have made a leap that will have made the invention of the iPhone look modest. But the important thing will be that every piece of iOS software, every last detail from the graphics for the satnav to the diction of the car's voice, will be upgradable. It is fitting that Apple will be paying unintended homage to the car with which it all began: the 1956 Chevrolet Bel Air.

2

FOOD
Owning Fat and Thin

THE DEAL: The BMI index recalibrated by statistician Louis
Dublin at Metropolitan Life Insurance is adopted by
doctors and pharmacists across America.

AIM: To create a scientific measure for obesity, in so doing
inventing a health panic years before a genuine obesity
epidemic existed, and a market for the diet industry

WHERE: Metropolitan Life headquarters, New York

WHEN: 1945

When you walk around a supermarket, what do you see? Walls
of highly caloric, intensely processed food, tweaked by chemi-
cals for maximum "mouth feel" and "repeat appeal" (food scientist speak for addictiveness). Pure science on a plate. And
next to this? Row upon row of low-fat, light, lean, diet, zero,
low-carb, low-cal, sugar-free, "healthy" options, marketed to
the very people made fat by the previous aisle and now desperate to lose weight.

There is a deep, symbiotic relationship between the dieting
industry and the food industry. Weight Watchers was bought
in 1978 by Heinz, who in turn sold the company in 1999 to

investment firm Artal for $735 million. SlimFast was bought in 2000 by Unilever, which owns Ben & Jerry's and Wall's sausages. Jenny Craig was bought by Swiss multinational Nestlé, which also sells chocolate and ice cream. In 2011, Nestlé was listed in the *Fortune* Global 500 as the world's most profitable company.

The business story of food and dieting is a strange and remarkable one, marked by fierce battles between rivals, bizarre experiments, skewed data and dirty tactics, and in the middle of it all, scientists and businessmen who set out to alter the nature of what we eat—in the process, making deals that transformed the way we eat.

The Origins of Obesity

In 1945, long before a true obesity epidemic existed, a statistician at Metropolitan Life headquarters in New York named Louis Dublin was on his lunch break. He was down on his numbers and needed to impress his bosses. Dublin began looking at the health premiums being paid by MetLife's life insurance customers and realized that they were hugely influenced by the customers' weight. Then he had an idea.

By lowering the threshold weight at which policy holders would be categorized as both "overweight" and the more health-critical "obese," Dublin discovered, he could raise premiums for tens of thousands of customers overnight, since the health risks associated with their weight would be deemed greater. Dublin needed a scientific metric to justify the shift, however, and stumbled upon body mass index (or BMI), first developed by nineteenth-century Belgian statistician Adolphe Quetelet.

BMI could provide a simple measure of a body's weight in proportion to its height, calculated by expressing body mass in kilograms and height in inches as a fraction, then multiplying that fraction by a conversion factor of 703 kg/m squared. At the time, BMI had a sheen of scientific validity, but some of its flaws have subsequently become apparent. Most significantly, BMI confuses muscle density and fat; according to his BMI reading, Usain Bolt, the world's fastest man, is obese.

Using Dublin's new technique, half the American population could now be defined as either overweight or obese. "It wasn't based on any kind of scientific evidence at all," according to Joel Guerin, an investigative journalist who has analyzed Louis Dublin's methodology. "Dublin essentially looked at his data and just arbitrarily decided that he would take the desirable weight for people who were aged twenty-five and apply it to everyone."

The picking of the most desirable weight as that of a twenty-five-year-old was not as arbitrary as it might seem. The older you got, the less likely you were to hit this ideal twenty-five-year-old-self weight, and the more you could pay in insurance.

The significance of the MetLife BMI cutoff was to create a health benchmark for obesity. Whether the motivation of Dublin and MetLife was to maximize returns on their customers or to standardize a health condition, the result was to create anxiety in the US public.

MetLife began to position itself as a brand that could be trusted to deal with this new health crisis. Grocery stores, doctors' offices and supermarkets across America began installing scales with the MetLife logo on them. Concerned housewives and businessmen who weighed themselves and found themselves overweight visited their doctors, who confirmed that their BMI readings were troubling. This extra weight, they said, is a ticking time bomb.

Newspapers reported a nationwide fat panic. People with an especially high BMI were told they were at imminent risk of a heart attack or stroke. But help was at hand.

In 1960, the *New York Times* first reported on a strange phenomenon sweeping America. Mothers were mixing up their baby's formula milk to drink themselves. They had discovered that a liquid diet made them lose weight. Chemical giant Mead Johnson & Company spotted a gap in the market and launched Metrecal, the first powdered diet drink. Johnson's head of marketing, C. Joseph Genster, had come up with the name by blending "metre" and "calorie." Genster then hired celebrity TV dietitian Sylvia Schur to front Metrecal.

The Louis Dublin BMI recalibration had inadvertently invented the first mass market diet industry. Diets were no longer a fad but a science, with companies like Mead Johnson keen to be first to capture the huge potential market of customers. Like BMI, Metrecal sounded scientific. And the infant diet industry did have some genuine science under its belt, but it was less than keen to share it with the public.

The Minnesota Experiments

Six feet beneath midfield of the Minnesota Golden Gophers football stadium is a network of underground cells and tunnels. In 1944, as Europe was being gripped by malnutrition, the US government wanted to find out what would happen if America was faced with a similar chronic food shortage.

Esteemed nutritionist Dr. Ancel Keys gathered thirty-six

conscientious objectors to monitor the effects of being systematically deprived of food. During World War II, Keys had been responsible for creating the K ration for soldiers: a highly calorific boost bar and, in effect, the first energy snack. In the 1960s, he would gain international fame promoting the "Mediterranean diet." He appeared on the cover of *Time* magazine and was hailed as the new guru of nutrition. But in 1944, he was working in secret for the US government.

For a year, Keys kept his subjects in the underground cells beneath the Minnesota stadium, limiting their calorie intake to 1,500 a day, 300 calories more than the average woman on a diet in the US consumes today. They were also given an extensive exercise regime, periodically dropped into tanks of cold water and forced to stare at food to see how they would respond.

The men quite simply went mad. In their diaries, they obsessed about food, fantasizing about meals they would have when the experiment was over. When allowed onto the football field above the cells, some tried to eat the grass; one of them bit a scientist; another chopped off three of his own fingers with an ax.

But Keys was most amazed by what happened when he began feeding them again. They began getting fat, and fast, not just replacing the weight they had lost, but surpassing their original baseline and continuing to gain. Dieting, he realized, had altered their metabolism, giving them a propensity to be fat where none had existed before.

Dr. Traci Mann works for NASA at the University of Minnesota, studying the physiological effects of dieting on the body, only a stone's throw from where Keys carried out his experiment. "The more and more I look at Keys's findings, the more remarkable I find them." Keys had provided compelling evidence that diets, as people generally think of them, do not work, Mann says. And he had found that dieters steadily gain pounds each time they go through the yo-yo cycle of dieting, becoming incrementally fatter over time. Then, because these weight gains are not seen as a consequence of the dieting, they return again to the same diets.

Keys's science could have spelled the end of the diet industry before it even started; instead, it provided a potential business model. Before the war, diets had existed as fads, but dieting had never been a coordinated, multibillion-dollar business. Keys changed all that, giving the diet industry the scientific confirmation that there could be a long-term business here.

"If you buy a car and it does not work," Mann says, "you take it back to the dealer and get a new one, but if a diet fails, you tell yourself it is your fault and keep going back."

I Just Had Those Two Words: "Slim" and "Fast"

Metrecal didn't catch fire. But the idea of a powdered diet product did, with the help of New York chemist Danny Abraham. Danny grew up above the pharmacy his dad owned; the smell of antiseptic is one of his earliest memories. Danny became a chemist himself. In his early twenties he began Thompson Medical, a chemical company dedicated to researching and launching new products. Danny tried several novel new lines but nothing quite worked. Then, one morning, he bolted upright with two words in his head: "slim" and "fast." Those two words would be the foundation of a diet empire, SlimFast, which would one day sell to Unilever for $2.1 billion.

I meet Abraham at a giant William Randolph Hearst–style castle residence in Florida, where he has a superyacht, *Netanya 8,* parked in the lagoon. "I always wanted a boat when I was a kid. Now I've got one."

How did Danny come up with SlimFast? "I just had those two words. No product. But I figured anything called Slim-Fast is going to sell." Abraham experimented at the development stage with Metrecal-type drinks, but they tended to taste chalky and medicinal. So he tested out some milk shakes instead. Abraham was seeking something all-American that tasted like an indulgence, minus the calories.

Danny is now in his nineties, but looks fighting fit, taking me to his gym where he shows me how much he can still bench-press. He then theatrically takes a SlimFast milk shake from the fridge and swigs it. "Damn. Tastes as fine today as the day I came up with it."

Danny maintains that the goal of losing weight through a SlimFast-centered diet is obtainable. He turns to me with a question. "Who's in charge of you, Jack? Huh? You are. No one else. If people blame other factors for failing to lose weight, they're looking in the wrong place. Get on the scales, go to the gym, it's up to you, no one else."

As I drive away, Abraham waves good-bye and shouts: "Remember, Jack, you're in charge of you."

Is this true when it comes to dieting? Are you "in charge of you"? The diet industry was created as a conscious business decision to take advantage of a health panic that—at the time—was not real. But now that obesity is a real health crisis, the diet industry has struggled to solve it. People trying to lose weight tend to be highly motivated, yet while a few succeed, the majority continue to fail. Over 95 percent of dieters are returning dieters. Are these people simply weak-willed, or is something else going on?

Kelly Brownell is dean of the Sanford School of Public Policy at Duke University, and one of the world's leading epidemiologists in the field of obesity. I put Abraham's point to Brownell. "Of course we are in charge of ourselves, but when it comes to losing weight, it's not quite that simple," Brownell says. He points out that each person's genetic makeup is different. A person with genes that predispose them to put on weight will find dieting harder, and the heavier they are when they begin dieting, the harder it becomes.

Brownell also points out something else. The body, he says, has its own thermostatic control, like a heating system. Once we go over a certain weight, our thermostat is reprogrammed. To lose weight after we have crossed this tipping point is doubly difficult, because the body's thermostat is fighting even harder against the diet, to reset to the new, heavier thermostat weight. So the truism that "in every fat woman there is a thin woman trying to get out" is the exact opposite of the biological truth.

For a planet becoming obese at unprecedented speed, conventional diet products are not the solution. But the message of self-empowerment—you can do it, as Danny Abraham shouted to me—is key to the insulation of the diet industry from criticism. If your diet fails, try again, because you did not try hard enough the first time.

The Weight Watchers Model

In New York, I meet with Richard Samba, the former finance director of Weight Watchers. Samba is a jovial man in his seventies with luxuriant hair and a relaxed swagger. From 1968, when he joined the company, to 1983 when he left, Samba transformed Weight Watchers from an $8 million-a-year franchise operation to a $300 million-a-year global brand.

Weight Watchers was begun at a New Jersey kitchen table in 1963 by housewife Jean Nidetch, who, for years, had binge eaten chocolate-coated marshmallows and sugary snacks. She had tried pills, hypnosis and fad diets but nothing worked. One day, she saw some commonsense advice on a poster pinned to the wall of a local clinic run by the health department: cut out carbs, exercise a bit and form a support group to keep motivated.

Nidetch began following the first two pieces of advice but they weren't working. Finally, she decided to focus on point number three, inviting six overweight friends to her home, where they had a group confessional about their overeating and problems. The friends invited more friends and within two months, the meetings had forty people attending. Al Lippert, a neighbor and fellow dieter, had seen Nidetch speak and was convinced there was a business model in utilizing her motivational skills. Before long, Nidetch had become a polished, inspirational speaker, and it was time to go into business.

In 1963, Nidetch turned her following, now in the thousands, into an actual company that could be rolled out as a franchise across America, with lots of mini-Jeans using the franchise name to present their own weight-loss programs. They called the brand Weight Watchers, with Jean and her husband Mortimer, Al Lippert, and his wife Felice, all of whom had attended Jean's sessions and lost weight, as the business's founders. Al would handle the operations side while Jean would be the face of the business. The idea of exploiting Jean's talents nationally, franchising out her inspirational message to thousands of other Jeans across America and charging these franchisees for the privilege to speak, was a brilliant one.

Al Lippert and Jean Nidetch had identified that the key to the success of each Weight Watchers group was the mutual support and encouragement the members gave one another. By making each group a self-help group counseling itself, Weight Watchers could maintain the home-spun, intimate feel. The group would not feel corporate and impersonal but shaped by the people who turned up.

This business was an overnight success; by 1968, 5 million people had enrolled. In the same year, Richard Samba came on board as finance director, staying at Weight Watchers until 1983. By the time he joined, the company was already America's number one weight-loss brand, offering not just a diet but an entire lifestyle: group support, weight-loss logs, all working toward an objective Samba described as a "lifelong commitment" to Weight Watchers. But how could a multibillion-dollar business, now the number one diet brand in China and India as well as the US and Europe, be constructed on a high statistical probability of failure, as Ancel Keys discovered all those years ago in Minnesota?

Samba smiled and shook his head. "Well, you know. Sometimes we would ask ourselves that same question." He says they would see mothers bring their daughters, who would in turn bring their daughters when they became moms. Mothers who had spent a lifetime on yo-yo diets would be passing Weight Watchers on generation to generation.

After five years on Weight Watchers, according to the Oxford University statistical research unit, less than 16 percent of participants reach their goal weight. That leaves 84 percent who have failed. And yet they still come back for more. "Of course they come back," Samba says. "Because the eighty-four percent: that's where your business comes from."

Putting the Sugar into Obesity

In 1971, Richard Nixon was facing reelection. The Vietnam War had eroded his popularity, but another central issue for his campaign was the soaring cost of food. People demonstrated outside supermarkets with placards. To bring down food prices, Nixon needed the cooperation of the powerful farming lobby. He appointed Earl Butz, an academic from the farming heartland of Indiana and trusted friend of the farmers, to broker a compromise.

Butz opened up farms to start farming on an industrial scale, exhorting them to plant "fencerow to fencerow" and one crop in particular: corn. The surplus corn was plowed back into the feed of cattle, who in turn were fattened by the immense surge in corn production. Burgers got bigger. Fries fried in corn oil became fattier. Corn was now being used in everything and was the engine for a massive surge in cheaper food supplied to American supermarkets.

Butz's strategy was twofold: supply food producers with cheaper corn, which could in turn be used in a host of supermarket products, and boost demand for this cheaper food with the consumer. The key was production: if it couldn't all be eaten, it could be exported.

In 1973, the USDA (Department of Agriculture) under

the leadership of Butz secured a $700 million deal to export 30 million tons of grain to the Soviet Union. The deal was paid for with export credits, so Nixon's government effectively subsidized the Soviet purchase.

But there was a reason. Butz wanted to aggressively open up foreign markets to American corn and if that meant subsidizing the exports to capture the market, so be it. Subsidy would underpin both massive overproduction by US corn farmers as well as these overseas sales. As a result of Butz's reforms, US farmers went almost overnight from smallholders to businessmen with a global market.[1]

In the mid-1970s, Butz flew to Japan to investigate a strange new scientific innovation that utilized the waste from corn. Called high fructose corn syrup (HFCS), it was an intensely sweet, gloppy syrup that was also incredibly cheap to produce. HFCS had been discovered in the 1950s by the Clinton Corn Processing Company in Iowa, but it was only in the mid-1960s that a process was found to harness it for mass production at a scalable level. The scientist who made the breakthrough was Yoshiyuki Takasaki at the Japanese National Institute of Advanced Industrial Science and Technology, who in 1967 created an acid-enzyme process for the cornstarch extract derived from milled corn, making HFCS a commercial proposition for the first time.

A myriad of HFCS products—from HFCS 42, used in breakfast cereal, to HFCS 90, used in pancake syrup—scalable thanks to Yoshiyuki Takasaki, were soon pumped into every conceivable food: pizzas, mass-produced baked goods, even meat. They provided that "just baked" sheen on bread and cakes, made everything sweeter and extended shelf-life from days to years. But HFCS was also packed with sugar. And it was one of the most sugary items in the supermarket, soft drinks, that HFCS would most profoundly transform.

Hank Cardello is a tall man with a hesitant manner, who greets me with a businesslike handshake at a diner in downtown Manhattan. In 1984, Hank was head of global marketing at Coca-Cola, which was about to make the momentous decision to swap sugar for HFCS.

Coke was to use HFCS 55, an amalgam of HFCS 42 and the far sweeter HFCS 90 (90 percent fructose). It was supplied to Coke by CCBSS (Coca-Cola Bottlers Sales & Services), a limited liability company created, owned and authorized by Coca-Cola. With something as important as the key ingredient of their drink, Coke could not rely on an outside supplier.

As market leader, Coke's decision to endorse corn syrup sent an unequivocal message to the rest of the industry, which quickly followed suit. It was the papal puff of white smoke that they needed.

At the time, Hank says, it was a risk worth taking, even given the possibility of altering Coca-Cola's iconic taste. The benefit to the bottom line was undeniable, as HFCS was two-thirds the price of sugar. When it was first introduced, a slight metallic tang in the first test batches was reported. Some US consumers began buying Coke from Mexico ("Mexicoke") because it tasted more like the old Coke they were used to. But they continued to buy Coke. And in 1984, Hank says, "obesity wasn't even on the radar."

But another health issue was: heart disease. Since the mid-1970s, a fierce debate had raged in the medical profession over what was causing it. The debate divided the medical establishment, and battle lines were soon drawn. The most prominent leader of one camp was Professor John Yudkin, a researcher at University College London, who blamed sugar for heart disease. Ancel Keys, of the Minnesota starvation experiment, spearheaded the opposing view, and believed the primary issue was fat. Keys was an internationally renowned nutritionist, a titan in his field, while Yudkin was a relative unknown, an outsider with an unorthodox and unpopular view within the bulk of academia: sugar is not only harmful, but potentially lethal.

Yudkin's colleague at the time, Dr. Richard Bruckdorfer, remembers that "there was a huge lobby from the industry, particularly from the sugar industry" against Yudkin's research. Endocrinologist Robert Lustig at San Francisco Hospital describes a concerted campaign to discredit Yudkin, including academic papers published to systematically cast doubt upon Yudkin's conclusions.

Yudkin was beginning to gain a popular following outside academia, however. In 1972, he published the book *Pure, White and Deadly*, which made a systematic case for the deleterious health effects of sugar.[2] It was a bestseller and became a key text for the growing health-food movement of the 1970s, but it was criticized by Yudkin's academic peers. Keys's campaign against Yudkin was successful. Yudkin eventually became a pariah, ostracized and forgotten. But according to Lustig, Yudkin had predicted the future by identifying the dangers of sugar, not just its connection to heart disease, but to a potential obesity epidemic as well.

Where Yudkin saw danger, food producers saw an opportunity. The public was keen to embrace a new product to fight the very obesity epidemic Yudkin had predicted. The food industry had just the product ready: a brand-new concept called "low fat."

The Rats Get Fat

Low-fat products were an industry dream: a new type of food forged in the panic around heart disease that could now be rolled out to deal with the coming catastrophe of obesity. But there was a problem. "When you take the fat out of a recipe," endocrinologist Dr. Robert Lustig says, "food tastes like cardboard, and you need to replace it with something—that something being sugar."

In 1983, the report of the Framingham Heart Study on cardiovascular disease clearly linked a high-fat diet to heart disease, and suggested a low-fat diet for everyone as a preventative measure. Miraculous new products arrived on the shelves that seemed too good to be true. Low-fat yogurts, spreads, even desserts. One low-cal candy, the oddly named Ayds, which took a major commercial hit as the AIDS epidemic unfolded in the 1980s, tasted far sweeter than its full-fat counterpart. And there was a reason: all these foods had had the fat stripped out and replaced with sugar.

Nutritional wisdom in the 1980s became beholden to what food historian Gary Taubes calls "the low-fat dogma," with sales of these incredible wonder foods rocketing across the globe. And as low fat took grip, so too did obesity. By the mid-1980s, doctors were being visited by larger patients than any they had seen before. The food industry began stressing that individuals must be responsible for their own calorie consumption, but even those who exercised and ate low-fat products were gaining weight.

In 1966, the proportion of people with a BMI of over 30 (classified as obese) was only 1.2 percent for men and 1.8 percent for women. By 1989 the figures had risen to 10.6 percent for men and 14 percent for women. The more sugar people ate, the more they wanted, and the hungrier they became in the process. Sugar appeared to be a new kind of addiction.

A professor at New York University, Anthony Sclafani, began to investigate. Sclafani was particularly interested in the connection between appetite and weight gain, and began to notice something strange about the lab rats he was testing. When they ate rat food, they maintained a normal healthy weight. But when they were given processed food from a supermarket—sugared cereal or snacks—they ballooned in a matter of days. Their appetite for sugary foods was insatiable; the rats continuing to eat long after their bodies were physically full. Sclafani had identified a paradox of obesity: the more you eat, the hungrier you get.

This, Sclafani believed, was unlike any nutritional attack the human body had faced before: a three-pronged assault on the metabolism that alters it in the process. Sclafani observed his lab rats not only gorging on sugar, but on low-fat products too. And if he put them on a diet, they got fatter when the diet stopped, exactly as Ancel Keys had observed in those cells beneath the Minnesota football stadium. It is possible, Sclafani concluded, for the obese to cross a line of no return, when their metabolic thermostat has been reprogrammed such that weight loss is a near-insurmountable challenge.

Professor Jean-Marc Schwarz is now trying to understand the physiology of obesity. Schwarz studies the precise way in which the major organs metabolize sugar and calls the momentum it builds in the body "a tsunami."

The effect this has on our primary organs is only now being understood. Around the liver, it coalesces as fat, leading to type 2 diabetes. Sugar may even coat semen and result in obese men becoming less fertile. But the organ of most interest is the gut. According to Schwarz, the gut is a highly complex nervous system—the body's "second brain"—and as it becomes conditioned to want more sugar, it sends messages back to the first brain that are almost impossible to fight. There is growing scientific evidence that fructose can also trigger processes that lead to liver toxicity and a host of other chronic diseases. Schwarz says this assault on the body is so comprehensive, it is analogous to an attack on the nervous system.

Dr. Tony Goldstone at Hammersmith Hospital in London is mapping out the specific parts of the brain and neurological pathways stimulated by sugar. When a person becomes obese, a hormone called leptin ceases to work properly. Normally, leptin is produced by the body to indicate fullness. However, in obese people, it is generally severely depleted, due in part to a high intake of sugar. When the leptin does not work, the body simply doesn't realize it should stop eating, just as Scalfani's lab rats could not stop gorging on sweet snacks.

These scientists are independently homing in on the causes of obesity. Yet any one attempt to begin questioning the food industry's role in that obesity epidemic faces a steep hill to climb. As one K Street lobbyist in Washington put it to me, the food industry is up there with oil and weapons in terms of access to the White House. "When you can get the President of the United States on the phone in five minutes, then you don't need people like me to lobby." The food industry has real power.

A joke, she said, that made the rounds in Washington in the late 1990s goes like this: How do you interrupt President Clinton when he's getting a blow job from Monica Lewinsky? Tell him Monsanto is on the line.

The reason the food industry is so powerful is simple. Food is an essential that has become a vice. And sugar has turned food into a vice by creating an unbreakable link between gut and brain. It is as addictive as cigarettes or alcohol. But unlike cigarettes and alcohol, the temptation cues are every ten yards, unregulated and unrelenting: in vending machines, coffee shops, fast-food outlets, supermarkets, cinemas, even gyms, libraries, swimming pools and train stations—just about everywhere.

The Magic Bullet that Backfired

Yet scientific causality between food manipulation and a fatter population has eluded the medical profession. Why? The reason has little to do with science and more to do with the fact that the same scientists researching the food industry's role in creating obesity are also funded by the food industry. With so little money set aside for independent research, and what little there is being cut, the food industry has become a vital source of financial support to researchers.

In an open letter to their colleagues in the *British Medical Journal* on April 21, 2016, professors of public health at the University of Liverpool Simon Capewell and Anna Gilmore urged researchers to come clean on the precise monetary amounts being given to obesity research by the food industry. "This funding biases research, and seriously constrains the fight against the obesity epidemic," they said. "Change will not occur until public health researchers refuse to take this ultra-processed food industry money."

However, other experts in the field disagree. Paul Aveyard,

professor of behavioral medicine at Oxford University, and Derek Yach, who has worked at the World Health Organization as well as at Pepsi and is now executive director at the Vitality Institute in New York City, argue that "even though industry promotes products that undermine public health, in many cases food industry and health goals clearly align and co-funding in-kind or in direct payment from industry is appropriate." Both assert that a standoff between public health and the food industry is simply unrealistic. "The alternatives are that the research [into better health] is not done, that it is done by the company itself, or the public pay."

When the world began getting fat, food companies and even the pharmaceutical industry looked at the escalating obesity crisis and realized there was a huge amount of money to be made. A multibillion-dollar cash cow emerged, encompassing not only low-fat foods, but diet drugs, home fitness, fad diets, crash diets and diet and recipe apps, with newly thin celebs promising an "all-new you" in just three weeks. Seen in terms of profit, the most lucrative market was not the clinically obese, it was the billions of ordinary people worldwide who were a little overweight and did not consider their weight to be a significant health problem.

To reach this market, the science needed to say they were at risk. And it all hinged on one deal on one day. On June 3, 1997, the World Health Organization (WHO) convened an expert consultation in Geneva, which formed the basis for a report that defined obesity as an "epidemic." The word "epidemic" is crucial because it categorized obesity as a medical catastrophe, in need of a "cure."

The lead author of the report was one of the world's foremost obesity experts, Professor Philip James,[3] who as a doctor in the

1980s had been one of the first in the world to spot obesity on the rise. In 1995, James set up a body called the International Obesity Task Force (IOTF), which reported on rising obesity levels across the globe and on health policy proposals for how the problem could be addressed. It is widely accepted that James first put obesity on the radar, and thus it was appropriate that the IOTF should draft the WHO report of the late 1990s that would define global obesity. The report painted an apocalyptic picture of obesity going off the scale around the world.

The devil was in the detail—the detail of where to draw the line between "normal" and "overweight." Several colleagues questioned the wisdom of lowering the cutoff point for being "overweight" from a BMI of 27 to 25. Overnight, millions of people across the planet would shift from the "normal" to the "overweight" category. Just as they had done when Louis Dublin first lowered the cutoff point in the 1940s.

Professor Judith Stern, vice president of the American Obesity Association, was critical and suspicious. "There are certain risks associated with being obese. But in the twenty-five to twenty-seven area, it's low-risk. When you get over twenty-seven, the risk becomes higher. So why would you take a whole category and make this category related to risk, when it isn't?"

At his London apartment, I asked Dr. Philip James about the origin of the decision to move the cutoff to 25, the decision that Stern questioned the motivation for. Dr. James is robust in his reply. It was, he says, based purely on medical evidence. "The death rates went up in America at twenty-five," he says, "and they went up in Britain at twenty-five and it all fits the idea that BMI twenty-five is the reasonable pragmatic cutoff point across the world. So, we changed global policy on obesity."

James's decision seemed sensible, so why had other health experts, such as Judith Stern, questioned it?

I asked James where the funding for his report came from. "Oh, that's very important. The people who funded the IOTF were drug companies." And how much were you paid? "They used to give me checks for about two hundred thousand a time. And I think I had a million or more [in total]." And did they ever ask him to push any specific agenda? "Not at all."

James says he was not influenced by the drug companies that funded his work, but there is no doubt that, overnight, his report reclassified millions of people as overweight and massively expanded the customer base for the pharmaceutical industry. Back in the 1940s, Louis Dublin had created an obesity epidemic on paper when there wasn't one, and fifty years on, Philip James had widened the net in the context of a genuine epidemic.

His critics, like Stern, alleged that the report was alarmist in order to benefit drug companies, but James countered that he needed the muscle of drug companies to press home the urgency of the unfolding obesity crisis. The problem was that the cure was not easily at hand. Since the 1950s, the drug industry's best option for weight loss had been amphetamines, prescribed to millions of housewives who wanted to lose pounds. But in the 1970s, amphetamines were banned for being highly addictive and for contributing to heart attacks and strokes.

Now drugs were once more on the agenda as a cure for obesity. The industry focused on one specific area: appetite suppressants called fenfluramines. After trials in Europe, the US drug giant Wyeth developed Redux,[4] which was approved by the US Food and Drug Administration (FDA) in spite of evidence of women developing pulmonary hypertension while taking them. When a Chicago doctor, Frank Rich, challenged the efficacy of Redux on US television, Redux was withdrawn from the market.

The search continued for a truly effective weight loss drug. British giant GlaxoSmithKline (GSK) found its antidepressant Wellbutrin had the handy side effect of helping people shed pounds. Blair Hamrick was a sales rep for the company in the United States tasked with getting doctors to prescribe the drug for weight loss as well as depression, a move that would considerably widen its market and profitability. In the trade, this is called "off-labeling."

"If a doctor writes a prescription, that's his prerogative, but for me to go in and sell it off-label, for weight loss, is inappropriate," says Hamrick. "It's more than inappropriate, people's lives are at stake."

GSK spent millions convincing doctors to prescribe Wellbutrin as a diet drug, but until Hamrick blew the whistle on his job at GSK, the practice of off-labeling escaped the scrutiny of law enforcers. As a result of Hamrick's going public on conduct relating to Wellbutrin and two other drugs, the company was prosecuted in the United States and agreed to a fine of $3 billion, the largest health-care fraud settlement in US history.

So drug companies, thus far, have failed to find a "magic bullet" for obesity. But simply medicating and managing the obesity crisis may be more lucrative than fixing it with a one-stop cure. Take type 2 diabetes, a by-product of obesity and also one of the pharmaceutical industry's most profitable medication opportunities.

A Possible Solution

Sitting in his MetLife office in 1945, Louis Dublin could not have envisioned a world in which obesity would become the global health crisis it is today. What he did do was create the scientific basis for a diet industry that took shape long before this obesity epidemic was real, but has shown scant evidence over forty years that it can actually provide a meaningful solution to the crisis.

It is naïve to imagine there is a magic bullet. But there is one area of research that has recently proved promising. Developments in cognitive behavioral therapy (CBT) suggest a possible long-term solution could come by reprogramming the brain to think about the routine of eating in a different way, and it's all to do with control.

Anorexics and binge eaters share an ability to exert control over their intake of calories that is detrimental to their health. Contrary to the common belief that the obese lack control, binge eating—like self-starvation by anorexics—is a well-maintained routine, just one that's damaging, and potentially life-threatening.

But if this dysfunctional routine can be switched to a functional routine of healthy eating and exercise, then the obese could be given a routine that works for them. A 2017 paper for the US National Institute of Health by psychologists Gianluca Castelnuovo, Giada Pietrabissa and Enrico Molinari, *Cognitive Behavioural Therapy to Aid Weight Loss in Obese Patients: Current Perspectives,* examined CBT's effectiveness.[5] "The literature on the psychosocial aspects of obesity has a long history," they write. "Granville Stanley Hall, the first person to earn a Ph.D. in psychology in the US, started studying eating behaviors and obesity in the nineteenth century (and) CBT is traditionally recognized as the best established treatment for binge eating disorder (BED) and the most preferred intervention for obesity." However, the report cautioned against seeing CBT as a new magic bullet for obesity.

"Although the comprehensiveness and the practical nature of the CBT approach are positive, this psychotherapy does not necessarily produce a successful weight loss."

The authors evaluated numerous examples of CBTs available to obese patients as well as their long-term efficacy, noting several promising evolutions of the psychotherapeutic approach that may appear to offer more sustained success.

HAPIFED (Healthy Approach to Weight Management and Food in Eating Disorders) was developed in 2105 by professors Palavras, Hay and Touyz, offering "therapeutic education" and CBT with emphasis on accompanying the patient through their weight-loss journey plus strong emotional support (interestingly, one of the key planks of the Weight Watchers approach).

Castelnuovo, Pietrabissa and Molinari also identify "third-wave CBT protocols such as acceptance and commitment therapy" as gaining traction with patients and support from clinicians. These include mindfulness and even the "sequential binge approach" (making food unappetizing and monotonous). Their conclusion is not so very different from the one I found for the diet industry: dieting works, but only for some, and not forever. Many factors are at play with obesity, and the solution is not readily to hand, raising an obvious if pertinent question: when someone does manage to lose weight and keep it off, is this because they have been given the right treatment or because they were going to succeed regardless of outside factors? If it's the latter, how can therapy tap into the inner strength and motivation of the few and pass it on to everyone else?

In the meantime, the baton for helping everyone else now appears to be handed to MedTech, where the use of health apps and even virtual reality may attempt to unlock the door to a solution that has eluded the diet industry for over half a century.

3

DRUGS
The Medication of Modern Life

THE DEAL: Henry Gadsden, CEO of Merck, proposes a plan for the pharmaceutical industry to deal with the potential crisis posed by the expiration of patents on its blockbuster drugs.

AIM: To expand the number of patients for which prescription drugs can be prescribed

WHERE: Interview with *Fortune* magazine, New York

WHEN: 1980

At 10:15 A.M. on October 14, 2008, I was in a meeting in London when something very odd began to happen. The floor began heaving beneath me. The walls started approaching me, then receding. I felt as if I were on a ship in a storm.

I went to the bathroom and splashed my face with water. The droplets in my hands wobbled. My reflection in the mirror was warping. Then my fingers began to tingle. The tingling moved through my hand, up my arm and into my shoulder. By the time I was on my way to the hospital, I felt as if a giant hand had come down from the sky and was crushing my body into a tiny corner of the ambulance.

I was having a stroke, but I was lucky. I could speak and I knew who I was. In the hospital beds around mine were seemingly fit and healthy men aged between twenty-five and forty. A refuse collector, who did the equivalent of a mini-marathon every day; a city trader, who went to the gym three times a week; a barman, who did salsa in his spare time; a criminal informer, visited by two policemen who brought grapes; and me.

We had all suffered strokes, years before any of us imagined we should decently have one. Why? Stress? Everyone has stress, but not everyone has a stroke. I had lost some feeling, but it returned in minutes. I was not blind or struggling to stand, as some of the other patients were. "When we had strokes," the guy in the bed next to me said, "we were hit by a hammer, but you ducked."

I left the hospital with a carrier bag of drugs. When I got home, I examined them. They were a chalky terra-cotta color and all had one word on them: "Simvastatin." I popped one in my mouth.

The Gray Zone

The United States has 320 million people. According to the US government's National Center for Health Statistics, roughly half of all adults go to their bathroom medicine cabinet every morning and take a drug like the ones I had just been given.[1] And prescription drugs are becoming more prevalent. In 2000, only 8 percent of adults took five or more prescription drugs, but in less than twenty years, that figure has more than doubled.

We do not magically have more illnesses than we did fifty years ago. Since 2000, we have become older and heavier as a society, but increased use of prescription drugs vastly outstrips these needs. Pills are taken by all socioeconomic groups, but especially by wealthy, non-Hispanic whites, who take roughly twice as many prescription drugs as poorer Mexican Americans, even though—with health needs normally dictated primarily by poorer socioeconomic background—the opposite should be true. Epidemiologists call it the "Hispanic paradox."[2]

The drug industry's backbone is built on the so-called Big 3 D's: depression, diabetes and dementia. But the fastest growing drug on earth is statins, used to lower cholesterol—the drug I was given when I left the hospital.

Statins are the key to understanding the rise in prescription medications. When I had my stroke, I entered the gray zone between the sunny uplands of health and the deep valley of the unwell. This gray zone is where much of the pharmaceutical industry's business increasingly lies. In widening this gray zone to the fullest extent possible, the pharmaceutical industry maximized the potential of illness and stumbled upon a revelation: many nebulous anxieties and neuroses of modern life could be reframed as treatable medical syndromes. And so—in fact—we do have more illnesses than we did fifty years ago.

By having a stroke, I put myself in the lower foothills of the gray zone in which drugs are taken as a "sensible preventative measure." But millions of people across the globe who take Simvastatin have not even had a stroke. So why are they being prescribed statins?

A few days after I was discharged, I asked the consultant who had been looking after me that question. "Do you want the official line or what I think?" Both. "OK. The official line is that even if your chance of another stroke is around 0.05 percent, you should take statins for the rest of your life."

So what about everyone else?

"About a decade ago, drug companies came along and were given *carte blanche* to hand out statins to doctors not only for strokes, but for everything. So we now prescribe them like sweets to anyone over forty as a preventative measure. It is sold to the patient like putting de-icer in your car or taking leaves out of the guttering.

"But we don't know who they work on," he continued. "It could be less than five percent with ninety-five percent popping them pointlessly. But there's one thing for sure. There's a winner here and that's the drugs industry."

I am not an anti-pharma person. Quite the opposite. I get angry with people who take a knee-jerk view that everything the pharmaceutical industry does is bad. Prescription drugs kept my grandparents alive. Drugs have kept my dad's high blood pressure at bay for forty years. The pharmaceutical business has prolonged life and alleviated pain on a daily basis for billions of people.

But here I was doubting that I needed to take a pill that I was assured would keep me alive. What was my problem? My problem was that I wasn't the only one in the new gray zone between health and illness. Everyone is.

A Stick of Wrigley's Gum

How was the gray zone created? The answer lies with a deal conceived of primarily by one man. In 1980, Henry Gadsden, the CEO of Merck Pharmaceuticals, was interviewed by *Fortune* magazine.[3] The six pharma giants were in trouble for the first time in their 150-year history. The postwar boom in prescription drugs, which had reached its apex in the 1960s with Valium, was now under threat. As the blockbuster drugs they had relied upon for decades lost their patents and went generic, customers would henceforth be able to choose cheaper alternatives. The drug companies' monopolies on these moneymakers would be over.

Gadsden's interview comments forewarned of the passing of the Hatch-Waxman Act in 1984, which effectively created the modern generic market by requiring producers of generic drugs to prove only that their generic had the same active ingredient, dosage strength and so-called pharmokinetic, or bioequivalence, as its brand-drug version. The very prospect of Hatch-Waxman was enough to threaten the guaranteed revenue streams of the drug industry for good. But Gadsden had a solution.

He put it like this. "The problem we have had is limiting the potential of drugs to sick people," he told *Fortune.* "We could be more like Wrigley's Gum . . . it has long been my dream to make drugs for healthy people. To sell to everyone."[4]

Gadsden's solution was genius. According to the Substance Abuse and Mental Health Services Administration, 18.2 percent of the US population is diagnosed as having some kind of mental illness in any one year. Ninety-five percent of the adult population will find itself ill from something, ranging from the most common ailments—flu and lower back pain—to severe PMT, migraine and asthma. Gadsden saw the potential for drugs to be taken by all as a preventative measure, or to deal with an illness not yet fully diagnosed, popped in the mouth like a stick of gum. And in order to make this happen, a raft of new illnesses and syndromes needed to be identified and diagnosed.

Modern Life Makes You Ill

Gadsden had a surprising fellow traveler. In 1960, psychiatrist R. D. Laing published *The Divided Self: An Existential Study in Sanity and Madness*.[5] Laing's fame spread quickly. He became the figurehead of the "anti-psychiatry" movement, advocating the end of mental-health labeling. Laing viewed madness as a construct, and it was during the Vietnam War that his popularity really grew. In a society, he said, that promotes carpet-bombing and the shooting of protesting college students on US campuses, the mentally ill can hardly be considered any more disturbed than society itself. In fact, labeling dissenting voices as "mad" was a way of silencing them.

The book became a countercultural bible, carried by hippies, beatnik poets and antiwar protestors, who quoted Laing's famous dictum that insanity is a "perfectly rational response to an insane world."

The Shakespearean idea of the mad as the only people who see the truth became a key tenet of the antiauthoritarian left, articulated by dystopian sci-fi writer Philip K. Dick, who summed up insanity as "an appropriate response to reality."[6] But R. D. Laing took this idea further by giving it medical credence. Laing said that imprisoning the mentally ill in psychiatric institutions and force-feeding them pacifying drugs was political oppression. By contrast, taking mind-expanding drugs like LSD could help people to see through the charade of modern life.

Laing first put his ideas on the incarceration of psychiatric patients into practice at Langley Hall, a community center in East London in 1965, where Laing encouraged therapists and patients with schizophrenia to live together and explore alternative treatments. The "anti-psychiatry movement" Laing spearheaded there gained international support, including from Jacques Lacan in France and Hungarian psychiatrist Thomas Szasz, who wrote *The Myth of Mental Illness* in 1961.

Though R. D. Laing had been exploring his ideas for over a decade, it was with the implosion of public trust following Vietnam and Watergate that they gained serious traction. Laing appeared on earnest TV discussion programs and was hailed as a genius at universities across America, where he often spoke against the capitalist society that forced people to degrade themselves with consumerism and office work. Anyone who broke out, according to Laing, was labeled mad. Laing's "LSD Marxism" was everywhere, until the counterculture collapsed and New Right ideas ascended in the mid-1970s. Laing suddenly fell out of fashion.

But then something extraordinary happened. In 1980, William Gadsden did his interview with *Fortune*. America was now in thrall to yuppies, Wall Street and power lunches. The drug industry looked at Laing's discredited theories and saw something no one else had picked up on before.

If, as Laing said, it was not individuals who were ill but capitalism that had made them ill, this was useful. Illness could be created by your job, your home, your friends and your children. By your anxieties around cleanliness, or your neighborhood. By sex, eating, pets, crowds, shopping, big spaces, small spaces, quiet places, loud places, your partner, your car, sunlight, darkness—just about anything. Illnesses could take the form of sweats, palpitations, irrational fear, dizziness, nausea, compulsive behavior, even the simple fact that your leg was restless when you watched television. All of this could be redefined as "illness."

R. D. Laing, the high priest of anti-capitalism, had inadvertently come to the rescue of the drug industry. Modern life could be shown to make you ill, but now there were prescription drugs to fix it. And the key to getting these drugs to market was to get them passed by the US government's highest regulatory body, the FDA.

The FDA

There has always been a deeply intertwined relationship between the food industry, the drug industry and the regulators of both. The Food and Drug Administration (FDA) was first created in 1862 by chemist Harvey Washington Wiley and was known originally as the Division of Chemistry within the US government's Department of Agriculture. As food and drug companies began to build familiar brands at the end of the nineteenth century—from soaps to cereals to painkillers—a new breed of specialist journalism arose dedicated to exposing the dangers of unregulated new products. Today, "muckraking" is either a pejorative term for shoddy tabloid journalism or radical polemical writing, but in the late nineteenth century, muck-raking was first coined to describe the pioneering investigative journalism of writers like Upton Sinclair in periodicals like *McClure's*. Sinclair and his fellow muckrakers would publish their findings and accusations of consumer malpractice with the specific aim of raising public awareness. They then began to lobby in their pages for greater federal regulation of pharmaceuticals and food stuffs.

In 1902, there was a catalyst. The death of thirteen children in St. Louis, Missouri, following their vaccination from a contaminated serum derived from a diphtheria antitoxin, prompted the passing of the Biologics Control Act. Four years later, President Theodore Roosevelt enacted the Pure Food and Drug Act, part of which made the inter-state transportation of potentially contaminated foods a criminal office. The drive for greater regulation in the 1910s and 1920s dovetailed neatly with the aims of the food and pharmaceutical giants, who themselves saw the need for greater regulation and standardization in order to build reputable, trusted brands.

In 1930, the Division of Chemistry was renamed the Food and Drug Administration, and eight years later the Food, Drug and Cosmetic Act gave the FDA the legal teeth it needed. It was no longer up to the FDA to prove a drug or foodstuff was unfit for consumption, but the responsibility of the manufacturer to prove it was safe. The FDA began to build a reputation as the toughest regulator on earth. When thalidomide was administered in Europe in the late 1950s as an anti-nausea drug to pregnant women, a drug that went on to cause terrible birth defects in newborn babies, Dr. Frances Oldham Kelsey of the FDA had already refused to authorize its license in the United States. An amendment to the 1938 act in 1962, the Kefauver-Harris Amendment, strengthened the FDA's regulatory power in light of the thalidomide tragedy, now requiring "substantial evidence" of a drug's efficacy and how it would add medical value.

While this was hugely beneficial to many consumers, it was an issue for the pharmaceutical industry. The lengthy process of getting a drug authorized by the FDA had created what pharma executives referred to as a "drug lag." As doctor and pharma industry expert John LaMattina explained in *Forbes* in 2013, "In the late 80s, drugs were being approved at a much slower rate in the US than in Europe. More than half of all drugs approved in the US had been approved in Europe more than a year earlier. As a result, patients, physicians, advocacy groups, and pharmaceutical companies were all concerned that access to important new medicines were being denied to Americans."[7]

The crisis Henry Gadsden had described to *Fortune* in 1980 seemed to be coming true. American pharmaceutical companies wanted to sell more drugs, and one way was to diagnose more illnesses to treat with these drugs, and fast. To make it happen, not only did these new mysterious illnesses need to be diagnosed and made bona fide, but the drugs for them needed to be approved in a far more streamlined way. The FDA was now the problem.

Help appeared from an unexpected quarter. In 1980, universities were given the means with which to potentially patent their own drugs and get them to market: the result of the passing of the Bayh-Dole Act. The intention was to allow any university, nonprofit organization or even small business with federal funding for a specific innovation or invention to be able to patent and then commercially exploit that patent. In theory, this meant universities could compete with drug companies by producing their own drugs, but the reality was different.

Senator Bob Dole was a friend of President Reagan and one of the most powerful men in Washington; he went on to become the Republican nominee for president in 1996. But in 1980, he was on the board of Verner, Liipfert, Bernhard, a law firm on a retainer to drug company Pfizer. Dole sponsored the Bayh-Dole Act, the immediate effect of which was to open up university departments for the first time in history to patenting their own drugs, which they could then license to the pharmaceutical industry. Senators Birch Bayh and Bob Dole were clear about their intention to commercialize federally funded research in public institutions, and open industry to a commercial relationship with these universities. And it could be argued that part of their intention was allow universities to capitalize on their intellectual property by maximizing what they could earn from it, especially important in a time of public funding cutbacks.

Researcher Catherine Kirby carried out a report on the impact of Bayh-Dole on universities for the McNair Center in 2016 and discovered that universities were already exploring patenting for their innovations prior to the passing of Bayh-Dole in order to fill funding gaps and monetize their discoveries, and the act itself made little difference to this trend. One very clear consequence of the act, however, she says, was to cement the financial relationship between universities and the pharmaceutical industry. It allowed universities to begin getting funding from drug companies in order to supply these companies with research to bolster their claims for a new drug seeking approval from the FDA.

Peter Rost was a drug-marketing executive at Pharmacia. Rost says that the safeguards against untested drugs being blocked by the FDA were circumvented by this new "partnership" of drug companies and university departments. A ping-pong game was created: a pharmaceutical company would invent a drug, the university would test it on behalf of the drug company with its "independent" hat on and give a heads-up on any possible FDA problems.[8]

More fundamentally, the degree to which the FDA had itself become beholden to the pharmaceutical industry became a furious debate within the medical profession. In a paper for the *Journal of Law, Medicine & Ethics* in 2013 entitled "Risky Drugs: Why the FDA Cannot Be Trusted," Donald Light of the Perelman School of Medicine at the University of Pennsylvania argues that the FDA routinely approved drugs with threadbare "proven" efficacy. He estimates that as much as 90 percent of FDA-approved drugs since Bayh-Dole are no more effective than existing drugs. Moreover, "since [the pharmaceutical industry]," Light says, "started making large 'contributions' to the FDA for reviewing its drugs, as it [also] makes large contributions to Congressmen who have promoted this substitution for publicly funded regulations, the FDA has sped up [this] review process."[9]

Not only, Light argues, does the FDA approve "drugs [that are] significantly more likely to cause serious harm, hospitalizations and deaths," it simultaneously puts the approval of drugs for experimental treatments of aggressive conditions such as multiple sclerosis and cancer in the go-slow approval lane.

In August 2013, pharma industry analyst John LaMattina responded to Light's accusations of pharma-FDA complicity, in *Forbes* magazine: "Unfortunately, as an academic whose work is supported by the Safra Center for Ethics [at Harvard], Light's word carries a disproportionate amount of influence," he wrote. "These comments perpetuate the view that there is an unholy alliance between the FDA and the pharmaceutical industry, an alliance that threatens the health of patients. This might make for a Hollywood movie plot. Truth be told, such a conspiracy doesn't exist."

These are the specifics on the financial relationship between big pharma and the FDA. In 1992, Congress enacted the Prescription Drug User Fee Act (PDUFA). PDUFA provided a mechanism for pharma companies to be charged a tax for each new drug application filed. As LaMattina explains, "the revenues from these 'user fees' were used to hire 600 new drug reviewers and support staff. These new medical officers, chemists, pharmacologists, and other experts were tasked with clearing the backlog of NDAs [new drug applications] awaiting approval. Consequently the FDA was able to reduce review times of NDAs to 12 months for standard NDAs and to 6 months for priority applications that involved significant advances over existing treatment."[10]

Those within the pharma industry laugh when it's suggested they have it easy with the FDA. Drug after drug is rejected: in the year that Donald Light accused the FDA of being beholden to big pharma, Merck had an insomnia pill, Allergan had a migraine treatment and Aveo had a potential cancer drug, all flat-out rejected. All were potential blockbusters worth billions.

But the economics do point to the FDA relying heavily on PDUFA funding, and whether this creates a conflict of interest lies at the heart of the debate. The fifth iteration of the act was passed in 2012, nine years after the first act. In 1995, the "user fee" charged was $208,000 per drug. In 2014, it was $2,169,000. With approximately 50 NDAs submitted to the FDA per year, Congress is subsidizing the FDA with more than $100 million directly supplied by big pharma. This is different from paying a routine administrative fee to a governmental body, as we do when our passport applications are processed. The FDA relies heavily on these user fees to function. Without these funds it would be a shadow of itself. So the fees are a financial boon but create a potential conflict in the view of the FDA's critics.

Jessica Wapner of PLOS calculated in 2016, reporting to *Business Insider,* that the drug industry has contributed $7.67 billion to the FDA since the passing of the PDUFA. User fees now account for 68 percent of the FDA's review budget for pharmaceutical drugs and 58 percent of generics. Whether one views this degree of dependence on pharma funding as compromising or just the economics of a hugely costly process of drug licensing depends simply on which side of the garden fence you are standing.

The Invention of Illness

With the approval process significantly streamlined by Bayh-Dole in 1980, drug companies turned to the other side of the equation: broadening their base of potential customers. This was the purview of a Roche executive named Vince Parry. Parry described the process as "the branding of a condition." We meet in his New York offices where Vince now runs his own branding firm, utilizing his years of experience in the pharmaceutical industry. Parry explains to me how branding a condition works, using the example of how, while working for advertising agency Saatchi, he transformed the fortunes of Zantac, a heartburn drug, by helping rebrand heartburn as the far more serious-sounding GERD (gastroesophageal reflux disease).

"Instead of people going into the drugstore and asking for Rolaids, you want them going into a doctor's office and getting a prescription for a chronic condition," Parry says. "That's a vastly different behavioral change you're asking for."

So how did Parry achieve this for Zantac's manufacturer?

"We have to put a name around that [condition] and we have to put a serious rationale around that to justify the complexity of that transaction. In other words, we're going to go out there and make a big deal about this therapy but no one yet knows they need it."

To turn heartburn into the more serious GERD, and thus turn a prescription-only treatment (Zantac) into a mass market phenomenon, it was essential to tap into the customer's deep-seated desire for normality.

"People fear not being normal," Parry says. "Being sub-standard. When people hear they can go to a doctor and get a name for that condition, that takes the terror of not being normal away."

The rebranding of heartburn as GERD was a runaway success. By the time Glaxo's patent on Zantac expired in 1997, 240 million people worldwide had prescriptions to treat GERD with Zantac. And GERD was not the only condition to appear from seemingly nowhere to afflict the public.

Lo and behold, a raft of new syndromes was created, popularized and broadened in their definition to cover huge swathes of everyday life: ADD (attention deficit disorder), ME, bipolar affective disorder, OCD, HRD, PTSD, IBS, metabolic syndrome, PMDD (premenstrual dysphoric disorder), SAD (social anxiety disorder and seasonal affective disorder). On top of these acronyms were a host of oblique phobias and addictions ranging from fear of shiny surfaces to the anxiety created by missing out on a bargain at store sales.

Any nebulous feeling or anxiety could now become a medical condition authenticated by university research. The task was not to create something entirely spurious; many conditions had been around for decades and had genuine sufferers, for whom a diagnosis and medication could be valuable. But the business opportunity was in extending the diagnosis to millions of other people in the gray zone.

The key to making it happen was the creation of direct-to-consumer (DTC) advertising, which cut out doctors and targeted patients directly. In 1981, President Ronald Reagan appointed a new head of the FDA, Dr. Arthur Hull Hayes Jr. Drug advertising to the public had hitherto been framed by a 1969 act that kept the control of pharmaceutical ads under the strict policing of the FDA. Under the old act, advertising was primarily aimed at doctors, who could theoretically read between the lines of the sales spiel and then recommend what was best for a patient.

But with the rise of patient rights advocacy groups in the 1970s, the public began to see themselves as consumers, not simply patients, with a right to decide for themselves what was best for their own health. Advocates for reform, both within the drug industry and from patient rights groups, believed pharma advertising should reach patients directly, helping them choose between alternative drugs. Hayes saw an opportunity the pharmaceutical industry had been waiting for.

In the early 1980s, Pfizer launched a public relations campaign called "Partners in Health Care" that sought to publicize underdiagnosed conditions such as diabetes, angina, arthritis and hypertension. Pfizer believed that patient rights groups would lobby their doctors to prescribe new drugs. Pfizer's visibility in the Partners in Health Care initiative also put them above the parapet and on the "side" of the patient and against the medical "establishment" of experts and doctors.

In 1982, with the deregulation-minded Arthur Hull Hayes as head of the FDA, Merck and Dohme got in on direct-to-consumer drug advertising with Pneumovax, a pneumonia vaccine targeted at those over sixty-five. Eli Lilly launched Oraflex, an anti-arthritic in the same year. The ads for Oraflex made claims beyond the approved product label and the drug was pulled by Eli Lilly only five months after it was launched.

The *New York Times* reported in the same year that "the Oraflex case comes at the worst possible time for the FDA which has proposed changes in its procedure for reviewing new drug applications . . . [reducing] the amount of paperwork submitted by as much as 70% and in many cases bringing the drugs to market sooner." The FDA's stringent clinical process was interpreted in the early 1980s culture of deregulation as petty bureaucratic nit-picking that held up the progress of bringing new drugs to market. Direct-to-consumer advertising was seen as integral to the reform of this stodgy system.

Once DTC was up and running, many drug advertisements took on a particular narrative and aesthetic: A sun-dappled morning; a smiling couple in their mid-forties is walking across a field with their dog. A soft voice-over explains that unbearable back/period/migraine pain has been relieved by a magical new drug. Then there is the FDA bit: thirty seconds of accompanying legal voice-over explaining that side effects could include heart attack, stroke or sudden death in forty-seven other ways. As DTC advertising of this sort became more ubiquitous on American television, the patient rights groups that had first advocated DTC ads on TV started to turn against them.

The reason was simple. According to Dr. Dee Mangin, associate professor at the Christchurch School of Medicine and Health Sciences in New Zealand (the only country in the world, apart from the US, that allows DTC), "DTC is used to drive choice rather than inform the patient."[11] The patient rights groups that had called for greater information from their doctors and initially endorsed DTC advertising that supplied medical information now saw DTC ads as merely pushing one interchangeable drug over another. Both drugs might do the same job but the informational element had become negligible or exaggerated to make a sale.

In 1997, the FDA eased up on a rule obliging companies to offer the detailed list of side effects in their DTC ads, exacerbating patient rights groups' concerns further. According to Mangin, the result has been not to disinform the public but just to offer myriad brand choices. Patients go to their doctor, Mangin says, asking for the specific advertised drug without the requisite information on that drug. "In an era of shared decision-making, it's far more likely that GPs will just do what the patient asks [and prescribe]."

The result in the United States has been an increased overall drug bill. World Health Organization scientist Suzanne Hill, working on rational drug use and access in the United States, believes this drive to promote specific high-price brands using DTC has intensified the acute health-care affordability crisis in America. "Part of the reason the United States has a drug expenditure bill that is completely out of control is this kind of advertising."[12]

Under fire from the WHO, the pharmaceutical industry trade group PhRMA issued a statement in May 2009 rebutting the argument that DTC was exacerbating the US health affordability crisis by bumping up the drug bill. "DTC benefits the entire health care system in the USA," it read, "by encouraging patients to seek medical attention, manage their conditions and avoid unneeded hospital stays or surgeries."

Yet today, 75 percent of consumers themselves believe they are unable to make informed decisions about a drug based on information from a DTC ad. Sixty-three percent say they are unable to tell if a prescription drug ad is misleading.[13]

Yet DTC has been a huge success for the drug industry. In just one year—1998 to 1999—the prescription rate of DTC drugs rose 34.2 percent compared to just a 5.1 percent increase with drugs that weren't advertised directly to consumers. DTC did its job and opened consumers to the unfiltered sales pitch of pharma, even if the initial advocates for this had been consumer groups themselves.

"I Can't Prescribe a Better Husband"

Drugs don't sell without illnesses to treat, and one of the most medicated conditions of the Western world is depression. Dr. Marie Williams is a physician in Blackpool, Britain's most medicated city for depression. "I can't prescribe a drug for a better job or a better husband or better housing. There is a direct correlation between poverty and bad health and yet dealing with the underlying causes is not my job. It's beyond my remit."

I spend a couple of days meeting some of the people whom Dr. Williams sees. John (not his real name) is twenty-four and has envisioned committing suicide a number of times. He never goes through with it, because he can always see himself alive at the end and "I don't want to feel the rope cutting into my neck." When he is in an "episode," he needs antidepressants to help him out of the hole. But sometimes they take weeks to kick in and in the meantime, he is dependent on talking therapy.

I meet a number of people like John in Blackpool with clinical depression and suicidal tendencies. They all say the same thing: talking therapy—maintaining an ongoing connection with an empathetic individual—is what keeps them going, not antidepressants. Talking therapy costs a fraction of the ever-escalating cost of antidepressants and, according to Steve—a psychiatric counselor I meet who works in the North West of England—is the best long-term solution for the patients that will bring them back into the functioning world.

John agrees, and says that antidepressants are viewed in Blackpool like illegal drugs, "but just don't make you feel as good." They're traded with street drugs and simply provide another option for chemical desensitization, often in combination with temazepam or heroin.

Part of the self-fulfilling prophecy of an overmedicated society is that once the medication has been created, we demand it. Dr. Williams says she has patients who come in for antidepressants because their pet has died. They are sad, she says, not depressed, and feeling sad is part of being human. "People have an expectation," she remarks, "that happiness should be a perpetual state of normality. It isn't, but we've created an unrealistic expectation that it should be."

The story of the evolution of antidepressant marketing is a surprising one. When Vince Parry worked with Eli Lilly in the United States on the antidepressant Prozac, it was originally developed as a slimming drug. It wasn't especially effective, but then the company realized Prozac also had antidepressant qualities. Prozac could be remarketed far more lucratively as an antidepressant than as a slimming aid.[14] Prozac was not only going to treat depression, it would boot up the happiness industry.

Launching a new antidepressant was challenging, as the competition was fierce. For Prozac to stand out, it needed a unique selling point. Parry and Eli Lilly came up with one:

Prozac would take the shame and stigma out of depression and make taking a drug to deal with depression a positive lifestyle choice. It would make saying you were on Prozac almost aspirational.

The problem with depression, Loren Mosher, one of the world's leading psychiatric experts on schizophrenia, once said, is that it is depressing. If Eli Lilly could get users to brag about using Prozac, spreading its virtues by word of mouth, then it would have a major hit. Prozac was to become the first antidepressant drug you became happy to say you were on.

Prozac was first developed as an antihistamine by scientist Bryan Molloy and Robert Rathbun in 1971. It was known then by its compound name LY-110141 but soon given an actual name: fluoxetine. It exhibited boundless commercial potential, with properties for treating eating disorders and slimming, reducing blood pressure, panic disorders, even OCD. There were any number of ways the drug could be used, and at the time, depression seemed the least lucrative one.[15]

This was because in the mid-1970s, antidepressants were largely restricted to use in psychiatric units. "Anxiety" and nervous conditions rather than depression were more commonly diagnosed in the public outside these psychiatric units, and Valium was the go-to drug for these disorders.

However, at the very beginning of Eli Lilly's trials on fluoxetine, researchers realized its ability to concentrate serotonin levels to boost the depletion of neurotransmitters in the central nervous system made it a prime candidate for treating depression.

Prozac is marketed as an SSRI, or "selective serotonin reuptake inhibitor," and it was the potency of the drug in increasing concentrations of serotonin that first alerted Eli Lilly to its dramatic antidepressant potential. In 1974, scientist David T. Wong published a paper on fluoxetine's SSRI characteristics. But the market for antidepressant drugs was still crowded out by Valium, so Eli Lilly bided its time. In 1974, fluoxetine was still ahead of the curve: a treatment the world was not yet ready for.

In 1975, Eli Lilly gave fluoxetine the trade name Prozac. The company filed an NDA (new drug application) for Prozac in 1977 but it took a full decade to get FDA approval, finally launching publicly in the United States in December 1987. Prozac's rapid success after launch has been credited to Eli Lilly's handing the drug's marketing to a company called Interbrand, responsible for the rebranding of some of the world's biggest multinationals, including Sony, Microsoft, Nikon and Nintendo.

Interbrand's strategy focused on the aspirational and easy-to-use aspects of the drug. The name was cool. As Anna Moore wrote in *The Guardian,* "Prozac hit a society that was [now] in the mood for it." Depression was no longer a fringe medical condition but was on the lips of middle-class couples at dinner parties, who by the mid-1980s had therapists and discussed therapy as openly as they discussed changing the color of their curtains. The culture was ready for Prozac. "National campaigns," Moore says, "supported by Eli Lilly alerted GPs and the public to the dangers of depression. Eli Lilly funded a brochure entitled "Depression: What You Need to Know" and distributed 200,000 posters raising awareness. Previous antidepressants were highly toxic, lethal if overdosed. . . . Prozac was pushed as entirely safe, to be doled out by anyone. It was the wonder drug, the neurological Eldorado. When launch day dawned, patients were already asking for it by name."[16]

Within a year, US sales reached $350 million. Prozac dwarfed its antidepressant competitors and was soon to become as big as Valium had been in the 1960s, with global revenue of $2.6 billion.

Yet the company was also alert to the fact that Prozac, like most commercially developed drugs, would inevitably have to go generic in a matter of years, when its patent expired. This would leave the drug open to commercial exploitation by other companies. (In 2001, after a five-year multimillion-dollar court battle with drug company rival Barr Laboratories, Eli Lilly lost patent protection for Prozac and it did indeed go generic.) In the fifteen years it had the drug under patent, Eli Lilly worked doggedly on alternative revenue streams for Prozac.

Sarafem, for instance, was a rebranded version of Prozac aimed at premenstrual dysphoric disorder (PMDD) that got FDA approval in 2000. PMDD, though controversial as a diagnosis for what was in essence premenstrual pain, was lobbied for hard by drug companies.

Eli Lilly had its eye on the longevity for Prozac, yet its success as an antidepressant turned out to be unprecedented. Before it was even launched, Eli Lilly read the change in mood on depression, saw an opportunity emerging and then brought a drug to market that appeared to change the culture. In reality, it had pushed at an open door. But Prozac became the standard-bearer of this new, more open attitude to depression in the minds of the public and the media.

Dr. Marie Williams, in Blackpool, says a problem was also created. Happiness, she notes, is a universal human desire but the expectation that we need to be perpetually cheerful has made us more depressed and increased a sense in patients that they do not measure up. We demand medication to make it happen.

And for subtle or nuanced mood swings that do not fit this

soma state of bliss, we have definitive syndromes and drugs to put you on the cloud. Prescription drugs become a normalizing sedative for any state: manic euphoria, restlessness, boredom, depression, overachievement and burnout, poverty, and anything in between. Drugs for coping with modern life, as Henry Gadsden had dreamed of, and a pill to flatten and numb any sensation. And nowhere is this labeling and numbing with medication more widespread than with "difficult" children, millions of whom are diagnosed with ADHD.

DSM III, IV and V:
The Journey to ADHD and the Medicated Child

The journey toward the medication of children took a decisive turn in the early 1970s, mirroring some of the changes that medicated society as a whole. The psychiatric profession faced a reputational low. In the Soviet Union, psychiatry had been used to silence political dissidents by labeling them schizophrenic. Psychiatrists in the West began to examine the reliability of their profession's diagnostic practices. What they were to discover and subsequently propose would change the way we define "normal."

David Rosenhan, a social psychologist at Stanford, wanted to put psychiatry's diagnostic acumen to the test. While a student, Rosenhan had attended R. D. Laing's lectures at Stanford. At these lectures Laing argued that schizophrenia was "theory not fact," and he began to formulate his argument against the "medical model of mental illness." Laing was like a cult leader pronouncing before a rapt audience of devotees, and Rosenhan was as enthralled as anyone else.

In 1973, to test the medical basis for a diagnosis of schizophrenia, Rosenhan recruited a number of pseudo-patients, screened to exclude anyone with a prior history of psychiatric disorder. Rosenhan instructed them to show up at a local mental-health facility and complain that they were hearing voices in their heads saying things like "empty" and "thud." Otherwise, they were to behave normally.[17]

What happened amazed Rosenhan. All the pseudo-patients were immediately admitted as inpatients and diagnosed with schizophrenia, a diagnosis based solely on the patients hearing the word "thud." Even other patients spotted the fact that they were fakes, but the doctors did not. When eventually sent home, having ceased to exhibit further signs of psychosis, many were discharged with the label "schizophrenia in remission." One was refused discharge, however, and had to be rescued by Rosenhan after several weeks in confinement.

Two years after Rosenhan's experiment, Ken Kesey's book *One Flew over the Cuckoo's Nest* was released as a movie starring Jack Nicholson as McMurphy, a recalcitrant patient intent on disrupting the humiliating regime of the mental institution in which he's been incarcerated. The "anti-psychiatry" of R. D. Laing and Rosenhan was now mainstream, an antiestablishment message that meshed with America's widespread distrust of authority in the wake of the Watergate scandal. Politicians and psychiatrists were on a par in the minds of the public— equally distrusted and part of an institutional culture of lies.

Melvin Sabshin, medical director of the American Psychiatric Association, believed psychiatry needed to fight back. To reestablish its reputation, the psychiatric profession brought on Columbia University's Robert Spitzer to come up with a plan to devise "reliable" scientific criteria for all psychological conditions, a rock-solid, diagnostic bible that would leave no psychological condition unmapped or undefined.[18] The objective was to create a common label for all the people walking into a hospital hearing the word "thud" in their head.

In less than three years, mental illness shifted from being a broad series of symptoms subjectively read to a categorical model that equated these visible, measurable symptoms with the presence of disease. The "bible" was eventually titled *The Diagnostic and Statistical Manual of Mental Disorders,* or DSM.

The first two iterations of the DSM created a "clinical diagnosis" for basic mental conditions, but the team of clinicians drafting DSM-III, led by Robert Spitzer, vastly expanded the number of mental illnesses that were now identified. The scope of the diagnosable condition was hugely broadened from DSM-I and DSM-II. DSM-III also adopted a "tick the boxes" approach to assigning symptoms. For instance, in diagnosing schizophrenia, doctors could now look for any six symptoms from a list of ten.

Two more DSM editions have been published since 1980. Each new edition is thicker than the last, with new mental conditions. Dr. Allen Frances oversaw the creation of DSM-IV in 1984, and when we meet at his San Diego home, I ask him what the specific plan for DSM-IV was.

"I was brought on board," Allen says, "because the whole thing was seen as having gotten out of hand." Allen's job was "to rein in the number of conditions being diagnosed," though he's not sure he succeeded in that mission. He later issued a mea culpa, indicating that the epidemic of new diagnoses of autism, ADHD and depression that followed the issuance of DSM-IV were largely "iatrogenic"—the product of a series of well-intentioned mistakes.[19] Frances believes many of the doctors involved in the pushing of DSM overdiagnosis and overmedication have the same regrets.

In 2013, DSM-V was published. "Most of the changes made to the DSM-V," Frances says, "are based on limited data. The evidence is remarkably weak for changing anything. DSM-V opens up the possibility that millions and millions of people currently considered normal will be diagnosed as having a mental disorder and will receive medication and stigma that they don't need."

DSM-III created clear, standardized, psychopathological categories, which gave the drug companies an incentive to launch randomized controlled trials to test newly developed psychopharmacological drugs for the treatment of specific new DSM-III disorders. For any medication to be approved by the FDA, it needs to be proven effective in the treatment of a specific disease—and thanks to the DSM-III, there were many more diseases to treat.

In the years following the publication of the DSM-III, billions of dollars were allocated by government and pharmaceutical companies for psychopharmacological research. Throughout the 1980s, the federal research budget allocated to the US National Institute of Mental Health increased by 84 percent to $484 million annually.[20]

The ever-widening definition of mental illness, and its enshrining as medical fact in each new edition of the DSM, meant that millions more Americans each year found themselves medicated for conditions that had been newly created.

Drug companies and psychiatrists did not do this in isolation. Whether modern life became more stressful or not, adults began to perceive their lives as more stressful, and this willingness to accept a diagnosis made drugs an appealing solution.

But adults were not the only ones who were stressed, depressed and dysfunctional; so too were our children. Eleven percent of all American children have been diagnosed with ADHD (attention deficit hyperactivity disorder). The figure has doubled in the last decade, and increases incrementally year after year, with even two- and three-year-olds sometimes prescribed Adderall and Vyvanse for ADHD.

Before we had ADHD there was "hyperactivity," which was first described by Sir Alexander Crichton in his 1798 study of mental disorders, *An Inquiry into the Nature and Origin of Mental Derangement*. Crichton described hyperactivity as a subtle kind of "restlessness."

After World War II, however, with the professionalization of the psychiatric profession and the standardization of psychiatric conditions in the DSM, everything changed. With each new edition of the DSM produced by the American Psychiatric Association, the range and depth of this childhood "restlessness" was widened and deepened. With the publication of DSM-I in 1952 it was described as "minimal brain dysfunction." By DSM-II in 1968, as a "hyperkinetic reaction of childhood." By 1980, it had switched from mere hyperactivity to a full-blown disorder: attention deficit disorder (ADD) "with or without hyperactivity." DSM-III-R in 1987 and DSM-IV in 1994 added the hyperactivity formally to the disorder by rebranding it attention deficit hyperactivity disorder (ADHD) with three subtypes: inattentive; hyperactive-impulsive, and combined.

From the very beginning of its diagnosis, stimulants have been the prescribed pharmaceutical treatment. When Kurt Cobain was once asked when he began to be a drug addict, he replied that it was when he was first given Ritalin as a child to treat his ADD.

The active chemical compound in Ritalin is the stimulant methylphenidate, which was patented by CIBA, now Novartis, in 1955. With the huge increase in the 1990s in the number of children being diagnosed with ADD and ADHD, Ritalin became a blockbuster treatment. It was quickly joined by dozens of competitors. Richwood Pharmaceuticals launched Adderall in 1996 as an "instant-release" tablet, combining a mixture of several amphetamine salts. Then there are methamphetamines like Desoxyn, methylphenidates (Ritalin, Daytrana, Aptensio, Quillivant, etc.), not to mention the nonstimulant drugs, such as atomoxetine (Strattera), clonidine Kapvay and guanfacine Intuniv.

ADHD is big business and I wanted to find out exactly who these drugs are aimed at.

In San Bernardino, California, I sit in on a therapy session between a psychiatrist and a nine-year-old diagnosed with ADHD. He was first diagnosed when he was five, though the therapist sees kids as young as three. The boy fidgets nervously throughout. When asked why he is here, he mumbles that he doesn't know. Asked how he feels, he wrings his hands furiously. I ask his parents why he is like this. "He's medicated." And do you think that benefits him? "Definitely, he's far more focused at school." How did he come to be diagnosed? "We didn't think there was a problem, but when he started at school, the teacher said she thought he was ADHD, so he was diagnosed." You didn't think there was a problem before? "No." How many kids in his class are like him? "About thirty percent are ADHD."

Thirty percent of kids who now take drugs to treat a condition that has consistently widened both its attendant symptoms and the numbers of children diagnosed. ADHD has proved to be the realization of Henry Gadsden's vision over thirty years ago of a condition for which there's an ever-expanding customer base, treated with a drug taken like a stick of gum each day.

An Illness No One Is Immune From

By 1987, seven years after Gadsden's interview in *Fortune*, one final frontier loomed: finding an illness that no one was immune from. This is where my stroke drugs make a grand entrance. A disease was discovered that was bigger than cancer, bigger than heart disease, and one everyone would get. It was called "risk."

When the medical profession treats people who are actually ill, they are treating a tiny percentage of the population. By treating people at risk, the number of patients given drugs grows exponentially. If risk is defined by its widest possible parameters, the entire game is changed.

A similar conception of risk had helped to reinvent Wall Street; applied to illness, it could reap rewards that even those who pioneered its adoption in medicine could scarcely believe were possible. Risk has become the key medical concept of the last twenty years. It does in many ways the exact opposite of what Spitzer and the DSM sought to do with mental illness, to make diagnosis cast-iron. With risk, a clear, diagnosable illness becomes a fuzzily defined possibility of future illness.

In 1987, Merck launched Mevacor, a statin for cholesterol. Cholesterol had always been considered a factor in heart disease, but now it was deemed the main factor in heart disease.

In 1995, the National Institutes of Health (NIH) said 13 million people in the United States were "at risk" from high cholesterol. Risk was not a new medical concept but the numbers defined as at risk were about to grow dramatically.

Raymond Moynihan and colleagues at *PLOS Medicine* undertook a cross-sectional study of widening risk and the ties between experts and drug companies between 2000 and 2013. Of sixteen publications on fourteen common conditions, ten proposed changes widening definitions, and only one narrowing them. Among fourteen panels with disclosures, 75 percent of members had ties with the pharmaceutical industry.[21]

We might imagine a panel like the NIH, or indeed the FDA, to be independent bodies. But it is normal practice for a large number of panel members on an independent panel to have direct ties to one or another of the big six pharmaceutical giants. The pharma giants are developing drugs that need constant testing and reevaluation; they are inevitably and appropriately in consultation with the people deciding whether a drug gets a license. The question is when this closeness crosses the line.

Either way, the number of Americans defined as being at risk from high cholesterol nearly tripled overnight from 13 million in 2001 to 36 million. In 2004, it went up again to 40 million. In a classic case of "net widening," millions of people previously on the safe side of the line were now moved to the zone marked "at risk."

And 2001 was the jumping-off point. On May 16, 2001, the *Augusta Chronicle* reported that the NIH was suddenly "calling for more aggressive treatment of high cholesterol." Dr. Claude Lenfant of the National Heart, Lung and Blood Institute said that "we can now say with certainty that lowering a high blood cholesterol . . . dramatically reduces a person's risk." Dr. James Cleeman of the National Cholesterol Education Program estimated that 33 percent of Americans needed to lower their cholesterol.

NIH guidelines had previously stated that 200 milligrams per deciliter of total cholesterol was the "desirable" level, and 240 mgs was too high. In 2001, the NIH suddenly halved the cutoff risk point: 100 mgs was now "desirable," 130 to 159 mgs was now "borderline high," 160 mgs was "high" and 190 mgs was "very high."

Risk of cardiovascular disease had been analyzed by the Framingham Heart Study project, which began in 1948. These risk factors were then introduced into the public vocabulary by a landmark 1961 paper that sensibly outlined them as high blood pressure, diabetes and cholesterol. A risk scoring system followed, adopted across the globe as a simple, convenient method of achieving a readable and understandable score.

But what score constitutes risk is open to interpretation. Lowering risk cutoffs and thus net widening the number of people "at risk" is sold as progress; greater complexity of diagnosis must mean a better understanding of a condition. But it could equally be the exact opposite: a fuzzing of previously distinct medical terms to net more potential patients, meaning more people taking drugs.

It was not only the FDA that was finding more people at risk from disease; drug companies too were, according to some who worked for them, actively seeking out conditions that could be cleverly talked up.

Dr. Peter Rost's job at Pfizer was to identify illnesses that could be "astroturfed": supported by a fake grassroots campaign, or groundswell of public opinion, quietly funded by a drug company. The Boomer Coalition emerged from nowhere in 2004, a patient advocacy group highlighting the health-care needs of fiftysomething baby boomers. Henry "The Fonz" Winkler and "Wonder Woman" Lynda Carter fronted the campaign. But buried in their seemingly innocuous drive to get middle-aged people to do more jumping jacks to stay fit was a call to "know your numbers" on cholesterol. It turned out that a PR firm being used by Pfizer, which owned cholesterol statin Lipitor, had orchestrated the grassroots campaign.[22, 23]

Joe Dumit, associate professor of anthropology and science technology at MIT, has made a study of net-widening practices, which, he says, work in two ways: genuine well-established conditions like high cholesterol, or osteoporosis, are used to scoop up millions of people with far milder versions under a single banner. But "I wouldn't draw such a clean line between manufactured and real diseases," he says. And the ambiguity is what makes it work for business. By creating an infinitely expandable medical condition with numerous offshoots and subcategories of that condition, the chances of partnering a drug to any one of the numerous diagnostic categories that have been created improves dramatically.

It would be both simplistic and wrong to blame the pharmaceutical industry alone for inventing or augmenting illnesses and conditions we then found ourselves taking prescription drugs for. We played our part too in the medication of modern life.

When Joe Dumit says the line between real and manufactured illnesses has no clear definition, patients helped fuzz that line by seeking medical diagnoses for the infinite array of subtle anxieties, emotions and pathologies we find ourselves daily prone to. Once upon a time, these would have been merely things to put up with or even facets of our personality commented upon by friends and family—a tendency to be absent-minded, or stressed-out or excitable. Now these are all conditions with acronyms, or parts of an umbrella condition taking in a number of subcategory conditions, such as ADHD or "on the autism spectrum."

The irony is that much of this overdiagnosis and medical labeling of subjective psychological traits was itself the result of a desire on the part of patient advocacy groups in the 1960s and 1970s to want greater dialogue with, and diagnosis from, their doctors. Nowadays, access to the internet means that our ability to self-diagnose is greater than it has ever been before. In addition to suffering from chronic fatigue, we say to our doctor on a routine appointment, perhaps I am gluten-intolerant and celiac into the bargain?

Whether this is good or bad is not the point. We believe ourselves to be suffering from a greater number of afflictions than at any other moment in history and this is not just because we have greater medical knowledge, but because our expectation to be healthy and live longer has never been greater too. In the past, we would put up with illness because life expectancy and the expectation to be happy were limited. Happiness is itself a relatively recent Western construct, coinciding with the decline of the Protestant work ethic and Calvinist sub-summation of the desire of the individual before duty to God, and the emergence of the Enlightenment, when Alexander Pope famously declared the new priority for a citizen: "Oh happiness! Our being's end and aim!"

Today, we aspire to perpetual perma-health and anything

that makes us fall short—things going against us causing un-happiness, or tiredness, or lack of ambition—could be said to have a medical or dietary cause at root. Perhaps this aspiration to total health is the one true condition we cannot escape, and for which there is not yet a drug.

4

CASH
Killing Physical Money to Monetize the Internet

THE DEAL: Peter Thiel, Elon Musk and Max Levchin sell
   PayPal to Pierre Omidyar of eBay for $1.5 billion.
AIM: To create the first billion-dollar platform for online
   transactions
WHERE: eBay headquarters, San Jose, California
WHEN: Monday, August 12, 2002

In 2014, we tipped into a new world. It happened without fanfare, a mention on TV, or a spike on Wall Street; it did not even trend on Twitter. But for the first time in history, card and contactless payments overtook cash transactions.

By 2025, even drug dealers will not take cash. South Korea plans to have no cash at all by 2020.[1] In Sweden, the European country going cashless first, street performers already use contactless machines. A new app, BuSK, lets Americans do the same thing. In Holland, a coat developed for the homeless allows people to give money by swiping a card on their sleeve.[2]

Physical money in your hand—a system of payment that began six hundred years before the birth of Christ—could be coming to an end. Apple CEO Tim Cook says the next generation "will not even know what money was."

Coins, a technological innovation even more transformative than the iPhone, first began circulating on three continents in the sixth century BC. Coins were a physical embodiment of trust, a simple way of doing something astoundingly complex: creating an agreed value for a trade of goods with nothing but small metal discs. Manufacturers in Southern India could cut a deal over a shipment of silk. Cash created "globalization" two thousand years before the world had a word for it.

By the 1860s, there were over eight thousand separate currencies in operation in the United States alone. Different banks, railroads and retailers all had their own forms of money: bonds, exchange systems and numerous forms of credit. The National Bank Act of 1863 tried to end this fragmented chaos and unify the United States under one currency: the dollar.[3]

Now, that world of eight thousand currencies is returning. Mobile money, Bitcoin, digital vouchers, Apple Pay, Android Pay, iTunes, exchangeable shop credits, everything from overseas currency transfers to billion-dollar deals with the digital handshake of block chain. All of it is money.

But the death of cash is not simply part of the natural evolution of payment, making it ever more seamless and consumer-friendly. The death of cash, if it happens, will be the result of a prescient business deal between a small clutch of tech visionaries twenty years ago, who remain close associates and investors in one another's ventures. From the beginning, these deal makers saw the revolutionary potential of what they were doing: ceding control of money away from the banks and even governments and placing it instead in the hands of the new players—tech companies.

And this deal was formulated at the very moment that an experiment was being carried out proving something blindingly obvious to anyone who has ever used cash, but also an observable neurological process: paying with physical currency causes actual pain.

The Deal and the Experiment

When we pay with cash, our neural pathways light up like a Christmas tree. This is the flinch moment we experience when our hands are forced to part with money. In that instant, the brain is telling the hand to not let go. We are torn between wanting to buy an object we desire and avoiding the neural pain, and this creates the flinch.

Having cash in your hand is not, as we might assume, a license to spend irresponsibly. In fact, cash does the opposite: it stops us spending. So creating a payment system that eradicates cash removes the neural pain—the flinch moment—and encourages the brain to spend. Which is exactly what two men decided to do in 1998.

Max Levchin and Peter Thiel met in an empty lecture hall at Stanford University. The meeting was not by chance. "I basically went there," says Levchin, "to see this guy Peter Thiel, who was giving a free lecture about currency markets. I figured it would be a filled auditorium, but actually it turned out to be a lecture with six people. So it was fairly easy to make contact afterward. . . . I came up and said: 'Hi, I'm this guy Max. I've been in Silicon Valley for the last five days and I'm going to start a new company and how are you doing?'"[4]

Levchin was a wild, directionless ball of energy. He had run a few start-ups that had "sort of blown up in catastrophic ways where people started the company and it was sort of like marrying the first person one met at the slot machine in Las Vegas. You might hit the jackpot but chances were things would just blow up."

Thiel was different. Now one of the Silicon Valley's titans, Thiel is famous for his uncompromising vision of the future: one in which mortality is a thing of the past. Thiel believes acceptance of death is a sign of Western "complacency" and has invested significantly in immortality projects, including $100,000 in disinterring a woolly mammoth to see if it could be brought back to life. "Almost every human being who has ever lived is dead," he has said. "Solving this problem is the most . . . important thing we could possibly do."

It has also been reported that Thiel injects the blood of eighteen-year-old girls to keep himself looking young (he doesn't). In 1998, he was already legendary in Silicon Valley for a different reason. Thiel believed he was going to create the future, even though he wasn't yet quite sure how. Levchin wanted to get into business with him, because Thiel was one of the few people on the planet who shared his ambition to make anything happen.

Thiel grew up in a fundamentalist evangelical Christian household. He still describes himself as a Christian but does not, he says, feel compelled to "convince other people it is [true]." Even at an early age, Thiel showed a formidable strategic intellect. He was given a chessboard when he was just six years old. By 1979, aged twelve, he was ranked number seven in the US under-13 category.

But his childhood was disrupted. Because his father, Klaus,

worked as a chemical engineer in the mining industry, Thiel and his brother moved from continent to continent. Thiel attended numerous schools and, in South Africa, was sent to a strict boarding school where pupils were struck for the pettiest transgression of the rules. His unpleasant experience there instilled in him a deep hatred for what he considered to be mindless conformity.

At Stanford, Thiel studied philosophy, and after seeing French philosopher René Girard speak, became a follower of Girard's mimetic theory: the idea that imitation destroys genuine innovation. Only by stepping outside the mimetic prison of trying to be like other people, Girard argues, does one truly succeed. Be yourself, he advises, however strange that might appear to anyone else.

When Thiel heard Girard, everything clicked. Thiel founded the *Stanford Review* to challenge the politically correct orthodoxy that he believed was stifling debate on the campuses of America. It was a big success and made Thiel a prominent thinker on the libertarian New Right, though Thiel eschewed any label. He was already a force to be reckoned with, and he hadn't even gone into business yet.

When Levchin approached Thiel in that empty lecture theater in 1998, Thiel had the self-assured mimetic mindset to take over the world, but did not yet have the vehicle. Following Stanford, Thiel had worked as a derivatives trader at Credit Suisse and as a speech writer for US Secretary of Education William Bennett. But he wanted to strike out on his own.

In 1996, returning to Silicon Valley, he could see the dot-com bubble building and raised $1 million to set up Thiel Capital as a venture vehicle to get in on the boom. But it did not begin well. He plowed $100,000 into a web-based calendar project dreamed up by future business partner Luke Nosek. It failed.

Thiel needed to hit a home run. In 1998, when Thiel met Levchin, the internet was still new; no one had truly figured out how to monetize it yet. The holy grail in Silicon Valley was finding a secure online payment system.

The internet had in fact existed in one form of another for twenty years, and security had always been an issue. At first it was a closed system for the military and the computer experts they worked with. At 10:30 P.M. on October 29, 1969, the first message was sent from the UCLA computer lab by the Pentagon's Advanced Research Projects Agency to a networking pioneer named Leonard Kleinrock.

The Pentagon was using a so-called packet-switched network (small pieces of information, called "packets," sent over the closed network). The system was called ARPANET, the precursor to the internet. But there were concerns ARPANET was hackable. In 1973, an engineer named Robert Metcalfe noticed that a group of high school students had managed to gain access. Computer scientists Vinton Cerf and Robert Kahn were tasked with building encryption technology, which was launched in 1976 as TCP/IP (Transmission Control Protocol/Internet Protocol). This became the protocol for what would later become the internet, and was first successfully adopted by the Department of Defense in November 1981.

On January 1, 1983, so-called Flag Day, the internet was officially born when access to ARPANET, using TCP/IP, was expanded to include the National Science Foundation and Computer Science Network, with universities then added to the network.

As the network expanded, so too did fears that the existing security couldn't hold the traffic. In 1986, Congress passed the Computer Fraud and Abuse Act, establishing a clear legal framework for data theft, unauthorized network access and "computer crime."

The act didn't prevent the first virus in 1988—the so-called Morris worm—created by a Cornell graduate named Robert Tappan Morris, who with just a dozen lines of code was able to infect thousands of computers across the planet. According to the *Washington Post*, about 10 percent of the sixty thousand computers linked worldwide to the internet were affected.

The democratization of the internet for the public and away from exclusively military and academic use brought with it increased security fears. In 1993, Mosaic was launched, the first browser, allowing anyone to access the so-called World Wide Web, which had been revolutionized and propelled into a global network by Tim Berners-Lee. In November 1989, Berners-Lee made the first successful communication between a Hypertext Transfer Protocol (HTTP) client and server using the internet. The internet as we now know it had been created.

With the use of animation tools such as Macromedia's Flash in the late 1990s, the dynamic potential of the internet was transformed yet again, but with it came the ability of hackers to take control of computers remotely via the internet. In 1998, when Max Levchin and Peter Thiel meet, the opportunity to turn this all-singing, all-dancing internet into a huge global platform for commerce is irresistible. Silicon Valley is enthralled with the idea of cracking a secure encrypted payment system for online shopping.

Max Levchin was an encryption genius, but it was Thiel who knew finance. After Thiel finished his lecture, he and Levchin talked privately for less than ten minutes, but it was enough. They decided to start a business they later called Confinity. They realized they'd both spotted a gap: developing the software to make online payments possible. The following day, they met for breakfast, and got down to it.

"Max and I spent a lot of time brainstorming different ideas on different types of markets," Thiel explains. "We finally decided that we wanted to try something with encrypted money on PalmPilots. We thought this was going to be the future of the world."[5]

The truth was, that for all their ambition, Thiel and Levchin were just like all the thousands of other tech entrepreneurs standing in queues in various coffeehouses across California: prospectors sifting through pans in the great internet gold rush. But in PalmPilot, they saw something no one else saw: a proto-iPhone, and one that could be used for buying and selling.

Three thousand miles away, an experiment was being carried out by a Serbian neuropsychologist at MIT into what happens to the human brain when people pay money in different ways. Drazen Prelec was fascinated by the irrational behavior people demonstrate toward money: why do we buy lottery tickets and insurance at the same time? Prelec says that we accumulate random rules and ideas about money throughout our lives that then coexist irrationally in our heads, such as buying the cheapest brands at the supermarket, but insisting on getting a cab home because we do not like the bus. Or using cheap cosmetics, but having a monthly spa massage.

Prelec was curious how fiscal irrationality changed when we paid with cash versus credit. He asked five hundred students on the MIT campus to make sealed bids in a silent auction for a sold-out basketball match. Half were asked to use cash; and half, cards. Prelec had an instinct that the credit-card bids would be higher, but not to what degree: the credit-card bids were on average twice as large as the bids made with cash. Some were six times as high as the average cash bid.

Prelec was stunned. "That's got to be crazy, right? It suggests the psychological cost of spending a dollar on a credit card is only fifty cents." This is because credit cards give the pleasure of buying with none of the pain. "The moral tax gets blurred. When you're consuming, you're not thinking about the payments, and when you're paying, you don't know what you're paying for."

So the appeal of credit cards is clear, but Prelec wanted to know why we had such a problem paying with cash. Is this resistance to spending cash hardwired? So Prelec set up an MRI scan for the students who had bid with cash. What he found out next would change the future of money.

When we pay for something with cash, Prelec discovered, a specific neural pathway lights up. Prelec had discovered the "flinch moment," the nanosecond in which we feel measurable neural pain as the brain registers the hand parting with money. Those bidding with cards in the experiment had felt no such pain, only the pleasure of shopping. Cash, Prelec concluded, does not enable but actively hinders spending. By removing it, and making payment instantaneous, the brain has no time to register pain.

Peter Thiel and Max Levchin were working on cracking the holy grail of Silicon Valley: an encrypted payment system. But Prelec had discovered the real holy grail: pain-free shopping for the consumer. Deliver that and you owned the internet.

Stage Left: Enter Iron Man

In 2000, Levchin and Thiel's Confinity had an office just a few doors away from another entrepreneur: Elon Musk. Twenty years on, Musk has turned his attention to revolutionizing the world with electric cars and colonizing Mars. But in 2000, Musk was looking for the Big Idea, like Thiel and Levchin, and was sure there was something in delivering a new way of paying, just as they were.

Like Thiel, Musk had grown up in South Africa, and like Thiel, Musk forged a fiercely ambitious and antiauthoritarian spirit from childhood trauma. Musk had been the victim of horrific bullying in school, once having to be hospitalized after a beating left him unconscious.[6]

Musk had made modest money from his first venture, Zip2, and then began operating his next venture, X.com. But looking at these guys, just a few doors down from him, Musk could see they were all going to get further, faster, in Silicon Valley if they worked together. He proposed a merger with Thiel and Levchin's Confinity. They too could see the logic of joining forces with Musk. The race to create an online payment system was a race against everyone else in town. More to the point, money was tight, and pooling resources was a way to win. Separately, they'd all lose.

If they could crack secure encrypted payment together, Musk said, they held the keys to the kingdom of limitless spending. But to sell this to the consumer as a way of removing neural pain—in other words, to turn it from a clever but small Silicon Valley tech innovation that could be stolen by other clever, small Silicon Valley tech companies into a globally recognized brand that would take over the world—they needed to do something very important. Promise the consumer that payment would be instantaneous: "one click away."

Thiel brought in a bright Wall Streeter named Jack Selby. I meet Selby in the Thiel Corporation's offices in San Francisco, next door to those of George Lucas, decorated in mid-twentieth-century Scandinavian furniture and with rows of bookshelves filled with philosophy: Kierkegaard, Ayn Rand, Marx, and the collected works of Donald Trump. Jack swans in looking like the title character in *The Great Gatsby*, with slicked-back hair and smashed-up boating shoes. He has on monogrammed cuff links.

"You make it sound like it was all going to happen—a fait accompli," says Jack, "but these stories get made up. The truth was, it was touch and go [whether] we'd survive. It was tremendously risky. We had a burn-rate of over a million dollars a month."

Sorry, can you just say that again? And you were supposed to be in charge of the money?

Jack laughs. "Yes. It was kind of hairy."

The truth was that they weren't sure they'd have a roof over their heads at the end of the month, let alone create a multibillion-dollar business. The dot-com bubble had been building and building but it was going to burst. And this, Jack says, is where Thiel's brilliance really came into its own.

"Peter realized we needed to get into business before the whole dot-com bubble burst. When that popped, it cleared away the deadwood and Peter knew the guys left standing were going to be huge. We needed to make sure we were those guys." Thiel had a very simple observation to make about the potential market: a few people have PalmPilots but vastly more people have email addresses. Make this work and you have the world in your hand.

They called their new company PayPal and "one click away" was the promise. PayPal now had the key that would unlock the internet. I met Eric M. Jackson, hired as PayPal's vice head of marketing. "It was a very funny place. When you arrived, you were given this task, which was to literally build your own desk from scratch. It was like a test of your ingenuity."

But behind the quirky makeshift offices, something amazing was going on no one, least of all those at PayPal, could quite believe. "It was phenomenal," says Eric. "The growth went from a million dollars a week to a million dollars a day to a million dollars an hour, just like that."

PayPal's meteoric success put it on a collision course with two huge established money players: the banks and the regulators. Jack recalls the bafflement of the established money players at PayPal's arrival. "Were we a bank or a payment system? They didn't know. We didn't fit into any neat regulatory box, and because we were still relatively small compared to the banks, we were like this little speedboat that could dart around and run rings around them."

Thiel said PayPal wasn't a bank because it didn't engage in fractional-reserve banking. But the banks saw it as a threat, and, Jack says, they had ammunition. PayPal had been taken up enthusiastically by online gambling, and this allowed PayPal's enemies to tarnish its growing reputation as a trusted mainstream payment system with the taint that it was an illicit payment method with dubious connections.

It seems laughable today, but PayPal was feeling the heat as a fly-by-night purveyor of vice. Moreover, financial regulation is a minefield and PayPal had a problem because the financial laws differed hugely from state to state. What was okay in Arizona was not necessarily allowed in California. Because PayPal was not a bank, it was forced into state-by-state agreements not just across America but in Europe and its new territories across the world.

It was expanding at ferocious speed, and the problems were expanding with it. In short, it was a nightmare. Selby recalls one politician in particular who had it in for PayPal and made it his mission to try and make life difficult at every turn. And because PayPal did not have the muscle of the banks, it could be easily thwarted by someone with the right connections on Capitol Hill, which the PayPal Mafia, as they became known, didn't. Yet.

If that weren't enough, the company was losing millions of dollars a month to online fraud. Because it was still unclear what PayPal actually was, the FBI could not march in and treat it as straightforward bank or credit card fraud. It was a crime, but what kind? PayPal itself was forced to find risk management solutions to fraud: another huge drain on cash, as well as massively stressful.

If PayPal was to survive, let alone grow, it needed a big-time partner.

In 2002, PayPal cut a deal with eBay for $1.5 billion. "By today's standards, it was a paltry sum," Jack says. The deal was bittersweet. On the one hand, it secured PayPal's future and took it out of the regulatory hell it had been in by getting some muscle on board. But it also sold PayPal short. "You could have held on," I say to Selby. "You could have been Google if you'd only held your nerve." "People say that but they don't understand the pressures we were under. When you know those, you'll see that it was a pretty good deal."

The internet now had a marketplace with which to trade through PayPal, and PayPal was now accepted in over 70 percent of all eBay auctions. The PayPal founders were Silicon Valley legends. The PayPal Mafia had gone legit.

Back at MIT, I meet with Drazan Prelec, the guy who first discovered that paying with cash causes neural pain. What did he think this new faster, frictionless online payment meant in terms of our tendency to spend? "It was a giant social experiment, and like any social experiment it's hard to know what will happen." One thing looked clear: cash was heading for the exit and Drazan was far from convinced it was a good idea. Cash, he told me, is the one thing that firmly tethers us to spending within our means. "You want to know how out of kilter we are with our spending? Try using only cash for one week. Buy everything with it. Pay your mortgage with it. Look at a thousand dollars as a mountain of cash. You will never treat money the same way again."[7]

The Glamour of Spending

PayPal was revolutionary on many levels but one of the most interesting things to come from it was its cultural effect on payment. Today, people fall over themselves to use the latest app to pay with—the whizzy new app is almost a fashion accessory, like a handbag or pair of shoes. Speed is a given but when PayPal launched, speed was the selling point.

Speed and security made PayPal new but PayPal was not the first payment system to utilize speed, convenience and modernity as a selling point. In the 1950s, credit cards moved out of the exclusive domain of business and began being marketed to the general public. They were sold as giving greater speed and efficiency to a transaction than cash. Their true appeal lay in giving the illusion of wealth, magically conjuring whatever you desired—a new sofa, fur coat, car—but without a genie and a puff of smoke, merely the wave of a signature. In early ads for American Express, a card was taken coolly from the pocket of a suave businessman and flashed impressively like VIP ID to a breathless air stewardess. Credit cards turned failing middle managers into James Bond.

Concerns were soon raised at the highest levels of government. President Johnson's special assistant for consumer affairs, Betty Furness, believed the aspirational dream the credit card offered was a mirage. In 1967, she said pushing credit cards on a general public of "compulsive debtors" was as responsible as "giving sugar to diabetics."

But were members of the public "compulsive debtors"? The great myth of the masses and especially the poor is that they cannot manage money or budget and therefore demand new technologies that "help" make precarious lives more "manageable."

The truth is the opposite. The poor have a tighter rein on money than anyone else. But what we have all done from the advent of credit cards onward is become habituated to ever more debt. In 2016, the average American family owed $16,061 on credit cards.[8] Seventy percent of Americans own at least one card, but 50 percent have two and 10 percent more than three, with the average American family carrying $40,000 of debt.

When the economy boomed in the 1950s, debt was encouraged, but was tethered to paying it back. In the mid-1980s, credit cards replaced installment payments, and by the 1990s they were given out freely. Each time credit has become easier and faster, we have normalized ever-higher levels of debt. And every time the economy goes into recession (the early 1980s, the early 1990s, post-2007), credit cards take on a new role—enabling people to survive.

Credit cards are now a tool for subsistence, used to pay for heating, food shopping and the monthly mortgage. Debt is also the *modus operandi* for governments claiming "growth" by factoring credit-fueled consumer spending into GDP. Debt provides a politically expedient role, window-dressing a stagnating economy by faking a healthy balance sheet.[9]

Enter eBay: Turning the Web into a Machine for Selling

When PayPal connected with eBay in 2002, the aim was quite simple: to broaden the very idea of what the internet could do. Web 1.0 had been a static-page forum for the circulation of ideas within academia, the government and the military. By transforming into Web 2.0, the internet became a living thing, fed, cultivated and grown by every human on earth with a connection.

Beneath the grand promises that this new living internet would deliver "empowerment," "decentralization," "connectivity," even a new kind of "democracy," was the economic reality: the potential of Web 2.0 to make the internet a giant slot machine offering up nonstop purchasing opportunities.

With the union of PayPal and eBay, the first true behemoth of Web 2.0, the internet clicked. On a beach in Honolulu, eBay's reclusive founder Pierre Omidyar now whiles away his time funding the Honolulu Civil Beat, an online investigative journal. In 1998, at age thirty-one, Omidyar set up eBay. The apocryphal story is that it was a speculative punt trading Pez dispensers. The truth is that Omidyar had much more foresight than that. With eBay, he consciously re-created the bustling marketplace in which coins were first traded two thousand years ago. A space in which everything is up for barter and value is infinitely fluid and market-driven.

Now every tech platform is a marketplace: Google is a marketplace for information, Uber for cabs, Airbnb for space, Seamless for food. But the first of these big digital souks was eBay. An empty space to be filled with the detritus of Planet Earth: shoes, furniture, concert tickets, vacuum cleaners, holidays, sex, old cameras, spare human organs, an unwanted husband.

eBay is capitalism in its purest form: one giant peer-to-peer trade in which value is determined entirely by what someone is willing to pay: $1,209 for a Dorito shaped like the Pope's hat (bought by the same buyer as a grilled cheese sandwich with the face of the Virgin Mary); Kurt Cobain's chair; Britney Spears's chewing gum; $55,000 for a ghost in a jar; ad space on someone's forehead; and, perhaps most poignantly, the meaning of life, which was worth just $3.26.

eBay offered something that cash did not: the addictive thrill of the online auction. The endorphin rush of gambling. In comparison, cash was boring. Online shopping exploded in the early 2000s at the same time as online gambling, and both shared the binge quality of an addiction without constraints that could now be indulged privately behind closed curtains.

Online shopping opened up, according to political theorist Benjamin Barber, a "candy shop of instant gratification." It re-infantilized the adult consumer, turning us back into children who get whatever we demand without concern for the cost.[10]

And because the neural pain of cash is gone, we can shop without a psychological boundary. The parent figure is removed.

The New Currency

If I hand you a ten-pound note or a dollar bill, no third party is making money from that transaction. It is cash from one hand to another. But if I make the payment digitally, someone has to facilitate it. The space between you and me becomes a place where money can be made. This is the space the tech giants—Facebook, Apple, Google, Amazon and Microsoft—all want to own, and it is a race to own money itself, and thus redefine what it is.

The value in that space is not even the charge for the transaction—which is generally free, at least to the consumer—it is the data that can be mined. Data is the hidden price tag in any transaction we make. It is a price we are willing to pay, because we are not handing over our cash. What we hand over instead are numerous details of our lives: from the euphoric or mournful playlist chosen to suit our mood to a preference for Chinese over Indian food, whether you are straight, gay or Mormon, surf or knit, have attention deficit disorder, go on vacation to the Caribbean or Florida.

In 2016, data was used to hone the profiles of potential swing voters in the US presidential election. Critics describe such data mining by businesses as a privacy issue, but the public is less alarmed. As the *Harvard Business Review* pointed out in 2015: "Our research shows that consumers are aware that they're under surveillance . . . [but] consumers appreciate that data sharing can lead to products and services that makes their lives easier and more entertaining, educate them, and save them money."[11] We are, however, more concerned when data mining strays into the realm of our health.

In 2007 came the moment of crystallization: year zero for this new world. The banking system began to crash and the iPhone was launched. Subprime lending set explosives beneath the banks that had controlled the ebb and flow of money for centuries and were now about to implode like derelict tower blocks.

These financial institutions had ridden boom-and-bust cycles for over a century: through the Wall Street Crash, Glass-Steagall and regulation, Reagan and deregulation, the 1990s recession, the longest bull market in history and the hidden time bomb of subprime lending. They were momentarily vulnerable, and tech companies were poised to strike.

These giants call themselves "tech" companies, but tech is really just a stepping-stone to becoming integral and indispensable to the running of our everyday lives through the myriad applications of technology. And one of the obvious places to begin is in displacing the banks.

In 2008, the iPhone propelled shopping off the laptop and onto the phone—the first stage in moving control over money away from banks and toward tech companies. But first base was shopping, and for this, they had a new weapon: the app.

Initially, Steve Jobs did not get the app. It took a venture capitalist called John Doerr and the activities of a group of "jail-break" hackers getting into the phone to turn Jobs on to third-party apps and what they could truly do for the potential of the iPhone. Jobs had been a steadfast believer in web apps, but less than a year after the launch of the iPhone, at the special iPhone Roadmap Event, Steve Jobs announced an about-face. Developers could create native iPhone apps and sell them through something called the App Store.[12]

Third-party apps justified the Apple boss's claim that once in a while a technological advance comes along that "changes everything." They proved pivotal in propelling the iPhone from merely attaining phenomenal success to becoming the defining invention of our time.

Apple was first to plant its flag on a new moon: the space in the middle of a transaction. If you prized this space open, you would walk out onto an infinite plain of information—the data on one specific purchase connected by gossamer digital threads to millions of other purchases made by you, your family and everyone you know. And new purchases could be suggested via algorithm: the things you, your family and everyone you know might buy in the future. The race was on to own this space, and it was to be fiercely fought over.

In the summer of 2013, Apple embarked on a highly confidential new project with what would to prove to have significant ramifications for the way we pay. The tech giant may have wanted to own the future of money but knew the only way to get there was to partner with the big existing players. Apple approached the five major banks as well as American Express, Mastercard and Visa. The plan was to create wide and comprehensive support for Apple Pay from the infrastructure of these big established financial players.

At the time of the deal, Nathaniel Popper of the *New York Times* analyzed the rationale for both Apple and each of the players in wanting to cooperate. "For the banks and credit card networks, Apple Pay could threaten some revenue streams as the technology giant looks set to assume a more central role in the financial universe," he surmised. "But the eager participation of banks and credit card companies suggests both Apple's clout, and the recognition among financial institutions that they face broader challenges from upstart technology ventures, many of which are not as eager or willing as Apple to work with the incumbent financial industry."

This incumbent industry may have perceived Apple as a competitor in the long term but Apple could be an ally for now, and help shore up the industry against new tech innovations such as iZettle, the mobile contactless payment system launched in Sweden in 2010, or even Bitcoin.

In spite of the fact that Apple was partnering up with every big player in the financial industry to maximize the ubiquity and presence of Apple Pay on its launch, only those at the very top of each organization knew the full extent of the plan.

According to a *New York Times* account of what happened behind the scenes, "From the beginning, the project was top secret, with what one person involved called a 'code name frenzy.'"[13] In London, I asked one of the key people involved in the deal, James Anderson, vice-president of Master Card, what these code names were.

"I think our code words were superheroes or types of metal. I'll be Krypton, you can be Zygon, that type of thing." The *Times* described the level of secrecy involved at another key player, JPMorgan, which "set up a war room in a windowless conference room in San Francisco, where the most sensitive work was done. Only about 100 of the 300 JPMorgan employees working on the project knew that it was a partnership with Apple."

I asked James Anderson how difficult it was to maintain secrecy and coordinate the multiple participants with the single goal of launching Apple Pay. "It was really a huge logistic task.

Getting all the ships—the different organizations involved—to cross over the horizon at the same moment . . . it was very difficult."

According to the *Times* account, when launch day—September 9, 2014—arrived, a smoothly choreographed pincer movement was carried out by Apple and JPMorgan Chase on the West and East coasts simultaneously. As Apple's Chief Executive Tim Cook made his announcement in California, Marianne Lake (JPMorgan Chase's chief financial officer) addressed the media in New York. "When Apple's chief executive, Tim Cook . . . finally brought up Apple Pay in California . . . one of Ms. Lake's deputies in New York took a green apple out of her bag and put it on the table on the stage, signaling that Ms. Lake was free to discuss the service."

I asked James Anderson, who was there, about the apple-on-the-desk story and he smiled. "Huh! I didn't know that." No one told him.

This was not "disruption." This was an earthquake, shaking the businesses that had run money for a century to the core. James said the Chase Apple Pay deal did not entirely "respect and honor the payment networks." Even though James had been one of the key players involved, clearly the deal didn't suit Mastercard. Apple had been at the hub of the deal with numerous other big financial companies, and everyone else, even the most senior figures involved, got only what Apple decided they would.

I ask James about this and he smiles, as if that's an end to it. But I persist. "Apple, and not just Apple but the other big tech companies," I say, "have reached an accommodation with banks and credit card companies because they need you for now, but ultimately they don't."

James sips his water. "I think the future is the future, who can say what it will bring but I still think the banks and card companies will continue to have a central role."

There is an awkward silence.

"I think you know far more than you're telling me, James."

"I couldn't tell you everything, Jacques. That wouldn't be ethical."

The Apple Pay deal was an accommodation with the banks and credit cards but the reality was Apple and Chase had parked their tanks in the middle of the prime real estate of America's oldest financial institutions, and those companies could do nothing about it.

More important, Apple was going to give away its service for free. The space in the middle of a transaction where the money was was no longer where the money was. Apple was gaining a leg up on its competitors by deliberately vacating it. Why? Unlike Google or Amazon or Facebook, Apple is not bothered about your data. It is interested in you using Apple products and transacting on multiple Apple devices. For the companies that bother about your data, however, it's all about the data. As the *Financial Times*'s Izabella Kaminska puts it, "data is the new oil and data on spending is the best grade oil there is."

In 2012, an angry man marched into a Minneapolis branch of superstore chain Target demanding to know why the superstore was sending his teenage daughter maternity shopping suggestions. "My daughter is still in high school," he said, "and you're sending her coupons for baby clothes and cribs." Target statistician Andrew Pole had identified twenty-five products that when purchased or searched together indicate a woman is likely to be pregnant. The shopping data culled meant Target had known the man's daughter was pregnant before he did.

The data is everything when it comes to targeting a consumer precisely. And to find out how this convergence of spending and spending data could be brought together seamlessly into a single whole, one tech giant has been looking to a surprising place for inspiration.

Africa, Not Silicon Valley, Is Where It Is Truly At

In December 2016, Facebook CEO Mark Zuckerberg's jet touched down in Kenya. Zuckerberg was interested in the fact that culling data from spending patterns, rather than charging to facilitate a transaction, was the future. But also that the plains of central Africa, not Silicon Valley or Wall Street, might hold the key to winning ahead of Facebook's rivals.

In 2007, M-Pesa, a mobile money system allowing Kenyans to transfer money directly from one phone to another, was launched across the country. Not through an app or a complex encrypted payment system, but by text.

M-Pesa was a revolutionary exercise in the democratization of money, using an entire nation as the laboratory. It not only cut out transfer fees, but made banks—as well as cash—extinct. It did not require an iPhone or a bank account, just a twenty-year-old Nokia. Within a year of its launch, M-Pesa had 17 million users in Kenya, 40 percent of the population. By 2010, more people used M-Pesa than had a bank account. It proved that Kenyans did not need one.

I visited Twiga Foods, the same banana-storage depot outside Nairobi that Zuckerberg had visited months earlier. Twiga has used M-Pesa to become one of the fastest growing companies in Kenya, and Zuckerberg wanted to find out how. He met with Edna Kwinga, head of human resources, and Kikonde Mwatwela, the COO.

"We didn't even know we were meeting Zuckerberg until ten minutes before he came in," Edna told me. "We were told it was the regional head of Facebook, and then in walks Mark Zuckerberg." What did he want to know? "He was very interested in how we'd used M-Pesa to grow. He was very nice. He'd been in West Africa the previous day and was off to South Africa in the evening."

Mwatwela is under no illusions that the big tech companies are muscling in on M-Pesa's innovation and sensing an amazing opportunity. "Silicon Valley often looks up to the top of the pyramid to see where money can be made, but Zuckerberg is incredibly clever." Zuckerberg is facing the other way and seeing that it's at the bottom of the economic pyramid that far more money is to be made.

Twiga pays everyone through M-Pesa. On a banana plantation near Mount Kenya, farmers pay their employees not with cash, but through their mobiles. People who do not have a mobile get a lesson from the boss in how to use one. Did he foresee a time when he wouldn't use cash? I asked him. "What? We don't use cash now. No one does. It's heavy and difficult to transport, it's unsafe, you can be robbed, you can be extorted. That is gone. I might use cash to buy a tea."

M-Pesa has allowed Kenya to leapfrog the standard twentieth-century stages of development: infrastructure and banks. Once you needed a bank account to get a business, but not anymore. M-Pesa loans money as well.[14] The company has genuinely disrupted money, and has done it with the most basic technology available.

M-Pesa is the creation of Vodafone, one of the biggest mobile networks on the planet. Vodafone had developed M-Pesa after, bizarrely, winning a tender competition with the British government's overseas development ministry to create an inclusive and secure payment system for the poor of Kenya, part of the UK government's development remit. Nick Hughes was the Vodafone executive in charge. "Inclusion was a sexy issue then, and we got a million pounds to develop it, which would have been harder for me to raise within Vodafone for such a speculative project. We began by almost overdesigning it to start with and then realized it needed to be simpler. Something that could just be used on a fifteen-dollar phone."

M-Pesa was as simple as texting. It took off like wildfire and basically created a new currency running through the Kenyan economy—the Vodafone unit. Izabella Kaminska says Vodafone was able to monopolize money across an entire country because the banks in Kenya were "asleep at the wheel." They were complacent and M-Pesa had staged a financial coup.

But Zuckerberg can take it to the next level, opening up the poor half of the planet to a money revolution by folding an M-Pesa–style payment into Facebook. And if it has worked in Kenya, it could work across the world. It's easy to envision M-Pesa as a gateway to digital consumerism, offering everything a bank does: big loans as well as small ones and everything else on the side: food, cars and holidays, even alcohol and online gambling. A one-stop shop.

But the money transfers using text M-Pesa pioneered also garner as much information about someone as their online shopping footprint. In 2016, a group of Kenyan police officers were arrested for making huge M-Pesa money transfers. They were not using Bitcoin as drug cartels do, or banks to launder cash, they were using text. Zuckerberg realized that M-Pesa offered micro–data surveillance on transactions in much the same way Facebook can, but it could also potentially access billions of people that Facebook presently cannot.

When digital money arrived in 2000, the likeliest scenario seemed to be the cementing of global inequality. The wealthy half of the planet would use digital and mobile money, while the poor would continue with cash. In fact, M-Pesa proved the complete opposite.

Is Cash as Irrelevant as We Are Told?

The subtext—and in many cases the text—of the drive to kill cash is the eradication of the black economy. Kenneth Rogoff, former chief economist at the International Monetary Fund, says the global end of cash is both an inevitability and a good thing.

We met in his office at Harvard, where Ken showed me the extraordinary mountain range of a graph detailing the boom and bust cycles of Western capitalism for the last two hundred years. The tax revenue generated, coupled with the devastation of the black economy—an economy fueled by cash—would make a cashless world the greatest leap forward in fiscal management since the end of fixed exchange rates. It would also provide, he said, far more effective immigration controls than building walls. But something perplexing is going on, said Ken. He demonstrated with his hands, crossing in midair. "As governments attempt to decrease the availability of cash and phase it out, there has never been more cash in circulation. People just keep using it, and it's not apparent why or for what."

The black economy—the cash, or "shadow," economy—is

really a euphemism for the livelihoods of the poor. Economists Ceyhun Elgin and Oguz Oztunali, using a data set for 161 countries between 1950 and 2009, estimated the shadow economy to account for over 22 percent of the world's GDP.[15]

Nearly a quarter of the planet's entire wealth is cash in hand. Criminals use the shadow economy, but so does someone cleaning an office, working on a building site or keeping a business afloat waiting to be paid. I asked Rogoff how likely it is law-abiding people, as opposed to criminals, will stop using cash. He shrugged. "Cash isn't going to disappear as quickly as anyone might want it to, and I'm not saying it should. It serves a purpose for sure."

In 2016, the Indian government suddenly and unexpectedly withdrew 500- and 1,000- rupee notes (the rough equivalent of a $7 and $15 note) from circulation. Its explicit aim was to cut the legs away from the huge Indian shadow economy, but the results were disastrous. Cash shortages lasted for weeks: twenty-five people collapsed and died after queueing for hours outside banks. The legitimate economy suffered a stock market crash, there was an agricultural crisis and trucking stopped. The black economy, the intended target, remained untouched.

Block Chain—the Nuclear Key

In April 2014, the Secure Sockets Layer—or SSL—encryption protocol providing watertight security for millions of online transactions carried out every second, and used by millions of businesses across the globe, was hacked. SSL was generally regarded by security experts to be the most secure payment system yet devised.

So how does it work? SSL is a new generation of "block chain" payment. Block chain was originally developed as a way of allowing huge corporations to do billion-dollar deals securely. It now works for everyday transactions carried out by you and me, and is based on the principle of the nuclear key.

In a nuclear submarine, with missile capability to destroy an entire continent, control does not lie with one person but with a number of individuals, each of whom has a separate key. These keys need to be inserted in the control panel in the right order and at the right time for the missile to go off. The crew does not know who has the keys, and thus there is theoretically no way of overriding the system.

With a financial transaction carried out using block chain, computers take the role of crew members. Each algorithm is primed to play its role inserting a password at the correct moment. No one party can override the system. It is an interlocking process with layer upon layer of security. It appears impregnable. Block chain is so trusted that the Pentagon is researching the use of it to encrypt nuclear weapons.[16]

Yet in 2014, SSL was hacked. Millions of people all over the world were told to change their passwords—the first nuclear key. After millions of passwords were changed, Walmart in America and the Chinese restaurant chain PF Chang both reported a further security breach. The very act of changing passwords had made the system easier, not more difficult to hack.

In 2015, a year later, the entire TalkTalk mobile network went down, because a teenager in a bedroom in Northern Ireland figured out the company's key passwords. The hack destroyed TalkTalk's credibility, resulting in thousands of customers leaving and the stock value of the company collapsing. When PayPal launched itself as a secure online payment system, the promise of security was integral. But twenty years on, the inherent fragility of this security is now a given.

When coins were first created two thousand years ago, their value was dependent on mutual trust between the two parties involved in the transaction: the buyer and seller. Today, that trust is one way. Yet this is not to underestimate the efforts being made to stay one step ahead of the criminals.

A parallel can be drawn with terrorism: for every large-scale cyberattack or fraud event you hear about, there are hundreds of thwarted attempts that you do not. On this basis, the battle with fraud could be argued as well fought; the write-off, simply the unavoidable collateral.

The Empty Bank Vault

In Sweden, where cash is set to disappear in the next five years, a debate rages over the merits of its extinction, a debate no other country is openly having.

In 2016, cash made up less than 2 percent of all payments in Sweden. Cards are the main payment method: an average of 207 swipes per person per year, three times more than in any other European country. And mobile phone apps, primarily Swish, developed by the country's four biggest banks, are fast taking over from cards.

Nine hundred of Sweden's 1,600 banks do not even keep cash on hand, or take cash deposits. In April 2013, a bank robber found this out the hard way. At 10:32 A.M. on a Monday morning, CCTV footage picked up what police described as "a single culprit, male, entering a bank in Öster malmstorg, central Stockholm, with a gun-like object." After demanding the staff open the safe, a woman behind a screen informed the robber that the bank held no cash. The vaults were empty. CCTV footage captures the moment the robber exits the bank less than two minutes after going in, penniless.

In 2012, there were only twenty-one bank robberies in Sweden, half the number reported in 2011, and the lowest total ever recorded.[17] Yet as physical bank robberies become all but extinct, online fraud in Sweden is at a record high.

Björn Eriksson, former president of Interpol, now runs Cash Uprising—a pressure group lobbying to keep cash flowing to stop fraud. However bad the banks and credit card companies have been with fraud, Eriksson believes, they will prove to be paragons of vigilance when cybercrime begins being perpetrated on the thousands of new tech payment options coming online that don't have the protection machinery of a Mastercard or Visa. Eriksson knows of what he speaks; he previously ran the biggest anti-fraud police force in Europe.

The cash divide is also generational. The older generation trusts cash and the young trust digital money. "Cash-free" businesses like coffee shops across Sweden are run by young entrepreneurs who use a sole trader app called iZettle.

The watershed for this divide between the young and the old in Sweden is the banking crash of 2008. The old remember a time before the crash when the banks could be relied upon. The young have a vague memory of the banking crisis and how it torpedoed the banks. They are happy to put their trust in contactless and digital money because that's how they run every other aspect of their lives: using social media and technology to organize everything. To them, cash looks medieval.

The risks managed by banks in 2007 were a spread bet, but one breached block chain is enough to wipe digital money off the face of the earth with the single press of a button. We could live without a Lehman Brothers, but we cannot live without Apple, Google and Facebook, because they are the infrastructure.

The Contagion

A decade ago, as the digital revolution got under way, a mountain was drilled through in order to produce a high-speed internet connection that increased the speed of transactions on Wall Street by one-thousandth of a second. This extra thousandth of a second translates to a billion extra dollars transacting through Wall Street every hour. But as speed becomes the God of new money, the dangers of an entirely digital economy being wiped out because a rogue algorithm decides to sell instead of buy, now falls beyond human control. It is simply too fast for a human to keep up.

I went to Pret A Manger for a sandwich the other day. The card machines had mysteriously stopped working and the cashiers were taking only cash. Staff politely asked customers to take money out from the ATM machine next door, but no one did. Instead, people preferred to wait for the card readers to come back online. Staff said it could take up to half an hour— but customers had habituated to a new way of paying.

My Pret experience showed perfectly the irrational behavior we demonstrate to paying cash that Drazan Prelec discovered at MIT.

When and if cash finally disappears for good, it will have been the result of a meeting in an empty lecture hall twenty years ago between two men—Peter Thiel and Max Levchin—

who wanted to erase the pain of payment by revolutionizing money, and succeeded. It was a bold, almost an insane idea—to attempt to replace traditional banking with digital cash transactions. But today it is so commonplace we don't even think about it.

Yet the freedom afforded to us by greater convenience and speed has been mitigated, Prelec says, by a paradoxical loss of freedom. "In medieval times, we all carried around with us a small bag of coins. Today that bag of coins is in our phones but we don't see the coins." We no longer have sovereignty over the sovereigns we have earned. Is that a bad or a good thing? Well, it's a thing—and the test will come not when everything is normal and we're waltzing around a department store phone in hand looking for a present for our husband or wife, but when that phone screen suddenly goes black, and stays black, and no one—least of all the phone network—knows why.

5

WORK
From What We Do to Who We Are

THE DEAL: McKinsey and the 7S Framework deal with Siemens and PepsiCo

AIM: To create an entirely new system of organizing companies and incentivizing employees, devised by McKinsey analysts Tom Peters and Robert Waterman

WHERE: Siemens headquarters, Munich, and PepsiCo global headquarters, Purchase, New York

WHEN: November 1979

Every night, approximately one in ten of us will wake to check our email. Once we've woken properly in the morning, half of us spend more time checking work email than eating breakfast. It's hardly any surprise therefore that throughout the day, seven out of ten of us check our mail every hour, and one in ten every ten minutes.[1] The fact we are not even surprised by these statistics is proof in itself of the degree to which we have embedded work into our lives.

The line between work and personal time has eroded. And according to Professor Adam Alter of New York University's Stern School of Business and author of *Irresistible: The Rise of*

Addictive Technology and the Business of Keeping Us Hooked,
our fixation with remaining wired to work, whether checking email on weekends, on vacation or during our kid's sports
day, has the paradoxical effect of making us less productive.
Interviewed by *Business Insider,* Alter explained that "we check
our emails six seconds after they arrive, which is a staggering
number."

And it's staggering because the email discombobulates our
brains and defocuses us from the task we were carrying out
prior to the ping in the inbox. "It's going to take you twenty-
five minutes to get back into that state of productivity you were
in before you checked your email," he says.[2]

Interrupting valuable sleep with work can have long-term
repercussions for our health. The blue glow that phones emit
wreaks havoc with melanin, the sleep hormone, tricking our
brain into thinking it is day. Scrolling through a phone and
checking email in bed creates "active" shallow sleep by reac-
tivating the working memory. Technology puts the brain in a
state of borderline anxiety, prepped to wake at any moment.
This means we never truly switch off when asleep. Three-
quarters of all adults are now failing to get adequate rest at
night, so we are exhausted when we wake. Consistent lack of
sleep could also have more serious consequences: higher blood
pressure, increased risk of heart disease and diabetes, anxiety,
depression, even a drop in fertility.

Work is a key ingredient of well-being. Roman philosopher Seneca listed work, home and love as the three elements
that constitute a basis for happiness. We need, Seneca said,
to have at least two in place for a modicum of happiness to
be achieved. But for many people, work is connected to all
three of these aspects. It provides money to live and creates a

home away from home, where we may spend more time with our coworkers than with our real family. And work can provide fulfillment and a sense of purpose. In preindustrial times, people were defined by where they came from; today, they are defined by what they do.

So how did work come to define us?

The Invention of Efficiency

In 1888, a jeweler in Auburn, New York, named Willard Legrand Bundy invented a time clock. The Bundy clock did not simply tell the time, it allowed employees to punch in the exact times they arrived at and left work, "clocking" in and out.

Unlike previous time clocks, the Bundy time recorder had individual keys for each employee, so no one could cheat the system by getting one person to mass-punch a bunch of cards. But to understand the need for such a thing, why Bundy—a jeweler, not a visionary—was merely filling a niche that employers sought, we have to go back a decade earlier to Frederick Winslow Taylor.

In 1878, Taylor, a law student accepted at Harvard and from a wealthy family, left school to become a machinist at the Midvale Steel Works in Philadelphia. Thanks to his eagerness (and his family connections to the owners), Taylor rose quickly from machinist to middle manager. Then, one day, Taylor approached his bosses with a plan.[3]

He had noticed that his colleagues were not working as hard as they might. In order to maximize efficiency, Taylor suggested a "scientific evaluation" of their work rates with a view to identifying the slackers. Over the next six months, Taylor was a blur of activity, racing around the steelworks with a clipboard, frantically making notes and using a stopwatch to measure the productivity of the workers. The Midvale management was impressed with Taylor's findings: he supplied "time studies" (later to become "time and motion studies"), exact calculations for the optimal length of shifts and breaks; he even analyzed the most efficient way to use a shovel. Taylor had a forensically detailed breakdown of every task of the labor force, including an efficiency evaluation of toilet breaks. There was only one problem. Taylor had falsified his data. He had worked late into the night drawing up charts to give "scientific" credence to his findings.[4]

Taylor is now widely credited with inventing "scientific management." But at the Midvale Steel Works, he had already applied the first rule of management consultancy: tell the client what they want to hear. Taylor knew that Midvale was keen on making cost efficiencies, which is why they hired him. After months of "scientific" evaluation, Taylor gave them the efficiencies they were looking for. If he'd come to conclusions at odds with their aims, would he have been listened to? Would we still be talking about Taylor today?

Taylor's real talent lay in using science to justify a plan already being implemented. But this was crucially important: by claiming the conclusions reached were scientific, the management had evidence that the workers could not dispute. Management could blame the expert, who could in turn point to the science. In this way, decisions appeared to cease being made by humans at all, but by an objective, God-like arbiter called data.

In spite of Taylor's falsification of data, he is still widely considered to have created the founding stone for scientific management. His revolutionary approach was to find patterns in seemingly random and disparate forms of work and put them under an umbrella "system." This was a completely new and transformative way of looking at work—and highly seductive to businesses looking to run more efficiently.

Following his triumph at the Midvale Steel Works, Taylor was hailed a genius and became the world's first management guru, thanks in part to his friendship with prominent Boston lawyer Louis Brandeis. Taylor's book, *The Principles of Scientific Management*,[5] became a bestseller, and in 1911, he toured America to packed houses explaining his science of efficiency and how it would change the world.

The public lapped it up eagerly. Science appeared to be able to solve anything. In 1886, Charles Darwin had used science to explain evolution; Freud had used it to decipher the subconscious mind. Taylor followed in their footsteps.[6] American industry was soon lining up at Taylor's door: coal, banking and the railroads all sought his expertise. He became a multimillionaire and one of America's richest men.

In 1913, he was invited to brief the government on how to implement his ideas for the benefit of America. But in 1908, when President Theodore Roosevelt said in his address to the first Conference of Governors at the White House that "the conservation of our natural resources is only preliminary to the larger question of national efficiency," he was already channeling Taylor.[7] A consultancy deal with the government would have cemented Taylor's place at the heart of power and pocketed him a further fortune. But in 1915, Taylor died suddenly. He never got to see his grand "science of management" take over the world. But that is what it did.

Peter Drucker: The Caring Corporation

In the 1950s, Peter Drucker, an Austrian sociologist, moved to the United States to reinvent himself as a management consultant. Drucker wanted to change the mentality of the huge corporation. Since the nineteenth century, companies had largely followed a model designed by sociologist Max Weber, who conceived of the corporation as something akin to the Prussian army: disciplined and hierarchical, with a CEO behaving like a general.[8]

Drucker believed a new kind of boss was needed, that productivity would be better harnessed by a kinder, more paternalistic leader, a father figure who would look after your long-term career interests, and with whom you would play golf on Saturdays to gain advantage over your colleagues.

This was the world of work my dad stepped into in the late 1950s. His father—my grandfather—was a Corsican immigrant who came to London in the 1930s looking for casual work. He played the cello and so began performing in café orchestras. Employed by a different café every night, my grandfather was paid cash in hand, but did not know from one night to the next if he had a job the following day. His life, and thus the life of his family, was balanced on a knife edge.

By the time my dad entered the workforce in the 1950s, the world of work had changed. Unlike his father, he could get a full-time job. He had the same state employer, the Greater London Council, for thirty years. Unlike his father, my dad got a guaranteed paycheck at the end of the month. He did not need to go out and hawk for coins with a cello. A career structure was mapped out before him, with a pension at the end of it.

But this security was a management construct, as the scientific efficiency of Taylor had been. The "caring company" did not mean the company was any less focused on attaining its monetary target. These could be better achieved by being paternalistic. Drucker advocated a new "science" of the workplace—one in which the manager was still God, but psychological coercion rather than the stick of efficiency was the way to get results.

Using Drucker's theories on psychological coercion, corporations would write to the wives of male employees, saying that Stanley would not be getting his bonus this year because Stanley had not worked hard enough: no bonus, no new fur coat for you. In this controlled environment, Drucker envisioned that wives could become secret agents of the company. Drucker reasoned that the husband was far more likely to do what his wife said than what his boss demanded.

This paternalistic company was not so nurturing after all. It was a total system: an all-seeing eye, determining not only what happened at work, but using the family to push work too. The company had seeped its way into the fabric of domestic life, keeping up the pressure when Stanley's wife poured him a drink at the end of the day and questioned why she had got that critical letter from his boss.

But then something happened that blew the world of Drucker away and brought efficiency into sharp focus. In 1973, the OPEC oil crisis plunged the world into global recession. Suddenly, companies sought profit not by finding new business, but by making internal cuts. The postwar boom, which had delivered a historical blip of stability and prosperity for millions, was over. The world of precariousness that my granddad had lived in was about to make a dramatic return, swallowing up my dad's job and defining the working world into which I would step.

The catalyst was swift. One morning in 1980, my dad arrived at work. A group of men he had never seen before, wearing what he described as "Willoughby suits," had taken over a floor and were walking around each department with notepads, asking people what they did. Three months later, the layoffs began.

These Willoughby-suited men were "management consultants" and were about to streamline the working world with a new "science" of efficiency every bit as persuasive as Frederick Winslow Taylor's. Their gurus were two men, Tom Peters and Robert Waterman, both rising stars at the world's most elusive and powerful management consulting agency, McKinsey & Company. On that day in 1980 when my dad went into the office, he didn't know that these men with notepads were following a brand-new business model developed by Peters and Waterman.

It was called the 7S Framework, and it was a remarkable piece of work. Peters and Waterman said the successful business model of the future would not be a rigid, hierarchical management pyramid, but would resemble a complex molecule.[9] The molecular business would have "seven interlocking elements, all of which need to be in perfect alignment," like stars in a constellation. These key elements all began with the letter *s*: "strategy, skills, structure, systems, style, staff, and the nucleus, superordinate goals (or shared values)." The boss would "walk around"—micromanaging and generally nosing about. In fact, this would be called MBWA (Management by Walking Around).[10]

This soft-carpeted panopticon was nothing new—Drucker's

corporation micro-monitored the employee—but Peters and Waterman's approach was about changing the employee's mindset. The new world, they said, was turbulent and employees were either productive or they were out.

Peters and Waterman: The 7S System and the Search for Excellence

For inspiration, McKinsey looked to Japan, where employees knelt on the floor of the canteen each morning and prayed that Hyundai or Toshiba be more profitable. The Japanese cult of work was extreme: employees regularly died at their desks from exhaustion. It was so commonplace, the Japanese even developed a word for it: *karoshi*. Outside Tokyo is a "suicide forest," where stressed workers go to hang themselves.

In the late 1970s, Japan was an economic miracle and the world was keen to learn its lessons. Peters and Waterman were as awed as everyone else, keen to mimic its formula for success. They knew the totality of Japanese work culture would not translate to the West, but wondered whether it was possible to incorporate pieces of it.

Employees in the West had an entirely different mindset than the Japanese. The Western sense of self-worth had been shaped not by subsuming one's identity into the company or the nation, but by Locke, Descartes and the Enlightenment. Individualism is as deeply embedded in the Western psyche as dutiful collectivism is in Japan. But Peters and Waterman had a plan. Instead of selling a cult, they would sell devotion to work as "creative" and "fulfilling." If the employee felt fulfilled by their job, they would be more likely to buy into the ethos of the company. The culture would naturally evolve without any top-down edict.

The first thing to do was to get rid of the idea of work as a nine-to-five drudge. Work needed to become "rewarding." The goal of work would cease to be waiting for five o'clock to come around so you could go home, but the completion of the task. People in the office needed to stop seeing themselves as mere employees and start acting as autonomous, self-motivated mini-bosses. They needed to become freelance in their heads, while still adhering to the culture of the company.

The aim of Peters and Waterman's new management approach was to create a "fun" faux-home environment in the office. This translated into open floor plans, and comfy, communal seating areas, which replaced hard, regimented rows of desks. By blurring the boundary between home and work, and making the work environment more pleasant, employees would be more inclined to work longer hours.

Today, most successful big brands have a cult of loyalty. I recently visited one of the world's fastest growing drinks companies. Its offices are self-consciously quirky, with bright fake-grass flooring, faux white picket fences and country-style signs directing you to corporate boardrooms. Every Monday morning, there is a team-building event designed to motivate staff for the week ahead with crazy games and prize giving. This company has cleverly incorporated elements of loyalty. It has a big red switch on the wall reminding employees to "switch off" and an arrow pointing "HOME" to encourage that the work/life balance be maintained. But not all companies get this balance right.

In London, I was waiting to go into the cinema recently when I heard screams and shouts of exaltation coming from one of the large adjacent conference halls, rented out for corporate events. I sneaked a peep around the door. A major coffee brand was hosting its annual employee-of-the-year event. Baristas from across Britain had come to London to share for a day what their jobs meant to them.

I watched in awe as men and women in identical purple uniforms bounded up to the stage and took to the mike stand. "Hi, I'm Mario from Italy." (Applause.) "I just wanted to say I have been working with my team for two years now, and you guys are my life!" (Whoops and hollers.) Hanging above Mario was a giant coffee-cup logo, brimming with exultant froth.

And the bigger the brand, the bigger the cult of loyalty, and secrecy. A food industry analyst I spoke to said that whenever he attends industry conventions, one group stands aloof from everyone else—"the McDonald's guys"—as if they know something no one else does.

In San Francisco, locals often see the "Google Bus" on a night out. Google employees from the "campus" at Mountain View are driven into the city and eat at restaurants or go to the cinema en masse (agreed to days before in a round of emails). Google employees believe in Google not as just any other company, but as the only company that matters.

Ask anyone with a serious stake in climbing the corporate ladder at these companies how critical they are of the company, and they will wince. Disdain and nonconformity are *verboten*. Criticism can be a useful tool of self-promotion, however— companies with a cult identity "welcome" criticism from followers, because constant "reevaluation of goals and aims" is part of today's corporate lingua franca. Just as long as the criticism is "constructive."

And now, technology makes it possible to create an environment of corporate unity that once would have been scarcely imaginable.

I am in Boston outside the office of the world's most advanced work surveillance system, waiting to be buzzed in. In the lobby, I meet Greg and Tony. I already notice something strange about them: they are both wearing small white boxes dangling from their necks emitting an intermittent flashing light. Greg explains that they are "socio-metric badges." Every employee in the company wears one from the moment they arrive at work till the moment they go home.

These are the offices of Humanyze, with the most advanced form of workplace surveillance anywhere on the planet. Humanyze is taking micro-tracking of the employee to the next level by amassing and then analyzing every single second of their day. It is Frederick Winslow Taylor's dream of total monitored efficiency of the worker come true over a century after he proposed it.

The small white boxes Humayze has created to capture data that hang around Greg and Tony's necks record everything they do every second of the day: who they talk to and for how long, whether these meetings are formal or informal "collisions"; how long they spend walking as opposed to sitting, on the phone or online, collaborating with colleagues in meetings or in isolation in a glass box. The badge can also detect subtle dynamics between colleagues. It registers speech patterns and assesses how dominant or passive the conversants are, as well as who in a group is controlling the agenda. In short, it creates a total digital data map of workplace character productivity.

Greg and Tony show me what happens once Humanyze, which is reported to have contracts with Deloitte and Barclays, has collected all this data on its employees. I sit in a glass room with a huge screen, on which various molecular structures appear and begin morphing into one another.

"These are algorithms that have crunched down on the group dynamic of the team. So what you are seeing is the group interactions and channels of communication, and how well they work." In March, the team was stoked because their San Francisco colleagues were in town, so there was a great deal of high energy "symbiosis" between the two offices of Humanyze. But then something went wrong in April: I can see the molecular structures suddenly drag apart. Greg and Tony frown at a single orange blob connecting two rather forlorn-looking groups of molecules. "That's a bottleneck," Greg says. "We know who it is," Tony adds. Because of privacy concerns, the data is farmed anonymously. Management is not told to whom specific data connects, but by looking at the patterns, they can generally work it out.

The data, Greg says, reveals unexpected patterns in productivity: who is and isn't pulling their weight, or doing their job properly. It has the potential to empower employees who feel they are discriminated against, because the data, at least in theory, represents a level playing field. Those in power in management who could previously rig the system of assessment to hide their own shortcomings and blame subordinate colleagues are as under the microscope as everyone else. There's no hiding place.

The primary interface for employees working with Humanyze is the "personal dashboard," where employees can access their own data to see how they can improve. This makes Humanyze the realization, not of the crude work panopticon, but of the Peters and Waterman managerial dream of the self-motivated worker self-policing their own productivity through a personal data "dashboard" and driving on to be ever more efficient.

"The Confession Is That I Didn't Go Far Enough"

Frederick Winslow Taylor could never have imagined such technology when he first drew up his efficiency tables at the Midvale Steel Works over a century before. Ironically, the two men who were to push his idea of efficiency to the next level in the late 1970s—Peters and Waterman—saw their new brand of work efficiency as an antidote to Taylorism.

In November 1979, Peters and Waterman flew to Munich, Germany, for a seven-hundred-slide presentation of their 7S molecular system to the technology giant Siemens. The Germans were impressed, and word of Peters and Waterman's new theory of work spread fast. Pepsi's chief, Andy Pearson, and his coexecutives at PepsiCo's global headquarters in Purchase, New York, asked to meet Peters and Waterman, to see how 7S could transform their empire too.

Both Siemens and PepsiCo were bowled over by Peters and Waterman's 7S vision. They did a deal to adopt McKinsey's system. It meant not just using McKinsey's management ideas and partnering with McKinsey in the long-term strategic planning for the company but taking the philosophy of 7S to heart. To this day the 7S framework is used as a template for the organizational structure and business strategy of both Siemens and PepsiCo. McKinsey's 7S model is used by hundreds of companies in different industries across the world, from Starbucks and Samsung to the State Bank of India. And the reasons are not hard to fathom.

Peters and Waterman said simply that big corporate structures were too rigid to handle innovation. "Structure," they said, "is not organization." In June 1980, Peters wrote an op-ed article in the *Wall Street Journal* called "The Planning Fetish." In it, he dismissed the entire idea of "strategy" as inherently flawed. By the time a company comes up with a strategy and this plan chugs laboriously through the cogs of an organization, it's out of date. 7S inferred greater autonomy for individuals, who could navigate as individuals around the ocean of a company far faster than the company could turn the whole ship around from one wheelhouse.

Some at McKinsey were reputedly angry with Peters and Waterman's revolutionary approach. Mike Bulkin, the head of McKinsey in New York, was rumored to have viewed the *Wall Street Journal* op-ed advocating 7S as "a frontal assault" on McKinsey, whose business model had been built on selling its version of "planning" to big companies. Peters and Waterman were effectively tearing up the McKinsey rulebook before McKinsey's eyes, while being paid by McKinsey to do it.

But business was lapping it up because this appeared a philosophical sea change in business thinking. As Tom Peters put it, "the picture of a thing is not the thing. An organizational structure is not an organization." The way you think your company works is not how it works.

Peters and Waterman distilled a seven-point version of the Siemens and PepsiCo presentation into a book called *In Search of Excellence: Lessons from America's Best-Run Companies*. It was to become the best-selling business book of all time. Peters and Waterman agreed to leave McKinsey. Peters/Waterman and McKinsey agreed on a fifty-fifty split on profits from the book, and McKinsey would get to sell 7S as a McKinsey idea. The revolutionary idea had become company orthodoxy.

The reason the ideas in the book chimed so perfectly with the times was clear. The global economy was in the midst of a recession, an opportunity for companies to rethink some of the guarantees and stability that they had once provided employees. By giving employees more creative autonomy, they could also pit them against one another for their own jobs in an "internal market." Employees would learn to become more competitive. They would in essence learn to be working for themselves. The "freelance" mindset was born. Even if you were working in a big company, you'd be thinking as if you were self-employed to survive.

In 1988, a film brought Peters and Waterman's philosophy to the big screen. In *Working Girl,* Melanie Griffith plays Tess McGill, a receptionist whose brilliant business ideas get stolen by her conniving boss Katharine Parker, played by Sigourney Weaver. On Tess's first day in the office, she takes her most prized belongings out of a box and places them on her desk. At the top is a copy of *In Search of Excellence.* It is her bible for survival, signaling to the audience that nothing will stop this character. She is a winner.

The movie was also a kind of allegory for what had happened to Tom Peters at McKinsey. Or what happens to anyone with truly radical new ideas confronted by a monolithic organization those ideas challenge: inevitable conflict and drama.

I meet Tom Peters in a plush Boston hotel. He bounds into the room like an excitable dog, raring to go. He asks dozens of questions in quick-fire succession and is dramatically engaged with everything I say, throwing his arms up in the air in frustration or stamping his foot in delight, depending on whether he agrees or disagrees. He is, as an ex-colleague at McKinsey told me, "quite a guy."

The 7S's emerged, Tom says, as a catchy way of encapsulating "the core requirements of any successful business": strategy (the vision and direction of the company); structure (the interconnections between management and employees); systems (the procedures and routines, and the way information passes through the company); staff (their caliber, their role and ability to fulfill it); style (the way key managers set goals and behave); skills (the distinctive capabilities of the organization) and shared values (the core beliefs underlying the founding and existence of the company)."The 7S's were not a plan as such."

Peters is very clear this was an analysis of the overall culture of a company, and indeed its advocates have said the brilliance of this analysis was to combine hard and soft managerial insight into an all-encompassing overview. "A company could do these S's well or do them badly, but no organization could ignore them," Tom says.

Yet the message the world took away from the book was different. It was "excellence" that mattered, not a series of words beginning with the letter "S." "Excellence" was the brand that turned the 7S's into the most successful business book ever written. And excellence—as interpreted in the context of a ruthless new business culture emerging in the early 1980s—was about individual drive and killing the competition.

Peters and Waterman were West Coast outsider intellectuals, the closest management consultants will ever get to being anarchists, who despised the management consultancy establishment. Management consultants obsessed about "systems."

They wanted to break this narrow-minded management thinking of the past—epitomized by Frederick Winslow Taylor and Peter Drucker—by tearing up convention and teaching managers to think "outside boxes" or systems. But the book was not taken this way; it was seen as a guide to creating a ruthless machine for productivity.

"I cannot legislate for the way big companies chose to treat their employees," Peters remarks, in discussing how businesses have interpreted *In Search of Excellence*. "Companies were going to rationalize workforces and drive for greater efficiencies with or without the book." But the book gave them a bible.

Then, in 2002, on the twentieth anniversary of its publication, Tom Peters gave a rather unusual if characteristically frank interview to *Fast Company*, admitting that "okay, I confess. We faked the data":[11]

> *In Search of Excellence* was an afterthought. . . . I had no idea what I was doing . . . there was no carefully designed work plan. There was no theory that I was out to prove. I went out and talked to genuinely smart people. I had an infinite travel budget that allowed me to fly first class and stay at top-notch hotels, and a license from McKinsey to talk to as many cool people as I could all around the United States and the world.
>
> So what? In *Search of Excellence* . . . said that from this point forward, the world changes . . . it's never going to be the way it was—and if you want to be a part of the way it's going to be, you have to read this book.
>
> Was our process fundamentally sound? Absolutely! Start by using common sense, by trusting your instincts, and by soliciting the views of "strange" (that is, nonconventional)

people. You can always worry about proving the facts later. But that's not the confession. The confession is that I didn't go far enough.

Why did Peters tell the world that the 7S system—the greatest reform of the working environment in the last forty years—was fiction? "Everything needs great packaging, right? That's what the 7S was: great packaging. People want to be told that other people know what they're doing. But the underlying principle was right: individuals need to take control of their own destiny. Read between the lines and that's what the book was saying."

"The Firm"

Like all revolutionaries, Tom Peters and Robert Waterman believed in themselves. They made history by reading its runes and working out a simple pitch: "if you want to be a part of the way it's going to be, read this book." They were a living embodiment of how to act if one is going to make it in the new world.

In a post-OPEC 1970s world of profound uncertainty, in which the old rules no longer appeared to apply to anything, consultants stepped into the breach because, as Peters says, people want to be told that other people know what they are doing. Government and economists no longer seemed to have the confidence in their own expertise to govern or determine the direction of the economy, and in the vacuum created, a huge business opportunity emerged. And the new arbiters of wisdom increasingly became companies like Peters and Waterman's own, McKinsey.

McKinsey was the world's most influential consultancy firm. It had commissioned the 7S study and in the late 1990s, it was to transform the work of world again with a bold new insight into success.

McKinsey is a "consultancy" firm in the way Google is a search engine. Its true remit is soft power, just as Google's actual remit is the control and real-world application of all data. McKinsey ranks only seventh in size among its global competitors, behind such organizations as Boston Consulting Group, Bain, PricewaterhouseCoopers and Deloitte. Yet McKinsey is more important than all the others put together.

McKinsey rose to power in part by counterbalancing the failure of nerve that beset career politicians in the 1960s and 1970s. In the early 1960s, young ambitious politicians were fired up by the desire for "change," the word that brought Kennedy to the White House. In this new political era, the machinery of government—bureaucracy and obstructive civil servants—often seemed to stand in the way. But McKinsey was there to help. The technocratic revolution—the "white heat of technology"—had delivered confident, new, smooth-talking experts from consultants like McKinsey, who looked far more dynamic than the old-fashioned civil servants.

They did not go for a long lunch, they talked the breathless modern management speak of flip charts and graphs. They were efficient and independent-minded outsiders untainted by the bureaucratic inertia of the career civil servant. In the 1970s, politicians like Gerald Ford began to work with consultants more widely. Dick Cheney and Donald Rumsfeld, who advised Ford, said the thirst for new ideas from these outside-the-box thinkers to breathe new life into politics was insatiable. The moment had come for outsiders to become insiders.

"The Firm," as McKinsey is known by its competitors and employees alike, was instrumental in restructuring the entire staffing and running of the White House.[12] It asked politicians to think the unthinkable—there was nothing that could not be radically reformed. Nothing was sacred. McKinsey now "advises" ninety of the one hundred biggest companies on the Fortune 500 list, and dozens of governments across the globe. New recruits are selected from Rhodes and Baker scholars at Oxford and Harvard, just as MI5 and the CIA once recruited spies.

As the *Financial Times* revealed in 2011, "When James Kondo (co-founder of Table for Two and former head of Twitter Japan) joined McKinsey, he says insiders offered two analogies to help him understand the Firm: the Jesuits, and the tailors of Savile Row, who 'unlike fashion houses and designers . . . are always in the background.'" Other management consultancies do not even refer to McKinsey by name; they call it simply The Firm.[13,14]

In 1997, fifteen years after Peters and Waterman had revolutionized the workplace with their 7S system, McKinsey was to transform it again with a new idea: the war for talent.

McKinsey's Ed Michaels, Helen Handfield-Jones and Beth Axelrod looked at seventy-seven flourishing US companies over a broad spread of industries, and made a surprising discovery. Talent was in short supply. Only 23 percent of the executives McKinsey polled believed that their companies attracted the best employees.

Talent, Michaels, Handfield-Jones and Axelrod said, is essential. If a company does not attract the very best people and pay top dollar, it will not survive.[15] A booming economy might hide inferior talent for a time, but eventually things will head south, and that is when companies need the very best people. And these talented people, Michaels, Handfield-Jones and Axelrod said, should be given free rein.

The Enron Connection

Enron was, according to the *Wall Street Journal* in 2002, the model for a highly aggressive, testosterone-fueled corporation on a mission to win at all costs. As the *Wall Street Journal* pointed out in a follow-up article on the culture of Enron in August of the same year, "Chief Financial Officer Andrew Fastow had a Lucite cube on his desk supposedly laying out the company's values. One of these was communication, and the cube's inscription explained what that meant. When Enron says it's going to 'rip your face off,' it said 'it will rip your face off.'"

Yet the numbers appeared to vindicate such a strategy: In Enron's annual report for 2000, the company boasted of "Astonishing success . . . An enormous increase of 59% in physical energy deliveries . . . Our retail energy business achieved its highest level ever of total contract value." The company's net income reached, Enron said, "a record $1.3 billion in 2000."[16]

Two books were considered bibles at Enron, according to Jamie Doward, who researched the Enron/McKinsey relationship for *The Guardian—In Search of Excellence* and *The War for Talent*. And Enron's extraordinary growth in the energy-trading business had been built in large part by Jeffrey Skilling, who had previously been a McKinsey consultant for twenty-one years.

In the mid-1980s, McKinsey and Skilling had advised Enron on how to smooth gas prices through the creation of forward contracts.[17] By the mid-1990s, Enron, with Skilling at the helm, was paying McKinsey $10 million a year for its advice, including over twenty reports by McKinsey. The relationship was symbiotic. Richard Foster, a McKinsey partner, repaid the compliment by interviewing a senior Enron executive in his book with coauthor Sarah Kaplan, *Creative Destruction*. "We hire very smart people," the executive said proudly, "and we pay them more than they think they're worth."

Then, in October 2001, Enron collapsed in spectacular fashion, the most dramatic implosion of a single corporation in US business history.[18]

Enron had really taken McKinsey's "war for talent" idea to heart: it had allowed flashy, fast-talking executives with little or no expertise to rise quickly through the company, making decisions of huge import because they seemed like they knew what they were doing. According to Julian Birkinshaw, professor of strategy and entrepreneurship at the London Business School, even if these guys came fresh out of McKinsey or Harvard Business School, they didn't necessarily have the boots-on-the-ground business experience to be making multimillion-dollar initiatives. To these inexperienced but headstrong recruits, "Enron was their sandbox." The place was utter chaos masquerading as a responsible business. But at the heart of this chaos was the principle that talent should be given its head. McKinsey's Richard Foster called it "creative destruction." In slavishly chasing the "creative," Enron had brought about its own "destruction."

McKinsey had to some degree unleashed a Frankenstein's monster with Enron. John Allario, a former Enron staffer, says McKinsey tried to rein in some of Enron's unrealistic ambitions but with little success. "I heard McKinsey contributed greatly to the early establishment of the broadband division. Once the business gained momentum, most of their ideas were ignored in favor of Enron management directives. It may have been that Enron listened only when it suited them."

The lesson of the "war for talent" as applied at Enron should have been to treat the claims of the uniquely "talented" in business with a hefty pinch of salt. It is not the "talented" who should be rewarded but those who don't put a self-aggrandizing label on their job title, just do their job, quietly and very well. But in the early 2000s, "talent" became an elixir not just at Enron but throughout business. And most pointedly in consultancy itself, uniquely placed to tell business how to conduct its own business. In spite of the fact that people in business might already know what they're doing.

The Valley of Death

John Bennett was a management consultant in the 2010s for one of the so-called Big Four: Deloitte, KPMG, PricewaterhouseCoopers and McKinsey. His specialty was the healthcare sector.

"Every time you go into a client, you are looking to find new problems to expand the job. It's like being a car mechanic who looks under the bonnet of your car, sucks in their teeth and says it is much worse than you think. We call this strategy 'land and expand.'" Bennett says that key to this management strategy is the initial rolling out of a piece of diagnostic work: a "template." This template is a foot in the door, often given away for free. The money comes in "landing and expanding" the job once you are in.[19]

David Craig is an intense man with horn-rimmed spectacles and a stick, which he uses to point at huge words in CAPS during his PowerPoint presentation. He meets me in a very large darkened boardroom in London, where the only light comes from the overhead projector. The first words that appear on the whiteboard are "VALLEY OF DEATH."

David worked for thirty years as a consultant selling millions of dollars in contracts to the private and public sector. He explains to me how he landed and expanded business. "You need to give the client a big shock. Something along the lines of: 'It's worse, far worse than you imagined.' You are sending them into what we call the Valley of Death. 'Only by correcting this immediately is there any hope of turning this around.'"

What happens after the Valley of Death? "Then you provide the sunny uplands of salvation in the shape of an IT project worth fifty million." Like the pharmaceutical industry, the serious money is not in a cure, but in medicating an ongoing critical condition. Bennett calls it the "fostering of a partnership." "You are looking to create a long-term dependency culture on your firm." Creating a permanent crisis situation in which government or the business cannot do without you.

This deeply cynical approach to management consultancy is not shared by everyone in consultancy and in fact, many of those who work for and with the big four would argue they do invaluable work in turning failing businesses and organizations in the right direction. The best consultants seek to minimize, not maximize, their role, enabling those within the organization to then take on their recommendations and do the work themselves.

In Wales, PricewaterhouseCoopers came up with an ingenious new kind of "partnership" with local government called a

"risk and reward contract" designed to deal with making politically sensitive cuts to services, such as basic support for the sick,
the old and the vulnerable. Instead of companies paying consultants up front to make cuts, consultants receive a percentage on
all cuts made that they have suggested. Critics of risk and reward
say that the more cuts made to public services, the more consultants stand to earn. But PwC argues that they are incentivized
to make the best decisions and do not receive money up front.

In many areas, consultants work constructively with local
politicians to make difficult budgetary decisions and have provided invaluable expertise at a time when government has had
its own expert staff hollowed out or made redundant. The reality is that both employers and management consultants now
operate in a world of work that is changing fast, and one that
is going to be revolutionized by one new player in particular:
Uber.

The Uber Revolution

On a freezing night in January 2008, two Americans stood
on the Champs-Élysées in Paris trying to hail a cab. Snow was
falling thick and fast, and the traffic was rapidly grinding to a
halt. They had less than an hour to make their flight to New
York. As the Champs-Élysées gridlocked, horns beeping, a
single, distant yellow light flickered—the one free cab on the
whole of the Champs-Élysées, trapped in traffic more than five
hundred yards away. They were never going to make it.

Then one of them, a thirty-four-year-old UCLA dropout
named Travis Kalanick, had a eureka moment. Imagine, he
said to his colleague Garrett Camp, if every car you see became

a cab. Not one flickering light, but hundreds of flickering yellow lights, all offering a ride to the airport.

Kalanick had invented Uber. He had not merely created a new cab service. He had transformed work by reconceptualizing the idea of who works for whom. On that night in January 2008, the world was crashing and rising simultaneously, like two tectonic plates. The subprime loan crash had plunged the world economy into unprecedented debt, at the same time as the iPhone and mobile devices were freeing the world to work in a brand-new way. Uber did not merely disrupt the economy, it reinvented the future. Within a year, it had signed deals with Google Ventures, Toyota and China's largest search engine, Baidu. We were now all our own bosses with a mobile device.

The Uber business model is remarkably simple, and far from new. Once upon a time, it was called a franchise, and the king of the franchise was McDonald's, 80 percent of whose locations are franchised.

McDonald's franchisees, after ponying up a hefty sum to license the location and purchase equipment, embark on a nine-month training period during which they are shown the McDonald's way of doing things: service, values, staffing and menu specifications. Then they're up and running. But how does McDonald's make its money?

Rather differently, of course, than Uber does. McDonald's takes 4 percent on all monthly sales at franchises, and either a flat base rent or a percentage rent of at least 8.5 percent of all sales. The average annual net sales at a McDonald's franchise is $2,700,000, with a gross profit of $1,782,000. After payroll, taxes and other controllable costs are taken into account, the average profit per restaurant per annum is $761,400. But after Mc-Donald's has taken its cut and other noncontrollable expenses are taken into account, that profit whittles down to $153,900.[20]

Franchisee profit varies hugely from location to location and according to footfall numbers, which is why the average franchisee has six sites or more to spread the risk. And the franchisee's overall business, of course, benefits from economies of scale. But the prohibitively high entry fee also makes owning a McDonald's franchise very different from being an Uber driver: a franchisee is typically a quite successful businessperson with capital assets to begin with.

Uber, on the other hand, offers an entry-level opportunity to run your own business, and sells itself as hyper-flexible. Do it whenever you feel like it. As with the McDonald's franchise, you are "buying a job" in the sense that you are the boss but working under the umbrella and receiving business as a result of the brand you have bought into.

Compare the McDonald's franchise with the Uber equivalent. You do not rent your car from Uber as you would a branch from McDonald's; Uber does not own anything but the brand. It will not lease you the tires and chassis. You can instead rent an Uber-ready car from one of a host of intermediary Uber-approved companies. You need just a clean driving license and an iPhone to access Uber's app connecting you with rides (if you don't have the phone, Uber will rent you one for $10 a week). You also need commercially approved car insurance. The rate for a hybrid personal/commercial coverage could well increase once the insurer is informed you drive for Uber.

To the IRS, you are a self-employed independent contractor. You receive a 1099-MISC form reporting gross income. You are fully responsible for all federal and state income taxes, and also for taxes an employer would normally cover, such as those for Social Security and Medicare. A *Washington Post* investigation into the hidden costs of being an Uber driver concluded that an Uber driver receives all the liabilities of a self-employed contractor and none of the benefits of an employee. "You don't get fringe benefits. No paid sick leave or vacation days, no subsidized health insurance and so forth." Things would be different if you worked at corporate headquarters for Uber Technologies. "You would receive a 401(k) savings plan, gym reimbursement, nine paid company holidays, a full medical/dental/vision package and an unlimited vacation policy. You might even get snacks in Uber's lunchroom."

In 2017, Uber's founder Travis Kalanick took another cab ride, and on that ride he learned firsthand what an Uber driver thinks of this business model. His ride was not on the Champs-Élysées, but wedged in the back seat between two women in San Francisco, playing distractedly with his phone and shimmying to Daft Punk on the car radio. As the ride came to an end, the driver suddenly and unexpectedly confronted Kalanick.[21] "I'm bankrupt because of you," Fawzi Kamel said. "Bullshit," Kalanick replied. "You're raising the standards and you're dropping the prices," Kamel continued. "People are not trusting you anymore. I lost $97,000 because of you. You keep changing everything."

Kamel's problem lay with the fact that drivers for the high-end "elevated ride experience" Uber Black are required to drive recent models of select premium luxury cars, so earning a higher rate, but still competing with the cheaper UberX rides. Kamel had bought or leased a car on the basis of projected income to cover its cost, only to have Uber slash fares and increase commissions. He'd been undercut by Uber.

Kalanick fiddled with his phone as Kamel explained his situation, and then Kalanick responded: "Some people don't like to take responsibility for their own shit. They blame everything in their life on somebody else." Then he got out and wished Kamel "good luck."

Less than a year later, Kalanick was ousted as the head of Uber. The Kamel confrontation was the last in a long line of controversies that had engulfed his leadership. It was the end of the ride for Kalanick, but his radical new vision of how employment could be configured was here to stay.

Uber had not been Kalanick's first foray into the "sharing economy." In 1998, a decade before he stood on the Champs-Élysées trying to hail a cab, he had dropped out of UCLA to create a peer-to-peer file-sharing service like MP3 music site Napster.

It was called Scour, and like Napster, it was destroyed by the music industry. Metallica and Dr. Dre sued Napster for infringing copyright, forcing it out of business. Scour faced a lawsuit from the American motion picture industry, the Recording Industry Association of America and the Music Publishers Association.

The idea of peer-to-peer seemed doomed. But Napster and Scour had created the germ of a new idea—one that Kalanick would resurrect eight years later when he found himself standing on a Paris sidewalk in the snow: peer-to-peer that shared employees instead of music.

In a peer-to-peer system, peers are both suppliers and consumers at the same time. There is no one-way client server. It is collaborative, with peers contributing by dropping in and out.

Optimists for the sharing economy refer to this free-market equality as "dot-communism." In theory, dot-communism undermines anyone who sets themselves up as an authoritarian boss, because it empowers the individual to choose where and how to work. Infinite demands for different services mean work will become infinitely diverse and varied. We can stick it to any one employer, because they have no monopoly on employment. It destroys hierarchical structures by replicating the egalitarianism of social networking in the workplace.

Here is the less optimistic view. Take an Uber cab driver. In theory, he has the opportunity to go and work for anyone. But in reality, he is tied in to Uber, because Uber has a virtual monopoly on cabs in many cities. He could always take another low-paid job, but he has already made the investment in his car. So he is trapped.

The benefit comes not necessarily so much for the driver as for the consumer. But this could be a chimera too. When hailing an Uber cab, you theoretically have an active marketplace of cabs vying for business before your eyes on the app. Prices are driven ever downward and this means cheaper transport. But there is a limit to how far these prices can be driven down. If competitors come in to the market, they can theoretically undercut the Uber cabs and keep a competitive cab market alive in your city. But not if Uber has a monopoly. If it gains that, it can raise prices again, as any monopoly can.

Airbnb and the Redefinition of Value

At the same moment Kalanick was inventing Uber, two roommates in San Francisco were struggling to pay the rent on their loft apartment. Brian Chesky and Joe Gebbia had only two bedrooms, which they slept in, so renting out another room was not an option. Then Chesky had an idea. "Why don't we turn the living room into a bed and breakfast?" They advertised their "Airbed & Breakfast" on a website for an upcoming design conference in the city, and quickly had three takers. Airbnb was born.

Like Uber, Airbnb was a conceptual shift in what constitutes value. It was peer-to-peer with beds instead of wheels. Uber redefined labor value, while Airbnb reassessed space, asking a profound question: what is the true value of any physical space and how can that value be extracted? Why can't a home be a hotel and vice versa?

In 2016, less than eight years after Chesky and Gebbia pumped up an air bed in their living room and invented Airbnb, it was worth $30 billion. Uber was worth $70 billion. But the potential value of both far exceeds that. Airbnb did with four walls what Uber did with four wheels, but its model is if anything even more radical and potentially far-ranging. Airbnb is reshaping cities, and also daring people to find the extractable value in everything they own.

Airbnb has driven down accommodation prices for consumers in cities across the world and altered the economics of those cities in the process. It's now possible to travel across the globe, as Airbnb says in its advertisements, ignoring the old circuit of homogenized, overpriced hotels and instead immersing oneself in the genuine lived city: staying with local people and experiencing what it is to be a local inhabitant.

Up to a point, at least. In Ibiza, Spain, Airbnb has exposed an affordable housing crisis and driven a wedge into an already precarious situation. Residents cannot afford the rising rents created by a demand for tourist accommodation and neither can the tourist industry's seasonal workers, who fly in to service the very industry dedicated to the people renting the Airbnb properties. In August 2017, the number of beds advertised on sites like Airbnb was capped by the regional government, keen to do something about escalating rents for local people. But the local response by residents highlighted the Catch 22 of muzzling the market: local businesses dependent on the influx of tourists for their livelihoods attacked the measure as detrimental to the Ibizan economy by potentially driving tourists to other holiday resorts with more supply.[22]

In 2016, in Santa Monica, California, Scott Shatford became the first person convicted of bundling a number of properties in a desirable area and renting them as an Airbnb host. Shatford told the *Los Angeles Times:* "The city came after me, to make me their little poster child and be able to promote their first victory . . . It's pretty silly." Shatford added that he planned to move to Denver, where authorities would be more tolerant. He now runs a data analytics company called AirDNA which takes the data from Airbnb as valuable investment intel for those seeking to get into the rental market themselves.[23]

Airbnb has both empowered consumers and exposed affordable-rental crises in dozens of cities across the globe. It has become a lightning rod for protests, even in cases where it could not reasonably be held at fault. In Barcelona in summer 2017, tourists were smoke-bombed as they sat at outside café tables enjoying cocktails by local activists blaming them for the housing crisis. Tourism is an essential part of the economic model of Barcelona, and one the city has cultivated since 1992, when it hosted the Olympics. Yet now residents say they are paying the price, and Airbnb is to blame.

But cash-strapped residents are also using this very same mechanism to survive. In Los Angeles, where the median annual wage is $28,000 and the median rent for a one-bedroom apartment $2,000 a month, a growing number of people use Airbnb on a near-permanent basis to subsidize their own housing by giving over their sleeping space to strangers. For them, Airbnb is a tool to keep renting, not a tool to prevent them from doing so.

Potential benefits aside, many big cities today have a fraught relationship with the company, in part out of concern for residents' skyrocketing rents, and in part due to concerted lobbying efforts on behalf of the hotel industry. In 2016, Berlin banned the letting of whole properties via Airbnb's app. London, San Francisco and Barcelona have all sought to create caps on how many properties can be used for short-term rentals, and for how long, in order to help local residents gain a foothold once more.

Do Uber and Airbnb face legal challenges because they are genuine disrupters challenging vested interests or because they threaten to make an existing problem—precarious employment in Uber's case, unaffordable housing in Airbnb's—worse? Both.

It is hard to restrict something when people see an opportunity to make money. In London in 2015–2016, the number of properties being advertised on Airbnb rose by 126 percent, and the story is the same in any big city where the basic laws of supply and demand apply.[24]

These laws apply to the brave new world of work too. The sharing, or gig, economy is the biggest transformation in our working lives since the Industrial Revolution and the advent of the five-day work week.

Freelance, or hyper-flexible, so-called contingent, work is growing at a tremendous rate—from 34 percent of the US workforce in 2017 to what is projected to be over 50 percent by 2020. The word "contingent" is interesting: it means that employment is "contingent" on there being something to do. The new sharing economy may offer new opportunities, but the number of people offering their services also has the potential to massively outstrip demand.

PayPal founder and tech billionaire Elon Musk has suggested a solution—a "universal basic wage" if automation delivers economic prosperity. Robots could be taxed on their labor and pay income tax, as humans currently do. The resulting revenue would then be used to pay humans and enable them to shop, as consumerism will continue to drive growth.

In ten years' time, a staff job like my father's will be rare and highly prized. Everyone else will be CEO of their own business enterprise, whether they are Warren Buffett or the person cleaning out the trashcan under his desk.

The Cheap Goods Equation

The global equation of low wages and zero growth depends on a third factor for its equilibrium: cheap goods. If things stay cheap, wages can stay low. Take the package I have on my desk. It is a pen with cartridges bought online for $2, less than the price of a coffee from Starbucks. It cost more to ship it from India to London than the object is worth.

This new age of flexible work is built on the founding stone of cheap goods made for next to nothing across the globe. Glancing up from my computer, I see a package that arrived this morning from China. It contains a single item—a phone cable—that cost 99 cents. My books sit on a shelf that cost $24 from IKEA. There are books on that shelf that cost twice as much as the shelf itself. I am wearing a T-shirt that cost, shockingly, $2. The coffee mug I drink from cost $4. The beans that made the coffee cost more than the mug.

We are so accustomed to buying things cheaply that we cannot imagine it any other way, but we should. Because should a substantial price rise come, we will not be ready for it, or be able to afford it.

Cheap imports began with the entrepreneurial vision of one man. In 1967, ex–trucking entrepreneur turned shipping tycoon Malcolm McLean, the CEO of US container company Sea-Land Service Inc., cut a deal with the US Army, which was desperate to get supplies quickly over to Indochina during the Vietnam War. Sea-Land began transporting millions of tons of food, cigarettes and medical supplies in huge, oblong metal boxes over thousands of miles of sea. At a stroke, McLean had invented modern containerization, and by 1971, McLean's deal with the US Army was worth $100 million a year.

McLean's innovation, improved on by engineer Keith Tantlinger, had been to create so-called intermodal containers, interlocking boxes that could be loaded and unloaded efficiently and at speed using cranes, thereby cutting down on labor costs and expensive harbor times.[25] These intermodal containers could be locked together with a secure twist-lock mechanism, allowing safe transportation by crane and secure positioning on long voyages. As important, containers could also be stacked high—meaning they could carry an unprecedented tonnage of goods—on ships like the SS *Ideal X*, the world's first modern containerized vessel: a refitted tanker.

Containerization of one sort or another had existed for nearly two hundred years, starting with the bulk transportation of coal in wooden containers by English entrepreneur James Brindley in the 1760s, but McLean launched the ultra-efficient modern mega-box ship we know today. And it was in Japan that he saw his opportunity, transporting goods back in the same containers that had delivered supplies to the US troops in Indochina. Between 1960 and 1973, Japanese industrial output quadrupled. American consumers hankered for one product above all, which Japan could suddenly supply on the cheap: home technology.

With the help of containerization, the United States was flooded overnight with hi-fis, radios and TVs. Once the preserve of the wealthy, technology was now "Made in Japan" or "Made in China" at a fraction of the price. These hi-tech luxuries were now affordable to anyone.

Cheap goods were a boon to consumers, but a disaster for Western industry. The rise of Asian imports coincided neatly with the collapse of Western manufacturing. Containerization was the killer blow. Marc Levinson has calculated that 300 million containers are now crossing the world's oceans each year, 26 percent of them coming from China alone.[26]

The downward price drive has only accelerated. TVs today cost 3 percent of what they cost in 1980. Cameras are 75 percent cheaper than they were in 2000, thanks to smartphones. Phones themselves are half the price they were in 2005. The first commercial mobile phone, the Motorola DynaTAC 8000X launched in 1983, cost $4,000. Technology, once the domain of the rich, is now owned by all of us as material recompense for stagnating wages.

And if wages don't pick up, can goods remain cheap enough

to be widely affordable? Perhaps not, as the world's resources become ever more strained. Steve Howard, IKEA's global head of sustainability, says there is potential for a global price hike.[27]

In the 1990s, before the internet took off, IKEA offered a cunning template for how the internet might look if it were laid out like a store. At IKEA, the layout ensnares you: you follow a winding path that dictates your route but allows you to think you are diverting off to look at a bed, a toast rack or some shelving. The layout of the store provides a hidden guiding hand. It gives the illusion of freedom, just like Peters and Waterman's 7S work model. Eighty percent of the people who go to IKEA have in mind a single big purchase they are either buying that day or scoping out. But they get home with a sponge shaped like a strawberry, a rubber-duck wine stopper, scented candles and some Swedish biscuits. What did all the things they actually bought have in common? They were cheap.

"How long can we expect to push the margin, as the consumer demands cheaper and cheaper?" Steve Howard says. Price inflation will make an economic model built on low wages and stagnant growth simply unsustainable. "At some point, prices will have to rise as resources get more expensive. This is the coming global price hike, and who's going to pay if it's not passed on to the shopper?" Steve says companies cannot pass it on because that will hit their customer base, so an impossible conundrum is created.

Prices and wages have been inextricably linked over the last twenty years. We have seen both travel downward in tandem. But if they need to be uncoupled, how? Perhaps with some good old-fashioned economic growth.

6

RISK
How Chaos Was Harnessed by Wall Street

THE DEAL: The OPEC oil states Saudi Arabia, Syria, Egypt, Iran and Tunisia agree to an oil embargo on the United States.

AIM: To use the Yom Kippur War as political leverage for a massive hike in oil prices

WHERE: Vienna, Austria

WHEN: October 17, 1973

In New York, overlooking Central Park, is an anonymous apartment block. On the fiftieth floor, Robert Dall is being moved from his bedroom to the chintz living area by a nurse. Dall uses an oxygen canister when he moves around the flat, but when I arrive, he greets me with a strong slap on the back.[1] Back in the 1980s, Robert Dall was the man who changed the world by teaching it to embrace risk, and in so doing, invented the mechanics for shorting the stock market. In *Liar's Poker*, Michael Lewis says that Dall shaped the world to come because "he began to think thoughts years into the future."

Robert Dall's lightbulb moment was "securitization." It was

a conceptual shift in the very idea of trading. Instead of trading with physical assets and their value now, Dall conceived that you could trade on what something would be worth in the future, and secure it against something that exists now, like a mortgage policy.

At Salomon Brothers, Dall loomed over the trading floor, a giant in a pin-striped suit, who by his own admission "worked hard, partied hard, did everything hard." He was "a down-and-dirty brawler. But I was coasting for a while there in Wall Street." Until something changed. Dall discovered the work of two economists named Fischer Black and Myron Scholes.

Black and Scholes were to stocks and shares what Copernicus was to astronomy. In the early 1970s, they took economic wisdom and turned it on its head. Everything we knew about the way the market works, they said, was wrong. They focused on risk, encapsulating it in a single equation, known as the Black-Scholes formula:

$$C = SN(d_1) - N(d_2)Ke^{-rt}$$

C = Call premium
S = Current stock price
t = Time until option exercise
K = Option striking price
r = Risk-free interest rate
N = Cumulative standard normal distribution
e = Exponential term

s = St. Deviation
ln = Natural Log

$$d_1 = \frac{\ln\left(S/K\right) + \left(r + s^2/2\right)t}{s \cdot \sqrt{t}}$$

$$d_2 = d_1 - s \cdot \sqrt{t}$$

This equation was to become the basis for options and derivatives, today worth $1 quadrillion, ten times the value of all goods produced on earth. The brilliance of the Black-Scholes formula was multifaceted, but in simple terms, it enabled traders to put a value on something no one had been able to accurately put a value on before: a stock option.

What the Black-Scholes formula does is this. Say a copy of this book is worth $10 today. No one can predict what the book will be worth in a year's time. It might be $12, it might be $16, it might be $8. The genius of the Black-Scholes formula was to pin this ambiguity down to a predicted value.

The price of a stock option for this book, Black & Scholes said, would be the difference between the expected share price for the stock option on the book set for a year's time ($12) and the actual price when the option comes due ($16). This book is worth, alas, just $4.

The more you think about the Black-Scholes equation, the cleverer it gets. Value resides not in the innate book-ness of this book. That value is an illusion, because people will continuously disagree on that true value. The important thing is not to chase the tail of the market and second-guess what people will think the value of a commodity is at any given moment but instead to embrace the inherent volatility of the whole enterprise of attributing value to thin air. To make the equation the underlying law by which to measure value concretely.

Black and Scholes looked to the molecular particle theories of Albert Einstein, Jean Perrin and Marian Smoluchowski for inspiration: theories that studied the random movement of liquids and gases, and attempted to create a unifying principle that could explain, even predict, this random movement of particles.

Black and Scholes appeared to bring system to chaos and revolutionized Wall Street. Nobel Prize–winning economist Professor Robert Merton at MIT Sloan School of Management remembers teaching Black-Scholes to a generation of students in the early 1970s before setting them loose on Wall Street. They created, he says, the "methodology, as 20-somethings, for what turned out to be a 40-year revolution in the financial services industry. It made possible an enormous amount of innovation across markets because it was a kind of universal methodology people could apply."

Black-Scholes was first adopted on Wall Street by the US company Bankers Trust under the chairmanship of Charles Sanford, who was enthusiastic about what the formula could do for his company to transform its pricing approach into something dynamic and risky. "Successful people," Sanford said, "understand that risk, properly conceived, is often highly productive rather than to be avoided."

Bankers Trust put Black & Scholes into action with a precisely quantified measure of risk called RAROC, or "risk adjusted return on capital." RAROC put a concrete value on the risk to a trade, the effect on profit, and how to optimize the return on the risk over a spread of trades and shareholdings.

Californian economist Hayne Leland took Black & Scholes one step further, rightly predicting that the options industry would be revolutionized and turbo-charged if Wall Street began adopting risk as a pricing strategy. Leland worked out that by assessing risk, he could "create a form of insurance against share prices dropping, not just one by one but across an entire investment portfolio."[2] Black & Scholes could open up a whole satellite industry.

It was an early form of "shorting." Pricing was speeding up at a meteoric rate in the early 1970s, and Leland had cleverly worked out that there was as much money to be made in providing a service for insulating Wall Street against risk as in risky trading itself. The genius of Black-Scholes was that it encouraged risk as a fundamental dynamo of business but also provided the tools for mitigating the dangers of risky trading by calibrating the level at which a business was prepared to risk.

MIT's Robert Merton argues that Black and Scholes's formula for pricing in the unpredictable economic climate of the early 1970s was spectacularly good timing. But Black-Scholes really came into its own when the world was plunged into severe uncertainty. One of the main causes for this deepening of uncertainty was the 1973 OPEC oil crisis. This crisis also turned out to be a breathtaking real-world lesson in how Black-Scholes could work when applied by a cartel who understood how to harness risk to their financial advantage.

On October 3, 1973, an Arab coalition of states led by Egypt, Syria and Iraq invaded Israel on the holy day of Yom Kippur. OPEC, the oil producers of the Middle East, used the resulting instability to hike the price of oil overnight. It was a massive gamble, dependent on the United States dithering over what to do about the invasion of Israel. With the eyes of the world on Arab tanks rolling through the desert, the price of oil smashed through the roof and, more to the point, stayed there.

The strategy was brilliant. The ostensible political reason OPEC gave for the 1973 price hike was solidarity with their Arab neighbors when Israel counterattacked, but the reality was pure economic opportunism.

Six days after the Arab coalition invasion, the Nixon administration supplied weapons to Israel to support Israel's counteroffensive into Syria. OPEC's leaders, meeting at its headquarters in Vienna, decided on October 17 to strike, using oil price increases as their weapon against Israel and its Western allies.

Initially, OPEC decided to raise prices 70 percent. But in December, OPEC met again—this time in Tehran—and prices were raised 130 percent. OPEC also imposed a total oil embargo on the United States, Canada, Japan, the Netherlands and the UK, industrialized countries heavily dependent on the Arab export of oil. OPEC had attempted an embargo before as a response to the Six-Day War in 1967, and it failed. But this time it believed it would work. The United States, Britain and the countries supporting the Israeli counteroffensive were some of the heaviest oil consumers on earth. These countries could not afford a prolonged embargo from OPEC, and OPEC knew it.

OPEC's was a double-edged plan. On the face of it, turning the tap off for Israel and its allies provided evidence its behavior was motivated primarily by political solidarity with the Arab nations. But this masked the economic opportunism beneath: grasping the moment to ramp up prices without any need to moderate the hike, and then keep prices at this new astronomically high level. The Shah of Iran told the *New York Times*, "Of course the world price of oil is going to rise . . . certainly! And how! Let's say ten times more."

OPEC then offered what looked like an olive branch. It gave conditions under which it would end the embargo: a negotiated settlement favorable to the Arab combatants. It created a catch-22 situation for President Richard Nixon. If he negotiated peace under these terms, the embargo would end but the price of imported oil to the United States, quadrupled from $3 to $12, would remain irreversibly high. A drop in price was not on the table, and Nixon would also be seen to be capitulating to OPEC's demands.

Yet the other option for the US government was no more appealing. If Nixon refused to entertain a negotiated settlement the political crisis would escalate, and oil prices with it. Either way, oil prices went up. Nixon initiated multilateral talks and on January 18, 1974, US Secretary of State Henry Kissinger negotiated an Israeli troop withdrawal from the disputed Sinai Peninsula. OPEC lifted the embargo, but not until March. And the price of global oil was now set at an unprecedented $12 a barrel.

The OPEC price hike was Black-Scholes in action. The received wisdom on business decisions prior to Black-Scholes was that they were finely calibrated judgments based on minimizing risk, not maximizing it. In a pre–Black-Scholes world, OPEC would not have used military action as an opportunity to make an audacious price jump. In a pre–Black-Scholes world, the Israeli counteroffensive would have probably resulted in a platitudinous statement of support by OPEC for its Arab neighbors, perhaps an embargo (as in 1966), but not the full embrace of a military and political crisis as a business opportunity. OPEC intuited what Black-Scholes had taught Wall Street about risk, made a high-stakes gamble of its own and pulled it off.

It was a wake-up call for Wall Street and Western governments. The OPEC oil crisis demonstrated perfectly the Black-Scholes view that the coming world was volatile, not controllable, and business needed to harness this volatility, like a skilled sailor harnessing a storm. A cautious approach in this new world of unpredictable jumps in price and value was untenable. A company that stopped taking risks that mirrored the new risky economic climate was like a shark that stopped swimming.

The Black-Scholes formula spread like wildfire through Wall Street. Its originators were hailed as economic prophets, heirs to Adam Smith and David Ricardo. But one man in particular took the equation and turned it into banking reality—Robert Dall. Dall homed in on one target: the mortgage. By taking a safe asset like a mortgage and using a complex series of "financial instruments" to turn it into a risky "liquid asset," that house could now be traded as a "security."

Wall Street was no longer trading tangible objects, but promises "securitized" or underwritten by real things owned by real people. "Securitization" was Dall's creation, but it was really Black-Scholes on the trading floor. Robert Dall believed the mortgage market had been made a perfect vehicle for securitization, and the drive, he said, had come unexpectedly from government rather than banks. A promise had been made to the American voter. "The political slogan of the time," Dall recalls, "was 'A Home for Every American.' It wasn't realistic, it wasn't what we should have been offering, but it caught on and that was then the expectation of the public."

As a result, the rapidly expanding mortgage market became an insurance policy of its own for those like Dall who wanted to use these loans for securitization. It guaranteed a giant pipeline of continuously flowing money with which Wall Street could mitigate the risk of risky trading. That's to say, while those that are lent to can afford to pay back their loans. One thing Dall and Wall Street knew was that the growing home-owning market wasn't going to dry up anytime soon. Mortgages were the base oil with which to securitize on an undreamed-of level.

By the early 1980s, Dall would walk into a downtown restaurant and brokers would come up to him and shake his hand or buy him bottles of champagne. "I'd turned them into multimillionaires. Of course they thanked me!"

Securitization dropped like a bomb onto the financial markets. If a house could be securitized, why not a bank? Or a supermarket chain or global corporation? Why not securitize a whole country? In 2000, the European Union shoehorned Greece into the Eurozone, taking a risk on the balance sheet of an entire nation that had flagged how risky it was as an asset. In doing so, the European Central Bank was risking the entire stability of Europe.

What the world did not know was that Goldman Sachs had been tasked with massaging Greece's accounts in order to make them "eligible" for entry into the Eurozone.[3] An entire country became liquid on the promise of a better credit rating sometime in the future. Goldman Sachs warned that it was risky, too, but we were now in a post–Black-Scholes world. Risk was good.

I wondered what Robert Dall thought when he woke on the morning of October 9, 2007, and heard that the entire banking system of the West had collapsed, built largely on a system of risk that he had conjured.

His nurse fusses about him. He rearranges himself in his penthouse apartment, and takes a brief hit from his oxygen mask. "I always knew it would go too far. That they'd push it too far." Dall spends a little time pondering his role in the whole arrangement and answers. "I was like Robert Oppenheimer," he says. "I invented the atomic bomb, but I didn't drop it."

A Surprising Inspiration for Subprime

In 2007, the Jenga pyramid of subprime mortgage bundles built on Black-Scholes risk taking was pushed to the edge. But years before this financial cataclysm unfolded, Wall Street had already been given a tantalizing glimpse of what could be achieved by bundling risky loans.

In 1982, as Robert Dall's securitization revolution was coursing through Wall Street, a health insurer down on his luck was sitting on his porch in Florida reading his local paper. Tucked inside was a story that piqued Peter Lombardi's interest—about gay men dying of a mysterious disease in San Francisco.

Lombardi ran a small Florida-based health insurance company called MBC, which, in 1982, was struggling. But when he read this story, he had an idea. Lombardi had discovered that gay men dying of AIDS could not access the money in their life insurance policies when they needed it: while they were still alive. This was money that could buy them better health care, pay off a mortgage for a partner, or fund a nice vacation. Money that could massively improve the remainder of their lives. So Lombardi offered them a deal: upfront loans on their life insurance policies in exchange for the full payouts upon their deaths. Lombardi came up with a name for his weird new loan: a "viatical." He had created the death futures market.[4]

The only reason Lombardi could loan all this money in the first place was because he himself had borrowed it at extortionately high interest rates. It was a rather unsavory idea, but undoubtedly clever. The insurance policies of a few men dying of AIDS amounted to little in themselves, but when thousands were bundled together into a viatical, suddenly the sum might be hundreds of millions of dollars, money that could then be used as leverage to make far bigger loans and deals. The viatical was about to make Lombardi a major player on Wall Street.

But viaticals depended on one crucial element to work: the men passing away quickly. The quicker they died, the quicker

Lombardi could collect and pay back whomever he had borrowed from. It was a shell game of debt, just as subprime would be. Lombardi's viatical pyramid was colossally risky, but Lombardi believed he could handle it.

In 1985, the first viable AIDS drug was discovered. Clinical trials on an HIV inhibitor called AZT began at Duke University, led by a Burroughs Wellcome virologist, Marty St. Clair. To the rest of the world, from the millions of HIV-positive people in sub-Saharan Africa to the men in San Francisco and their families, it was a miracle. But to Peter Lombardi and his business partners at MBC, brothers Joel and Steven Steinger, it was a disaster.

The money started slowing down and Lombardi became frantic. MBC was no longer collecting life insurance policies fast enough to pay its creditors. It had forked out over $100 million to more than 28,000 people with terminal AIDS. Now, with AZT destroying their business model, the partners doubled down on their original strategy, seeking out people who were ill with other diseases, such as leukemia or cancer. By the early 1990s, AIDS had dried up, but MBC had found new, deep wells into which to drop its bucket. Between 1994 and 2004, the company raised more than $1 billion from 30,000 new "investors" across the globe.

Then the IRS caught up with them after years of chasing. In 2003, the Securities Exchange Commission accused MBC of the largest health fraud in US history.[5] At the trial, Lombardi was accused of "purchasing life insurance policies from persons suffering from AIDS, the chronically ill and elderly. Having purchased the life insurance policies, MBC sold fractionalized interests in insurance policy death benefits, known as 'viatical settlements' to approximately 30,000 investors."

The prosecution alleged that MBC told investors viaticals offered a fixed rate of return with low risk but that it misrepresented "various important facts," including the estimated life expectancies of the insured persons and the supposed independent role of doctors determining those life expectancies. MBC's "fraudulent methods" didn't stop there but also encompassed downplaying the risks associated with certain policies, the amount and timing of payment of premiums and the real source of funds used to pay investors.

Lombardi was bullish in his defense. Given a positive spin, his behavior could have been interpreted as a public service to people who could not access money any other way—a kind of cash-based Dallas Buyers Club. But the court did not see it that way. They were sentenced to from fifteen to twenty years each.[6]

Lombardi's story, and the story of the thousands of people MBC signed to its extraordinary Ponzi scheme, would be a curious historical footnote were it not for what happened next. In 2004, the year Lombardi went to jail, viaticals got a surprise resurrection when Lehman Brothers, ACC Capital Holdings, Merrill Lynch, Wells Fargo, Countrywide Financial, HSBC, Lone Star, JPMorgan Chase and the twenty-five other biggest lenders in America looked at new models of bundling risky loans.

Robert Dall had embedded risk in the psyche of Wall Street, but thanks to Lombardi, Wall Street was about to take it to the next level by bundling a viatical for the home-owning market and calling it a "subprime mortgage."

The quiet, thoughtful bankers walking the hushed corridors of these banks in 2004 would have winced if you had dared to suggest to them that what they were doing had anything in common with an insurance scam by a group of convicted felons that exploited dying people. But the mechanism was the same. Subprime depended for its success on offering high-risk customers a loan, then bundling millions of these loans into a huge liability that could then be traded with.

In 2007, the housing bubble burst and the shaky pyramid of subprime came crashing down. Lehman Brothers went under and the entire banking system was taken to the edge of total collapse. The world went into recession, from which it has still not bounced back. This much is familiar.

But in an uncanny echo of the government's "Home for Every American" that Robert Dall recalls underpinning securitization back in the early 1980s, so Michael Bloomberg described the same impetus behind subprime in 2004. "It was not the banks that created the mortgage crisis," he told New York bankers at a business breakfast in midtown Manhattan on November 1, 2011. "It was plain and simple, Congress, who forced everybody to go and give mortgages to people who were on the cusp . . . they were the ones who pushed Fannie and Freddie to make a bunch of loans that were imprudent. . . . [members of Congress] were the ones who pushed the banks to loan to everybody. And now we want to go vilify the banks because it's one target, it's easy to blame them and Congress certainly isn't going to blame themselves."[7]

And a decade on, subprime is back. And the impetus is the same. Reaching beyond credit-secure borrowers to high-risk borrowers in an attempt to offer loans to all. A principle approved of by government.

In 2016, Wells Fargo, Bank of America and the very same banks responsible for the first crash began again offering mortgages with less than a 3 percent down payment though they did implement some safeguards. Wells Fargo had a new deal with the consumer. If you had no savings, you could be eligible for a lower interest rate. All you needed to do was sign up to a government-sponsored "personal finance class." Bank of America had a special low rate that could only be accessed if you could prove to them your income was below the national average.[8]

In August 2017, a portent of a second subprime crash appeared to Wall Street, and lenders began to get a foreboding sense of déjà vu. And this time, with car loans. Provident Financial, who had used the same subprime mechanisms for car loans instead of homes—called PCPs, or "personal contract plans"—saw repayment rates with customers fall alarmingly from 90 percent to 57 percent in the space of one year. Provident's share price plummeted and its chief executive resigned in the wake of the figures.

After the first crash in 2007–2008, car sales had driven the economic recovery. But now they threatened to bring about another crash. The difference from 2007–2008 is that the car loan market is worth just $1.1 trillion in the United States. The mortgage market is worth $14 trillion. And since the lenders for car loans are not banks, the risk is not considered systemic. If one lender goes belly up, it doesn't necessarily mean the whole system will.

But a recovery built on car sales as an indication of consumer confidence could turn out to be as dangerous as a boom built on subprime mortgages. "Without these car sales," according to economics correspondent Phillip Inman in *The Guardian*,[9] "growth in GDP, wages and all the other standard measures of economic progress stand still."

Shorting and the Arab Spring

Risk didn't just play out on the residential streets of America but across the globe. On December 16, 2010, a twenty-six-year-old Tunisian street vendor named Mohamed Bouazizi needed a loan to buy fruit and vegetables to sell at market the following day. As a result of a rise in food prices, Bouazizi, like many other street traders across North Africa, had no choice.

Bouazizi woke early the following day. He was at his usual spot at Sidi Bouzid market by 8:00 A.M., but by 10:30 A.M., according to eyewitness accounts, local police began harassing him to move on, ostensibly because he did not have a vendor's permit.[10]

An argument ensued over money. Officials had extorted bribes from Mohamed in the past, but this time he refused. As he stood his ground, Faida Hamdi, a forty-five-year-old municipal officer, slapped him in the face. She spat at Bouazizi and confiscated his electronic weighing scales. Two unnamed men with Hamdi then overturned Bouazizi's cart into the alleyway, and his goods were confiscated. He now had no means of making a living. Bouazizi—a quiet man who did bookkeeping and accounts for other traders—was enraged. He asked to see the governor—Hamdi's superior—but was ignored.

Bouazizi then left and bought a large container of paint thinner. On the pavement outside the governor of Sidi Bouzid's office, he covered himself in thinner. Onlookers gathered and took out their phones. Bouazizi is alleged to have shouted, "How do you expect me to make a living?"[11] He then set fire to himself with a match and a revolution began.

Days after Bouazizi set light to himself, a one-thousand-strong funeral procession was forbidden by the Tunisian government from passing the place where he died, for fear of inspiring copycat acts. But the Arab Spring had already begun. The crowd chanted, "Farewell, Mohamed, we will avenge you," and on social media, people were mobilizing.

The Arab Spring is often described as a "Twitter Revolution" but there were only two hundred active Twitter accounts in Tunisia on the day Bouazizi committed suicide. There were, however, 2 million Facebook accounts, and it was the handful of Twitter posts shared with these millions of Facebook users across North Africa that fueled the uprising. One image in particular went viral; not of Bouazizi, but of a woman in a hijab holding her BlackBerry aloft to film the growing mob. The fact that Bouazizi's act could be communicated was as important as the act itself.

In days, the Arab Spring had spread across the whole of North Africa, coming to topple governments like dominoes: first the Tunisian government of Ben Ali, then Mubarak in Egypt and Gaddafi in Libya, then Saleh in Yemen. In Syria, Assad was challenged by pro-democracy rebels, erupting into a complex civil war that drew in Russia, the United States and Europe.

The political vacuum created across North Africa was filled by the Islamic State, who unlike its predecessor al-Qaeda, saw territory gain in the crumbling regimes as an opportunity to create a continent-wide caliphate, a borderless Islamic State from the Atlantic to the Red Sea, wrapped in a black flag. When IS rolled into town, they didn't just terrorize local inhabitants into supporting them. They brought down the price of wheat to win hearts and minds.

Mohamed Bouazizi's death sparked the most dramatic reconfiguration of the Middle East since the Sykes-Picot Agreement of 1916 carved up the map of North Africa to create French, British and Russian "spheres of influence." Sykes-Picot enshrined religious conflict by promising homelands to both Jews and Arabs in exchange for support in the First World War. A century on, the Middle East is reshaped by a humiliated street vendor pushed over the edge by a sudden rise in food prices. Sykes-Picot fueled religious fundamentalism, and in 2010, the rise of wheat prices fueled the rise of the Islamic State and fourth-wave jihadism.

The Arab Spring was portrayed in the West as a spontaneous outpouring of anger to bring freedom and democracy. But that was not how it started. There was another factor at play. A little-reported financial maneuver that could be traced to a handful of US companies with an enigmatic acronym: ABCD.

ABCD

ADM, Bunge, Cargill and Louis Dreyfus are the biggest grain producers on earth, known by their initials, ABCD. They collectively control 90 percent of the world's wheat. As food writer Felicity Lawrence puts it: "wherever you are in the world, whether it is the corn in your flakes, the wheat in your bread, the orange in your juice, the sugar in your jam, the chocolate on your biscuit, the coffee in your cup . . . if you've eaten beef, chicken or pork, consumed anything containing salt, gums, starches, gluten, sweeteners, fats or bought a ready meal, ABCD have shaped your consumption."[12] In essence, ABCD feed the planet. In the early 1970s, President Nixon tried to win the Cold War by suggesting the food giants hike the price of corn sold to Soviet Russia and starve communism into submission. They refused and Nixon backed down.[13]

SOAS University of London Professor Jane Harrigan has extensively researched the control these companies exert on food prices and their influence on the Arab Spring.[14] Harrigan found that the Mena region of North Africa is the most "food insecure" region on earth: the gap between what is needed to feed the population and how much is imported to fill that gap is greater than anywhere else on the planet. Fifty percent of food is imported and 35 percent of those imports consist of wheat. In short, the entire region lives on bread.

But in 2010, the food giants ABCD faced a crisis of their own. Because harvests are unpredictable, pricing cereals is notoriously volatile, and in 2010 profits were down. Food pricing has always been unstable. In the 1960s and 1970s, according to food pricing experts C. L. Gilbert and C. W. Morgan of the National Center for Biotechnology Information, it was subject to extreme fluctuations. But in 2010, the food companies had a mechanism they had not employed in the 1960s and 1970s, a mechanism inspired by Black-Scholes and by which they could effectively control price: shorting.

ABCD started in effect betting against their own crops on the international markets. They would argue that this strategy was designed to bring stability to pricing. If a crop failed, then their hedge against the crop would insulate them against taking a hit. If a crop was successful, then they'd make money anyway. It's a win-win. They control pricing while cancelling out the risk to the bottom line from unpredictable harvests.

Their critics—including charities working on the ground, like Oxfam, argue that this is playing roulette with the lives of people affected by price changes. The stability, they argue, is not for the benefit of the consumers of wheat but for the investors on Wall Street.

The 2008 financial crash had a severe effect on the food companies, as it did on many industries. The global wheat price increase in 2010 was defended by ABCD as a renormalization of pricing following the damage caused to their business by the 2007–2008 crash, an attempt to get prices back to a degree of equilibrium.

As Rami Zurayk, professor of agricultural and food sciences at the American University of Beirut, points out,[15] "In Egypt, bread is known as *aish,* meaning 'life.' . . . In Yemen, there are over twenty different types of bread . . . the fertile crescent, stretching from the Egyptian Nile to the mouth of the Tigris and the Euphrates, is where agriculture began, where wheat, lentils, chickpeas, sheep and goats and olives were first cultivated."

In spite of the fertility of the region, it is also one of the poorest on earth. Forty percent of Egyptians and Yemenis live in poverty. Why? The richness of the soil should on paper make it one of the most self-sustaining. Since the 1980s, when the IMF and World Bank introduced policies that reduced farming subsidies and encouraged the export of fruit to the West, the region, rather than investing in local grain production, became increasingly dependent on the imported wheat of US food giants ABCD.[16]

Even when there is a bumper harvest, as in 2006–2007, a price drop is not necessarily passed on to the consumer. This is because, as with the oil industry, changes in the availability and price of raw materials are seen as "money in the bank" by ABCD rather than a benefit that should be passed on instantaneously through price cuts to the consumer. Like the oil industry, the food giants point to the relative price stability they maintain year after year as the true benefit to the consumer. They may not pass on price drops when the public expect them to, but neither do they pass on the volatility that comes with fluctuating supply.

But in 2010, as Mohamed Bouazizi prepared to go to sell fruit and vegetables at the market in Tunisia, there was a significant price rise. Professor Jane Harrigan puts this price rise in context. "One measure of a country's need is the food gap—the deficit between their food requirement and domestic production. Using that measure, the Mena region . . . has the largest deficit. Fifty percent of all calories consumed in the Arab countries come from imported food, and of that, 35% comes from wheat alone."

ABCD would argue that they encourage price stability in food-insecure regions such as Mena, but in 2010, as ABCD began "shorting" on food prices, that price stability disappeared.

In these regions, a tiny price rise does not have the same effect it would in the West. It cannot be absorbed by the consumer because disposable income is so low, and life is so close to what we in the West call the "breadline." A price rise can have catastrophic consequences. And as a result of the 2010 price hike, a food crisis ignited across the African continent.

There have always been "bread riots," but this was different. "The first protests of the Arab Spring in Tunisia were quickly dismissed as another bout of bread riots," Zurayk says. "Arab regimes responded by making adjustments to food prices and offering more subsidies. Increasing the subsidy slightly relieves the popular pressure, but also increases the profit margins for importers and manufacturers. But this time round, truckloads of flour did not do the trick."

In 2010, weeks before Bouazizi set himself alight, President Obama went to war with ABCD. Under pressure from the World Health Organization, UNICEF, British Prime Minister Gordon Brown and French President Nicolas Sarkozy, Obama attempted to pass legislation curtailing a food conglomerate's ability to short on grain prices in the poorest part of the world but failed. Part of his failure was a reluctance on the part of his administration to go nose to nose with the food industry, especially in the light of its attempt to impose a sugar tax on sodas in the United States to deal with childhood obesity. The subsequent climbdown by the Obama administration gave them a taste of what would happen if they repeated the fight with wheat pricing.

Aside from the political context, there is also fundamental disagreement between economists over the genuine culpability of ABCD. As food industry experts Sophia Murphy, Dr. David Burch and Dr. Jennifer Clapp observed in an August 2012 report by Oxfam on the volatility of wheat pricing, "there has been a particularly heated debate among economists over whether . . . agricultural commodities futures markets via new financial derivatives is [the] main driver of recent food volatility."[17] They noted, however, that ABCD had not taken a hit to profits post the 2007–2008 crash requiring a price recalibration. The authors also point to the passing of legislation curtailing ABCD's ability to short prices in the wake of the crash—primarily the Dodd-Frank Act passed into law by Congress in July 2010, calling for a regulatory agency in charge of commodity derivatives markets—as the real anxiety for the food giants, not a few bad harvests.

In its 2010 annual report to shareholders, Bunge (the B in ABCD) states that: "while it is difficult to predict at this time what specific impact the Dodd-Frank Act and related regulations will have on Bunge, they could impose significant additional costs . . . and could materially affect the availability, as well as the costs and terms, of certain derivatives transactions."

Before the Dodd-Frank Act curtailed ABCD's capacity to manipulate pricing artificially, the price of wheat rose sharply across Mena-region Africa, including in Bouazizi's Tunisia. The Arab Spring erupted and the Islamic State's fourth-wave jihadism rolled across border after border. In ancient Rome, the poet Juvenal described *panem et circenses* ("bread and circuses") as a strategy politicians use to buy the contrition of the masses. As the Islamic State solidified its power, it understood the importance of "bread and circuses" in winning the support of local populations.

ABCD were playing a risky game, and the people who lost that game were those who did not even know they were playing: the people of North Africa. They could now be "liberated" from the colonial West, and the black-flagged advance of the caliphate had leverage with the people they "liberated" when it came to food prices.

As North African states collapsed, refugee ships began sailing across the Mediterranean, sparking a crisis on mainland Europe. This in turn fueled fears of a migrant invasion, which in turn propelled the rise of anti-immigration parties across Europe. And all because some food companies shorted the price of wheat. On the June 8, 2017, the Dodd-Frank Act was repealed and the obstacles placed in the wake of the 2007–2008 crash to curtail the financialization of food by ABCD were removed.

China Gets Risky

In 2016, the world's second largest economy got in on risk. For Chinese banks, the strategy was to turn high-risk loans into what they would call investments. "Shadow banking" tactics would be employed to shift these loans off balance sheets and into "partnerships" with trust companies and securities brokerages. A way of masking the sheer scale what was going on.[18]

China's central bank governor, Zhou Xiaochuan, warned in 2016 that the world should not underestimate the levels of toxic debt being created in China. It mattered, Xiaochuan said, because China was underwriting the world's debt. China was the economy that the United States turned to when it sold $700 billion of bonds to bail itself out in 2008.[19] China had effectively granted a giant overdraft extension. A back-of-the-envelope calculation in 2016 by Dallas-based short seller Kyle Bass, of Hayman Capital Management, estimated Chinese debt at $10 trillion,[20] dwarfing anything even Western banks managed. If this toxic debt went belly-up, who would bail China out?

Yuan Yang and Gabriel Wildau of the *Financial Times* have investigated how difficult Chinese debt is to penetrate and quantify. Lenders use "assets that are in effect loans but structured to appear as holdings of investment products issued by a third party. Such financial alchemy allows banks to evade regulations designed to limit risk."

In June 2016, regulations designed to curb banking risk were blamed for encouraging greater risk taking. The Basel Committee on Banking Supervision was criticized by lenders for proposing safety regulations for banks aimed at making it harder for banks to cheat the rules.[21] These new measures might encourage banks to lend more, not less, to their weakest lenders.

We have now normalized risk to such an extent that it is synonymous with the financial system. As Black and Scholes first discovered in the 1970s when they formulated their equation, and OPEC discovered when it held the world to ransom over oil prices, risk can be highly lucrative. When the gamble goes well, it goes very, very well. But when it goes wrong, that's what most of us try not to think about.

It's difficult to remember back to a time before this risky thinking wasn't orthodoxy. Yet the Wall Street Crash of 1929 was due to the riskiest of circumstances: democratizing stock market speculation, away from professionals on Wall Street, to so-called "mom and pop investors." In 1929, just as in 2007, no one noticed until it was too late. By August 1929, on the cusp of financial meltdown, brokers had lent small investors across America two-thirds of the face value of the total stocks they were buying on margin. The amount of money out on loan was more than the entire amount of currency circulating in the United States.

The subsequent US Banking Act of 1933 (Glass-Steagall) was specifically designed to separate commercial and investment banking by law, bringing the system back under tighter rein to prevent another speculation-driven crash. Sixty-six years later, in 1999, Glass-Steagall was repealed as banks sought to have their hands untied once more (the truth was that banks had long found ways around Glass-Steagall but its repeal was a symbolically important act, sending out the message that business rather than regulation should call the shots in business).

This concertina of tightening and loosening the strictures on business is the story of capitalism. The Dodd-Frank Act was brought in to prevent another 2007–2008 crash, only to be repealed as Glass-Steagall was. The difference from 1929 is that now, the cycle of boom and bust has sped up. To some degree, Black-Scholes was less a blueprint for irresponsible business practice than a shrewd acknowledgment that this inherent volatility lies at the heart of the system rather than being an aberration. It was stability rather than risk that was the temporary illusion.

7

TAX
Why Everywhere Wants to Be the Cayman Islands

THE DEAL: Sir Vassel Johnson, financial secretary of the Cayman Islands Monetary Authority sets up a formal body called FINCOCO to plan tax strategy with the leading accounting firms on the island, including Coopers and Lybrand and Maples and Calder.

AIM: To send a message to global corporations that Cayman is a legitimate and tax-efficient place to do business

WHERE: Nassau, Bahamas

WHEN: November 1975

According to the two most recent US presidents—Obama and Trump—there has been a heinous crime perpetrated against the American taxpayer that the culprits have not yet been punished for. One they were both deeply angry about. Tax avoidance.

Yet it is a crime both governments were keen to enable. The twenty-first-century race to become the nation on earth offering the most advantageous tax breaks has replaced the twentieth-century race to become the most productive manufacturing economy.

When politicians decry tax avoidance, it can sometimes seem reminiscent of the old film *Casablanca*. When Captain Renault, the wily police officer, is confronted by gambling in Rick's Bar, he is affronted. "I am shocked, shocked to find that gambling is going on here!" he says, as the croupier hands him his winnings under the table. "Oh, thank you very much." Then he turns to the other tables. "Everybody out!"

No one knows exactly how much corporations have hidden off-shore, but a 2012 study based on International Monetary Fund data put the amount between $21 trillion and $31 trillion. The US Senate Homeland Security subcommittee claimed that one bank, HSBC, was alone responsible for "failing to monitor" billions going offshore. It turned a blind eye, just like Captain Renault.

It is not just the banks and tech giants—Google, Facebook and Amazon—who reroute their profits, but also decidedly lower-tech businesses ranging from Burger King to bus companies. Profits pass through a labyrinthine system of subsidiaries around the globe before ending up in Switzerland, Bermuda, Luxembourg, London or Delaware (appropriately nicknamed "the small wonder"). There are more than seventy tax havens tucked away in surprising locations around the world, from Malia, an autonomous part of Spain on the coast of Morocco, to the tiny island of Sark off the coast of France. Accountant and tax haven specialist Marshall Langer says the most important tax haven on earth is a small island, attached to the United States, called Manhattan.

This is how using a tax haven works for a business: Company X makes a billion dollars in the United States in one year but certainly doesn't want to be paying tax on a billion dollars. So it sets up a shell company in India called Company Y. Y buys "services" from X for the price of a billion dollars, and suddenly Company X's taxable gains in the United States are wiped out. But Company Y in India doesn't want to pay tax on these services it has supplied to X, so it sets up another shell company, Z. This company is registered in the Cayman Islands, beyond the jurisdiction of American or Indian tax authorities. The profits from Y are rerouted through Z and voila!—no tax bill to anyone. Company X, the actual company behind shell companies Y and Z, has gone offshore. This smooth-functioning system, oiled by an army of lawyers and accountants, is not merely taking advantage of existing loopholes in the increasingly borderless, frictionless global economy; it has rewritten the rules to make such maneuvers legitimate in the first place.

Who these tax havens are open to depends on where they are: the United States uses its tax haven mechanisms in different states to attract global business to America but doesn't offer the same tax advantages to its own citizens. Bermuda's rules on tax apply to residents and nonresidents alike.

The jurisdiction that led the way, providing the template for how the tax haven system could work for the rest of the world, was the Cayman Islands. Cayman is arguably more open and transparent a tax haven than say Switzerland, Hong Kong or the City of London, yet thanks to scandals like those at FIFA and HSBC, and the revelations of the Panama and Paradise Papers, Cayman has become synonymous for many with shady dealings. It's a reputation that was acquired long ago and Cayman has had trouble shaking in spite of considerable efforts by the island's financial industry to improve its image. Beyond tax, Cayman is a crucial intersection between foreign companies and the United States, allowing businesses to buy into the United States under the radar, and this is the curious tale of how Cayman acquired this role.

Using John Lennon to Legitimize Tax Avoidance

In 1975, Alfred Ernest Marples, an English baron, who had served as postmaster general in the Conservative government, boarded a night ferry, hours before the end of the tax year. According to a *Daily Mirror* account from the time, he had with him only "his belongings crammed into tea chests, leaving the floors of his home in Belgravia littered with discarded clothes and possessions. He had been asked to pay nearly thirty years' overdue tax. The Treasury froze his assets in Britain for the next ten years. By then most of them were safely in Monaco and Liechtenstein."[1]

At the very moment Marples was boarding the night ferry, two accountants in London were setting about changing the global mindset on tax avoidance—from criminality to clever accounting. Their story begins in London. It is 1969 and John Lennon is at a cocktail party in Mayfair. He is introduced to two men in suits, Roy Tucker and Ian Plummer, who have a very enticing proposition for Lennon.

Tucker and Plummer had worked for the big accounting firm Arthur Andersen, but now wanted to go it alone and believed that they had a new business model: creative accounting for the wealthy. When the Labour government under Harold

Wilson began taxing the rich at an unprecedented 90 percent, they saw their chance.[2]

That they sought out Lennon was not a coincidence. When taxes rose, Lennon was livid, collaborating with George Harrison on the song "Taxman," which decried the new policy.

When Tucker and Plummer began chatting with Lennon, they were in the process of creating a "bank" called Rossminster. But this bank was very different from an ordinary commercial bank. It would have a discreet entrance with a small gold nameplate, and would deal only with super-rich clients. If Lennon came on board, they bet they could then recruit a few of his peers: Roger Moore, maybe Mick Jagger and Bryan Ferry. And in return, they promised Lennon a tax bill of zero. In fact, they said, the Inland Revenue would be paying him money.

Lennon signed up and Rossminster had its first big-name client. Two men were going to change the British attitude toward tax.[3] Tucker and Plummer found all kinds of cunning places to spirit away large sums of money for their clients: charitable donations to needy causes or shell companies with no evident business or board directors. Fellow Beatle George Harrison plowed his royalties into the failing British film industry—a guaranteed money mineshaft—producing some great films like *Scum* and *Withnail & I* in the process. Tucker and Plummer had pioneered a new form of "creative accounting." Careful not to break the law by outright evasion of tax, they sailed to the very edge of criminality, finding loopholes or twisting the rules to within an inch of illegality.

Veteran tax expert Graham Aaronson says that Rossminster "transformed the tax avoidance landscape beyond recognition [but] before rushing to moral judgment it's important to see the context." In 1975, the government in the UK raised taxes higher still until the top earners were handing away 99 pence on the pound. British Chancellor Denis Healy famously said he would tax the rich until "the pips squeaked." "It's hardly surprising," Aaronson says, "that many high earners thought it more productive to call for help from Roy Tucker and Ron Plummer rather than howl with anguish or wait until their pips squeaked."

In 1970s Britain, the government was in fiscal crisis, twice going to the IMF for a bailout. Taxing companies and the richest at the highest rates government could get away with was its answer. But in the US, the postwar orthodoxy of high tax was being challenged. As the *Harvard Business Review* pointed out in 2014, a punitive tax for high earners began to look like a huge obstacle to growth in the United States in the late 1960s. Taxes had been hiked during the World War II—in 1944, the top rate hit 94 percent—and remained stubbornly high for the next two decades. "The theory was that most rich people were basically rentiers, rent-seekers, and their income from owned assets could—and should—be taxed at very high rates with no adverse impact on the economy. Financing WW2 would have been an excuse for these highly confiscatory rates, but rather than dropping after the war, they continued to rise."[4]

By 1963, someone earning a million dollars a year was still paying 89 percent tax. There was a bipartisan congressional attempt to lower taxes, and the cuts predominantly benefited those in the top tax brackets. In his 1963 State of the Union address, President John F. Kennedy made tax reduction a key plank of his legislative program. He planned a reduction for the top earners to 65 percent, a reduction of the bottom rate from 20 percent to 14 percent and a corporation tax cut from

52 percent to 47 percent. Following Kennedy's assassination, President Lyndon Johnson enacted part of his wishes in the Revenue Act of 1964, or the Tax Reduction Act, cutting taxes across the board by 20 percent.

Kennedy's plan, endorsed and enacted by Johnson, was to use tax cuts to raise personal incomes and increase consumption and capital investment, and it worked. Unemployment fell from 5.2 percent in 1964 to 3.8 percent in 1966. Fears that there would be a loss of revenue to the government from tax cuts proved unfounded. Tax revenue increased in 1964 and 1965. It seemed counterintuitive but reducing taxes had increased tax revenue.

The wisdom on tax had flip-flopped in a decade, and not as the result of an ideological crusade but because of bipartisan agreement that lowering tax would bring economic growth. A young economist from Stanford, schooled under the Kennedy-Johnson revolution in tax, named Arthur Laffer was keen on understanding the paradox of lower taxes increasing tax revenue and began to work on an economic theory of low tax. In the early 1970s, Laffer was to become instrumental in the next tax revolution—advising government behind the scenes on how the low-tax revolution could be taken even further and spread to everyone.

The Doodle on a Napkin

Laffer's ideas about tax were framed by the Kennedy era and shared the classic Kennedy position that low (or no) taxes would create a "rising tide that lifts all boats." In 1974, he had the first at what would prove to be a series of lunches at the Two

Continents Restaurant at the Washington Hotel, in Washington, DC, with two rising stars of the Republican party, Donald Rumsfeld and Dick Cheney. Jude Wanniski, a *Wall Street Journal* writer, was also present, invited by Laffer.

Rumsfeld and Cheney were part of the team managing the transition from the Nixon to the Ford administration. According to Rumsfeld, "the country faced a number of serious economic problems and what was coming up through the system was not what I felt the direction the country should go." America had just gone through the OPEC oil crisis of 1973 and felt the axis of global economic power shifting to the Middle East. Fixed exchange rates set by the Bretton Woods agreement were also coming to an end. Floating exchange rates were ushering in an era of globalization and a shift in business priorities from the national to the world stage. Business could no longer be dictated to about where it should invest. To woo business to one country over another, governments believed they could use low tax incentives as the carrot. A race was on. But no one had yet created a precise economic model for how low taxes worked, nor at what level low tax worked at an optimal level for both business and government. In other words, how low should you go?

Policy in the early 1970s was being dictated, Rumsfeld said, by "speech writers not economists."[5]

Ford was proposing a 5 percent increase in tax, but as Laffer explained to Rumsfeld and Cheney at the Two Continents lunch: "Look, you're not going to get a 5 percent increase in revenue from a 5 percent increase in tax surcharge."

Laffer got out a Sharpie pen and began drawing a graph on his napkin to explain. On one side was the level of taxation and on the other, the level of revenue collected from that taxation. If you tax people at 0 percent, Laffer said, you collect zero taxes. And if you tax people at 100 percent you get zero taxes, because there is no motivation to work.

But there was a sweet spot of low taxes, incentivizing greater productivity and thus generating more revenue as a result. Laffer drew a curve to illustrate his point. High taxes created a vicious cycle for business, he asserted, while lowering them did the opposite: it created a virtuous cycle in which growth and incremental reductions in tax worked in tandem, for the benefit of government, business and the public. If one followed the curve, one could determine the optimum level of taxation.

Rumsfeld turned to Cheney and said: "Arthur Laffer is absolutely brilliant." It was, Rumsfeld later told Bloomberg News, "so simple and compelling and contested the liberal and conservative view." It was brand-new thinking, but it dovetailed with the neoliberal thinking of the Chicago School of economists at the time, led by Milton Friedman. It was neoliberalism plonked right on Rumsfeld and Cheney's plate, and they liked what they heard. Wanniski, the journalist at the table, left and penned an article: "Taxes, Revenues and the Laffer Curve." The "Laffer Curve" was born.

Laffer's instinct to look for an optimal level of low tax had another impulse. Even though his economics fitted the new neoliberal thinking, Laffer was a Democrat of the Kennedy era. He believed not just the rich but the middle class should benefit from the low tax revolution, and the middle class thought so too. On June 6, 1978, two-thirds of Californians voted to pass Proposition 13, which cut and capped property taxes and mandated a two-thirds vote for any future taxes. On August

1, 1978, the *New York Times* declared the revolt of the middle class on tax to be gaining momentum across America. If the middle class—hurting from rampant inflation—was not appeased by its own tax cuts and given the same benefits as higher earners, America faced a new kind of political crisis. A middle class who demanded the same treatment on tax as the rich.

Reagan sailed into office in 1980 on a radical tax-cutting program for this middle class. By 1982, under his leadership, it fell to 50 percent, the top rate kicking in at an annual income of $101,000 or more. By 1988, the rate had dropped to 28 percent, triggered at $29,000.

The world was now prepped for a low tax culture but big business still needed a place to do business that was "tax neutral." A place to conduct post–Bretton Woods globalized transactions free of the burdens of tax.

Turning a Mosquito-Ridden Sandbar into a Trillion-Dollar Island

In the late 1960s, the British Empire was finally being dismantled, and the colonies were faced with a choice. Some, like Jamaica, became fully independent. But for others, the British government had another plan.

In 1969, a civil servant named John Cumber was called in to the Foreign Office. He was shown a map of the Caribbean and a circle was drawn around a small mosquito-ridden sandbar called the Cayman Islands. Pack your bags, he was told, because next week you are going to be the governor.

So-called treasure islands such as Switzerland and Monaco had long served as tax havens, and now the British government saw an opportunity to get in on the act with an actual physical island. Cayman could remain under British sovereignty, guaranteeing political stability, but act independently and write its own tax law.

Cayman owed its sovereignty in this respect to common law. As economist Jan Fichtner puts it:[6]

> The key difference between common law and civil law is that common law only stipulates what is prohibited, whereas civil law, as practiced in Japan, Germany or France, identifies what is permitted. The consequence is that new financial innovations such as hedge funds or CDO's [collateralized debt obligations] can be set up easily, because strict regulation is only put in place with conspicuous misconduct or strong pressure from powerful foreign actors—governments.

In other words, Cayman could do what it liked with regard to tax, until someone stopped it. Until Cayman was retooled as a tax haven, places such as Switzerland and Monaco were exceptions to the global financial system. But one man saw Cayman as a way for Britain to muscle in on the business of these hugely successful tax haven states, and in so doing validate the business model of tax havens. The key was creating a place with more advantageous breaks than those of Switzerland or Monaco, and with a geographical location that would suit America.

George Bolton was a director of the Bank of England on February 28, 1958, when he noticed something very strange. The British high street bank, Midland, was handling a transfer of $800,000 on the trading floor that had not been flagged. This was a large one-off transfer of unclear provenance, and crucially, it was not in dollars but Eurodollars.

Eurodollars were first used after World War II to fund the Marshall Plan: the rebuilding of Europe with American money. This led to the circulation of huge sums of dollars overseas that were not subject to the Federal Reserve's usual strict scrutiny regarding domestic bank deposits. Millions of dollars were routinely moved around and not too many questions were asked about where this money came from or where it was going.

The reasonable presumption was that this Eurodollar trade was for huge reconstruction works in Europe or for US banks to safeguard assets abroad. Normally, trades with Eurodollars were traceable, above-board and relatively small. The Midland Bank transfer was different. It was huge. So big that it looked like laundered money. Except it appeared it was being laundered in broad daylight through one of Britain's biggest banks.[7] In that moment, Bolton saw a whole new potential for Eurodollars, as a parallel trading system in its own right, not simply a way of making one-off deposits or safeguarding assets.

Bolton saw a potential for the Eurodollar market as a legitimate conduit for business conducted below the radar. To orchestrate corporate deals to move huge amounts of cash around the globe free of government and currency controls. And for this to happen, it needed a physical place where scrutiny wasn't an issue, an "offshore" jurisdiction, though Eurodollars were to some degree an offshore market before offshore banking even existed.

Offshore was to become real—a physical place, not just a concept—through a sort of wheel of financial contortion.[8] At the center was London, where legitimate deals could be carried out. But the spokes would extend to offshore havens thousands of miles away, where deals London would be unhappy to see go through their books could go through instead, under much less scrutiny.

When John Cumber arrived on Cayman in 1969, it was sparsely populated: only fishermen, their families, the Cayman crocodiles that give the islands their name and the mosquito-ridden swamps. A huge program was undertaken to spray the lagoons with insecticide and prepare the island for its new purpose.

Cayman's first clients were not big business as the British government hoped, but drug dealers, from Miami and Cuba, Colombia and El Salvador. Cessna planes would fly over the beaches dropping suitcases of cash to be deposited and laundered on behalf of the emerging drug barons of central America, who were flush with cocaine money but with few safe places to put it. In years to come, Pablo Escobar would become one of Cayman's most loyal customers.

But then Cayman hit a stroke of luck. The Bahamas, its neighbor and a leading rival for offshore business, descended suddenly into political turmoil, before becoming independent in 1973. The Bahamas' accountants fled en masse to Cayman, bringing their business with them.

The Bahamas had benefited hugely from the collapse of the Bretton Woods agreement in 1971. Bretton Woods had lasted twenty-seven years strictly controlling exchange rates and capital movements. But now, without it, currency was suddenly free to flow across the globe unscrutinized, exactly as George Bolton had imagined it would in the 1950s. And now that all the accountants had moved from the Bahamas to Cayman, it was Cayman that stood to benefit. Tax avoidance was still not widely accepted by the public, let alone government policy, but that was all about to change.

Cayman had hoovered up criminal money but South American drug barons were not the business the large accounting firms coming to the island wanted. They were keen on long-term relationships with the big corporations who could take advantage of Cayman's location and tax haven potential.

The first thing Cayman did to gain credibility with this kind of business was create its own currency: the Cayman Islands dollar, aligned to the US dollar.

Nevertheless, it was still difficult to attract legitimate business. Truman Bodden served as Cayman's acting attorney general in the early 1970s. "It was difficult getting people to have confidence in three little islands in the Caribbean. There was the stability of having Britain as the mother country but people wanted to know if they go somewhere to invest, that there is a proper court system to deal with disputes."[9] In August 1972, Cayman was given a level of independence with its own Privy Council. According to Markoff, this was crucial in giving potential clients a sense of Cayman's legitimacy as a place to do business.

Cayman now had legal and financial infrastructure in place to attract companies from across the world. Yet still they did not come. It was down to two men to put Cayman on the map as the go-to tax haven location for companies that don't want to be seen to be doing anything wrong.

Marshall Langer was a US tax attorney who was one of the first in America to understand Cayman's potential to US business. According to Cayman accountant Paul Harris, "Langer was the one who really promoted bank secrecy in those days." Harris himself traveled to Los Angeles, San Francisco, Atlanta and Miami to give seminars for lawyers and accountants about the benefits of Cayman's "financial services."[10] "I'd tell them the people in the Cayman Islands don't live in thatch huts . . . and try to instill a sense of security about the place."

Cayman was trying to pull off a difficult conjuring trick in those days, simultaneously attempting to attract legitimate big business from the United States by playing up its credentials as a respectable place to invest, while also giving a sly nod that things could be done below the radar if required as well.

One of the first bankers persuaded of Cayman's attractions by Marshall Langer was Montreal-based Jean Doucet, who moved to Grand Cayman to create the International Corporation of the Cayman Islands, later known simply as the International Bank.

According to Alan Markoff, Doucet arrived in Cayman and soon became evangelical in his promotion of Cayman to other American businesspeople. "Doucet commissioned Marshall Langer and an attorney named W. S. Walker to write a booklet extolling the tax benefits of Cayman. He mailed twenty thousand copies of the pamphlet to potential investors. He spent about $250,000 on printing and mailing it out in 1973 and 1974 alone." He even made a promotional film, shown to accounting firms and businesses across America, which he financed and distributed himself.

In July 1974, Doucet hosted a lavish party at the Holiday Inn Hotel, Cayman, celebrating the fruits of his labor with one thousand distinguished locals and business guests wooed to the island by his efforts. It was also the launch of his latest venture, Cayman National Bank Ltd. But on September 16, less than three months later, Doucet's bank collapsed due to a liquidity crisis and his $50 million empire imploded overnight. Doucet was nowhere to be seen. He had left for Monaco with his wife on a private jet three days earlier.

Cayman had only just begun to build its reputation with legitimate business and now faced a damage limitation exercise caused by Cayman's first high-profile scandal. In spring 1974, Cayman's governor, Kenneth Crook, convened a large conference on the island to offer a salvage plan. "We must seek to convert the concept of tax haven into that of a purely financial centre . . . and we must institute and keep under continuous review, the sort of control which is necessary, if we are to attract the right people and maintain the island's position."

The Deal

In November 1975, a plan was enacted. Vassel Johnson, one of the island's most respected financial figures, stood up at the Offshore Financial Centre conference in Nassau, Bahamas. Johnson is now widely regarded as the godfather of Cayman's success as an offshore center, largely because of what he was about to suggest.

"The Cayman Islands have never attempted to introduce legislation to attract the sort of business from highly-taxed countries," he said, "which would tend to promote the local economy at the expense of foreign tax evasion, as we think this is unethical."

A year before, Governor Kenneth Crook had spoken about rebranding Cayman as a place for reputable business, not criminality. Vassel Johnson saw the potential for making this real by creating an alliance of Cayman's government and the financial services industry. He proposed a regular strategy meeting under the aegis of the Financial Community Committee—known as FINCOCO.

FINCOCO would provide a place for a tax strategy for Cayman to be agreed between government and business in liaison, meeting fortnightly and planning strategy, especially to woo new business. This was important because Cayman was now in fierce direct competition with other tax havens across the world and credibility was key to gaining the edge.

Vassel Johnson's role in transforming the fortunes of Cayman is hard to overestimate. FINCOCO was a masterstroke, at once giving a sense of transparency to Cayman's activities while simultaneously providing a mechanism for developing policies that would subsequently be adopted by other tax havens across the world, something these tax havens were slow to implement themselves. It was Cayman's bid to become top dog, and it succeeded.[11]

Help was also at hand from the low tax doctrine being sold to Western governments by Arthur Laffer, which was shortly to go global and put booster rockets beneath Cayman as a hub for business. In 1979, an ideological revolution was led by the two most powerful leaders of the free world: Margaret Thatcher and Ronald Reagan. Both believed that government had become too big and, more to the point, both wanted to break the regulatory shackles that tied big business down. Markets, not government, should henceforth decide what was best for the economy, and at the heart of this revolution was low tax.

For forty years since the beginning of World War II, taxation had been seen as necessary, the price paid by citizens and business to have a functioning civil society. But if business was freed from this burden, it was now argued, everyone would benefit in the long run. Capitalism was about to change course, and Arthur Laffer's ideas, first doodled on a napkin for Donald Rumsfeld and Dick Cheney five years earlier, were now to become government policy, with tax havens—like Cayman—at the heart.

Laffer began to lunch with Ronald Reagan, as he had done with Rumsfeld and Cheney, again at the Two Continents Restaurant, discussing his vision of how Kennedy-era low tax theory dovetailed with the supply-side economics of Friedman and the Chicago School. When Reagan was elected in 1980, Laffer became a key economic advisor. His low tax doctrine was now government policy.

But it created a potential challenge for tax havens. Why would a business bother to offshore its earnings anymore when it had low tax breaks in its own country? Because Cayman also offers a benefit to globalized business that has nothing to do with tax avoidance.

Shadows Beneath the Water

When I arrive on Grand Cayman, it is very different from the island John Cumber landed on half a century ago. Today, the place feels like an affluent suburb of Florida. Low-rise buildings run along the main road that provides the island's spine: white sandy beaches and turquoise ocean on either side. Mega–cruise ships from Miami arrive daily, dispatching thousands of tourists who buy T-shirts and conch shells with "I Love Cayman" written on them, before reboarding their ships for a cocktail.

To look at the place, one would not think it a hub of global finance. There are no gleaming glass towers, like in London or on Wall Street; wealth here is hidden. Despite the lack of glitz, this single five-mile bar of sand in the ocean has more external assets than Japan, Canada or Italy. It is the number one legal domicile of choice for the hedge fund industry (60 percent of the world's hedge fund managers operate from this one stretch of sand). It is also the number one destination for asset-backed securities and collateralized debt obligations across the globe.[12]

But all of Cayman's profits and debts are housed in anonymous low-rise banks and offices staffed by casually dressed accountants in Bermuda shorts and flip-flops, who drive not Ferraris, but Toyota Priuses. And the thousands of corporations that have been registered in Cayman—from IKEA to HSBC, Starbucks to Vodafone, Pepsi to Disney—have no visible presence.

There is, however, one building tucked away at the end of the beach in which more than twenty thousand companies are registered. In 2008, President Obama singled it out as "either the biggest building in the world or the biggest tax scam in the world." At Ugland House, there are no big gates or security guards. It is all hidden in plain sight. I walk up to the glass doors to have a look inside. A relaxed doorman eventually saunters out to see who I am. "I wonder if I could have a look inside?" I am politely told to leave the property, but not before looking though the darkened windows. A lot of desks, but not a single person from those twenty thousand companies sitting at any of them.

It is very strange they have even let me in. After decades of secrecy, including a law forbidding journalists from even asking questions, let alone investigating anything, Cayman has now relaxed that policy significantly. With the race now on between Western governments to offer the lowest corporation tax, Cayman faces fierce competition. As companies seek out ever cleverer and more complex financial "arrangements," they also desire the veneer of transparency, and so Cayman is increasingly taking pains to open up and show the world it is legitimate. Currently, Cayman ranks number five on the financial secrecy index of least transparent tax havens.[13] In 2009, the IMF said the greatest danger to Cayman's future as a tax haven was not governmental interference or even outside investigation, but "reputational risk"—continuing to look dirty.

But if you ask Caymanians why they think their islands have such a bad reputation, it is not industrial tax avoidance or Pablo Escobar that is mentioned, but a 1993 movie starring Tom Cruise. At first, I thought this was a joke, but soon lost count of how many times it was mentioned.

The Firm tells the story of a sharp attorney working for a law firm who comes to realize his bosses are laundering money for the Mafia through Cayman. *The Firm* cemented a reputation that Caymanians say is unfair. Now they want to clean the slate—hence my invite. Unfortunately, the week does not start well for tax havens globally. Google is accused of siphoning 80 percent of its profits through tax havens in Bermuda. The IRS reveals it is chasing Amazon for $1.5 billion in back taxes stashed in Luxembourg (Amazon eventually won its case against the IRS), and Apple admits to moving $74 billion offshore to Ireland, paying an effective 2 percent tax.

I meet the island's governor, a woman in a pink hat who lives in a big colonial house, with whom I have tea. I am introduced to the elected premier, a polite if brusque man who clearly wishes he was not talking to me, and I speak with various prominent businesspeople, including John Cumber's grandson, who are all unfailingly charming. The message is clear: Cayman is an open book.

The place is a cross between a Caribbean island and Britain in the 1950s. I am given free rein to wander about asking anyone anything I want, as long as it is not about the corporations registering their profits here.

In the early 2000s, US, Dutch and British companies took advantage of Cayman because their governments enabled them to use it as a direct investment conduit, and now Brazil and China do the same. In 2000, accounting firm Pricewaterhouse-Coopers devised a legal "innovation" for Chinese corporations to list publicly abroad, thus getting access to foreign capital and circumventing China's restrictions on foreign investments. It is called a variable interest entitiy (VIE), a variation on the holding company.

In 2014, Chinese e-commerce giant Alibaba raised a record $25 billion with its initial public offering (IPO) in the United States, using PricewaterhouseCoopers's holding company innovation. The International Consortium of Investigative Journalists has revealed that the relatives of China's Communist Party elite also use VIEs to circumvent party rules to create shell companies in tax havens for the purposes of taking money out of China.[14]

Cayman is known to the world for tax avoidance, but its real function lies many layers beneath clever accountancy. Cayman provides the mechanism for foreign companies to buy up US companies and industrial infrastructure without appearing to be foreign, under the guise of "portfolio investment."

In 2015, Cayman reported "portfolio investment" assets to the IMF of $61 billion. Jan Fichtner at the University of Amsterdam drilled into the figures and put the real assets at $2,574 billion—forty-two times greater than reported, since the reported figures exclude hedge funds. Hedge funds are at the absolute heart of below-the-radar Cayman (which explains why 60 percent of the world's hedge funds operate here).

And the primary role of many foreign enterprises that do business in Cayman is to secretively buy equity in American companies. On the face of it, the true "nationality" of any port-folio investment is impossible to establish, because investment instruments cross-multiply jurisdictions, sometimes over dozens of countries. The only way to understand how they actually work, says Fichtner, is to look at two basic numbers: the money going in, and the money coming out.

This is called "inward" and "outward" investment, and the country with the biggest discrepancy in these figures on Cayman is Japan. In 2015, less than a tenth of Japanese portfolio investment of over half a trillion dollars went back to Japan; much of the remainder entered the United States, as Hong Kong and Japanese investors use Cayman as a conduit for portfolio investment into the huge American equity market.

Cayman is also a giant and crucial intersection for globalized trade. John Cumber's grandson, Marcus, who runs an aviation empire from Cayman, explains to me how it works, using a stick on a beach. He draws a circle. "This is, say, a Japanese company wanting to buy steel in the US." Marcus draws another circle. "And this is the company in the US selling the steel. Now where are they going to do the deal? In Japan, or in the US? They're going to do it by creating a holding company somewhere like Cayman." Marcus draws a third circle with a palm tree on it. "Cayman is the answer."

Railing against offshore is like railing at the ocean. It is there, and there is no changing it. Beneath that blue ocean, dark shapes move—the corporations waiting to come in. What started as a relatively simple mechanism for tax avoidance on a sand bar has mutated into an impossibly complex financial mechanism, with the moral complexities to go with it.

Offshore is how the world works, and this total global system operates beyond the control of any one government.

At tea in the governor's house, I asked her a question. "Could Cayman be shut down?" She looked shocked. "What do you mean?" Could the British government shut you down? "Good God, no. Cayman is an independent state."

I put the same question to the premier. "Ultimate sovereignty," he told me, "lies in London, with the British government."

So, no one is responsible. Cayman operates in a very convenient no-man's-land, beyond the remit of anyone. It is truly offshore in the way the entire banking system is offshore: operating somewhere out there in the middle of the sea, where dark shapes swim beneath the surface.

8

WEALTH
The Business of Inequality

THE DEAL: Tobias Levkovich chief equity strategist at Citibank, makes a presentation to the bank's biggest clients, suggesting a shift in business strategy.

AIM: To show these clients why global inequality was widening dramatically and how to take advantage of this inequality to make money

WHERE: Citigroup headquarters, 399 Park Avenue, Manhattan

WHEN: 2006

Imagine a golf cart that seats eight people. Then put the eight wealthiest people on earth on that cart. You would have Mexican telecom mogul Carlos Slim (worth $75 billion) riding up front. Next to him, Bill Gates ($75 billion). On the middle seats, Zara founder Amancio Ortega ($67 billion), Warren Buffet ($60.8 billion), and Jeff Bezos of Amazon ($45.2 billion). A row back, Facebook's Mark Zuckerberg ($44.6 billion) and Oracle's Larry Ellison ($43.6 billion), with Michael Bloomberg (a mere $40 billion) in the bucket seat at the back.

These eight people, with a combined worth of $426 billion, control as much money as the poorest 50 percent of the earth's population.[1]

Opinions on the severity of the crisis vary. Christine Lagarde of the IMF has called this polarization of global wealth the greatest threat the twenty-first-century world faces—the economic equivalent of global warming. But other economists, such as a group at the Institute of Economic Affairs, argue that overall global poverty is reducing, and that the widening gap between rich and poor is simply the inevitable price we pay for the planet as a whole getting richer.[2]

Regardless of one's moral response to inequality, many economists agree on a key factor that is at work: "rent-seeking." The wealth of the richest and poorest is connected so that even if the poor might become slightly less poor, the richer will become richer at their expense. Growing global prosperity is not, as John Kennedy put it, a "rising tide that lifts all boats." As the super-yachts rise on the tide, the little boats go under. This is because, as economists like Paul Krugman and Joseph Stiglitz have pointed out, the wealth of the very richest is "extractive": it extracts wealth directly from the poor. They are linked.

The first systematic attempt to understand inequality came from an Italian sociologist and statistician named Corrado Gini, who worked under Mussolini in Fascist Italy. Gini was a polymath intellectual and believed statistics, sociology, demography and biology could be merged to create a grand scientific understanding of human behavior.

In 1908, he published a paper on natal sex ratios, presenting evidence that a couple may be more likely to produce a boy or girl depending on certain hereditary factors. Though he was initially a collaborator and friend of Mussolini's, they fell out as the Fascist regime began to lean on Gini's work as academic evidence of its ideology.

Gini was above all an eccentric follower of his own path. He was a eugenicist and firm believer in using eugenics to "improve" the human race, as were many intellectuals of the left and right in the 1920s and 1930s. But he also had an insatiably inquiring mind. He led an expedition to study the Karaites in Poland, a sect of Judaism that holds the Tanakh alone as the supreme authority of Jewish religious law, because he genuinely wanted to understand Tanakh Judaism from the perspective of its scholars.

In 1912, as a way of measuring global inequality, he created the Gini coefficient, which he outlined in his famous paper "Variability and Mutability." A value of zero represents the most equal society—one in which every member owns the same amount—and the value of one the most unequal, one in which all wealth is controlled by a single person. The place a country falls on the zero to one scale is calculated by measuring the statistical dispersal of income of a nation's residents. The Gini coefficient became the standard by which inequality would be measured for the next century. While it can sometimes be an overly crude measure, it does makes a reasonable stab at measuring relative and absolute poverty.

In 2017, Oxford University academics used the Gini coefficient to estimate global inequality trends in the twenty-first century and concluded that while overall global inequality was reducing (the poor were getting less poor across the planet) absolute inequality was rising dramatically.

Dr. Laurence Roope of the Nuffield Department of Population Health at Oxford summarized their findings: "Over the past forty years, over one billion people around the world have been lifted out of poverty, driven largely by very substantial growth in income in countries such as China and India. This rise has been accompanied by a striking rise in absolute inequality, but it has changed the lives of many people."[3]

As one of the report's authors, Finn Tarp, explained: "Take the case of two people in Vietnam in 1986. One person has an income of US$1 a day and the other person had an income of US$10 a day. With the kind of economic growth that Vietnam has seen over the past 30 years, the first person would have now $8 a day while the second would have US$80 a day. So if we focus on 'absolute' differences, inequality has gone up, but if you focus on 'relative' differences, inequality between these two people would have remained the same."

But in March 2006, ten years before inequality was being written about in leader columns and discussed as cataclysm by the IMF and World Bank, a group of farsighted business analysts saw the whole thing coming. And they recognized that it would present some unusual business opportunities.

The Hourglass

Tobias Levkovich is a very smart man. He meets me in his vast office overlooking the Hudson River on the forty-ninth floor of the world's fourth-largest bank, Citigroup, where he runs the Global Strategy division. He tells me about one of his favorite books: *Leviathan* by Thomas Hobbes, a political treatise in which the most enduring message is that human beings will do whatever they can get away with, unless strong rules constrain them.

Informed in part by his seventeenth-century political philosophy, Tobias has a unique perspective on the contemporary world as well. And in 2006, he held in his pocket a photograph of the future, which, if he chose to share it with his clients, was going to make them a lot of money. A very large amount indeed.

In 2006, Tobias spotted something big. Three Citigroup colleagues—Ajay Kapur, Niall Macleod and Narendra Singh—had written an internal equity strategy report entitled "Revisiting Plutonomy: The Rich Are Getting Richer."[4] In it they argued that global wealth was polarizing, not merely a little or a lot, but in an unfathomable way that would eclipse anything seen in history.

Wealth at the top of the tree was going to be held in fewer and fewer hands. "We talk about the one percent, but to get technical, we're actually talking the zero-point-one percent," Tobias tells me. "We've always had the haves and have-nots, but now we would have the haves, the have-nots and the have-yachts."

In 2006, inequality was an observable trend. But what Tobias had was a strategy for how to capitalize on it. He revealed his blueprint at Citibank headquarters in Manhattan to a sea of stony-faced men and women in business suits. These people represented the biggest companies on earth: oil, steel, construction and hedge fund giants; food and chemical multinationals; supermarkets; aviation constructors; pharmaceutical companies and car manufacturers; mobile and internet providers on every continent.

"The coming decade will be marked by polarization and social unrest," Tobias said, "a direct consequence of growing economic inequality." The clients coughed and looked down at their notepads. "Many will be worried by this. We at the bank worry less."

Tobias predicted correctly at that meeting that inequality between different countries in the coming years would lessen as inequality within each country grew broadly. In 2016, Richard Baldwin at The Graduate Institute in Geneva wrote a book called *The Great Convergence* arguing that a combination of free-flowing information technology and low globalized labor costs is making countries more equal: poorer countries growing as the richer ones stagnate, until eventually we are all the same. Between 1820 and 1990, the share of the world's income going to wealthy countries soared from 20 percent to almost 70 percent. But in the last twenty-five years, that share has fallen back dramatically to where it was in 1900.[5] Countries across the world are starting to become equally unequal. But in 2006, Tobias Levkovich had already spotted this and told Citibank's clients what it could mean for their businesses.

Tobias used a simple analogy to illustrate his point: the hourglass.

Every country, as it becomes more unequal, will come over time to look like an hourglass. At the top, the super-rich global elite, who will buy Learjets and Bentleys. At the bottom, the global poor, to whom there will be new opportunities to sell poverty-related products: payday loans, zero-hour contracts, high-interest credit. As stress increases for the poor, gambling and alcohol will once again become boom industries. Pawnshops and discounting will become huge, as people fail to make ends meet.

It was a breathtaking vision, but I was intrigued by the hourglass. What was the deal with the tapered bit in the middle? "That's the middle class." They will be squeezed by diminishing income and cease to have the same purchasing power, and thus be of less importance as a market to sell to. Hence, the fact that they make the tapered part of the hourglass.

As Tobias painted this brave new world to Citigroup's clients, the room was silent. "You could have heard a pin drop," he says. At first Tobias thought this might simply be shock at the apocalyptic future he was predicting. "It must be true if Citigroup is saying it, right?" But then he realized it was something else. There was an expression of awe on their faces, Tobias said, as the scale of the opportunity opening before them began to dawn.

In the two years between the Citigroup presentation and the 2008 crash, the companies in the room diversified their portfolios exactly as Citigroup advised, focusing on businesses at both ends of the hourglass: high-end luxury for the rich and poverty-alleviating products for the poor.

But it was only when the crash happened that things really took off for Citigroup's clients. Tobias's prediction had come true faster than anyone could have dreamed.

A Family with $80,000 in 1986 Has . . . $80,000 Today

The people on my golf cart all think inequality is terrible. They say so all the time, as do the heads of the IMF, the World Bank, the Fed and every other financial institution that spent the last twenty years putting in place the mechanisms that allowed inequality to open up like a chasm.

In 2015, I interviewed French economist Thomas Piketty, the author of *Capital in the Twenty-First Century*, who believes that selling to the rich and poor spheres of the hourglass is merely a by-product of inequality; the underlying process that drives its perpetuation is wealth extraction from the poorest to the wealthiest.

This, Piketty argues, is uniquely dangerous for society as a whole, because it tests society's reason for existing. It pushes the contract of shared rules to the edge, which is when society begins to break down. So what can be done? Piketty shrugs his shoulders. "Perhaps retool the IMF, so it has transnational jurisdiction to prevent multinationals escaping their legal obligations." A kind of International Task Force like Marvel's Avengers able to swoop on unsuspecting corporations and slap them with a fine for tax avoidance. A bold solution, but an unlikely one.

Over the last thirty years, wealth has eroded in the United States for the vast majority of people. Economists Emmanuel Saez and Gabriel Zucman calculated in 2014 that the share of wealth for the top 0.01 percent has increased from 7 percent to 22 percent. For 90 percent of US families, a combination of rising debt, the collapse of value assets during the financial crisis and stagnant real wages has eroded their wealth. For US families outside the top 10 percent wealthiest—in other words, 90 percent of adult Americans—average household wealth is $80,000, the same level as in 1986, when adjusted for inflation. By contrast, the average wealth for the top 1 percent more than tripled between 1980 and 2012.[6]

Just as all countries are coming to look the same—equally unequal—so the makeup of the big city is becoming familiar. A mega-sprawl like Mexico City, Cape Town, São Paolo, Shanghai, Lagos, Los Angeles, London. An inner sanctum populated by the super-rich, living a gilded life of darkly lit exclusive restaurants, weekends in Monaco on the super-yacht, skiing in Gstaad, shopping in Dubai for $100,000 handbags and perpetual private-jet ("PJ") transit. This roped-off state floats above and beyond the masses like a fluffy champagne cloud, but is uniformly identifiable as the same place, with the same brands and schedule, wherever you are on the planet. In the other parts of the city, people living one payday away from broke and so stressed by this precariousness, they die ten years before the rich. Is this any different from the growing inequality of nineteenth-century England described by Friedrich Engels in his *The Condition of the Working Class in England*?

I live in the center of London and my local mini-supermarket is a microcosm of the new kind of city that is emerging. Seventy-five percent of the customers are fast-rising career people from Europe and the United States in their mid-twenties and early thirties, working for start-ups, big corporations such as Google or banks in the City. They come in to the minimart wearing hoodies and tracksuit bottoms after a run, buy some milk or quinoa salad and leave.

There are eight staff members, who work twelve-hour shifts, employed on zero-hour contracts. They are similar in age to the customers, but their lives are very different. Three of them live at least a ninety-minute journey from the minimart. One lives thirty miles away. They cannot afford to rent in central London, but cannot afford to give up their job either.

In 2015, Hannah Aldridge and Tom MacInnes of the New Policy Institute analyzed recent population movement in London to try to determine the level of interaction between these two groups.[7] They found a single city in which the rich and poor coexist in the same space, but are invisible to each other. The poor do not aggravate the rich, but defer to them—in public spaces and when they intersect (like at my minimart).

So why aren't the poor moving out? Moving means destroying everything. Key to surviving on a low income with highly precarious work is a social network of friends and family upon whom one can rely, allowing one to juggle these precarious jobs. This cannot easily be re-created elsewhere. The "working poor" cannot afford to leave, but neither can they really afford to stay, as rents continue to rise.

Growing cities are an insatiable machine that require people to service them. But if the people servicing that machine cannot afford to live there, what happens to the machine? In London, as in New York and Shanghai, the poor are bending their lives to make it work. If Corrado Gini were with us today, he'd be working on calculating the coefficient at which this machine breaks.

Who Stole the Parachute?

In 2008, the banks crashed. The answer was quantitative easing (QE). The US Federal Reserve, led by Ben Bernanke, bought bonds worth $3.7 trillion with money it had "printed." The Fed didn't print physical notes—it was electronically created—but "printing money" became the colloquial shorthand for QE.

This is how QE works in principle: in a crisis, printing money increases the overall amount of usable funds in the financial system, helping to restore liquidity. This in turn allows banks to lend, businesses to invest and consumers to spend. It's CPR for the economy, kick-starting a recovery.

That's the theory. When interest rates are close to zero, as they have been for most of the last decade, there's an argument that some QE also serves a purpose in creating some limited upward pressure on prices, stimulating growth. But not too much upward pressure. Inflation is seen as one of the dangers of QE.

In October 2014, Janet Yellen, the successor to Bernanke at the Fed, called time on QE for the United States. It was seen to having done its job. In combination with low interest rates, QE had freed capital and encouraged a steady rise in risk appetite, helping US stocks rebound since 2009.

But growth had stalled, and stubbornly remained stalled. Even though interest rates had remained at an historic low, Yellen began entertaining the idea that interest rates might have to go below zero. In 2016, at the annual economic symposium at Jackson Hole, Wyoming, she outlined a plan for negative interest rates that could effectively force banks to lend money. With negative interest rates, banks would pay to park their own money in their vaults. Anything but lending and spending would not be an option.

Negative interests were discussed in relation to another economic crisis, like 2008, but continued economic stagnation is a slow-motion crisis. Negative interest rates have already been employed in Sweden, Switzerland and Taiwan.

So did QE in combination with low interest rates function as intended? In the immediate aftermath of the 2008 crisis, QE as CPR kept the system alive and prevented a deeper recession, but long term, QE vanished. So where did it go? I ask Tobias Levkovich. "Ninety-five percent of quantitative easing, sold as bailing out the whole economy, went to the top of the hourglass."

In September 2015, the *Financial Times* investigated the real beneficiaries of QE. "Public pronouncements about the objectives of QE are deliberately shrouded in central bank speak.

Depreciation of the yen is quite obviously an indirect effect . . . but it would not do so for Shinzo Abe the Japanese PM to say so plainly. That would be politically toxic in the American heartlands. Nor would Mario Draghi, president of the European Central Bank, acknowledge that he is artificially distorting the bond markets so that the debt-ridden governments of peripheral Europe can continue to enjoy a low cost of capital (the Eurozone's very own Ponzi scheme). But that is what he is doing."[8]

QE covered a multitude of sins. But the biggest beneficiaries were the banks—with twenty or thirty times leveraged balance sheets. According to Marshall Wace, chairman of a London-based hedge fund, "asset managers and hedge funds benefited too."

QE also enabled the 1 percent to be able to invest in the poverty products from Citibank's hourglass that would widen inequality still further. In 2016, Scott Helfman, a Citigroup spokesman, said the bank doesn't comment on its relationship with clients but *Bloomberg Businessweek* obtained a leaked copy of its favored "secret client list" kept on the equity research desk. At the very top is a handful of hedge fund giants: Millennium, Citadel, Surveyor Capital, Point72 and Carlson Capital. The kind of super-class clients who receive advanced models and analytics, such as Tobias's hourglass model.

In 2006, the investment advice to diversify into luxury brands and services catering to the top of the hourglass was complemented by poverty products for the bottom orb—extended loans on cars, furniture, holidays, property, and bridging loans to cover heating and food bills. And this market depended for its growth on the acceleration of debt.

"Debt is really the key to the whole thing," according to

London School of Economics economist David Graeber. "The finance industry and the debt industry are really the same thing. To a large extent, 'finance' really just means 'other people's debts.' They're simply trading our debts with each other."[9]

But there was another option. Economist Anatole Kaletsky of the Institute for New Economic Thinking says QE was a fork in the road, and puts forward a radical alternative that has gained traction on the left and right.[10] Had QE not gone to the banks but to everyone else in the form of a one-off payment, every household in the United States would have received a check for $30,600. This money would have been spent on holidays, fridges and cars, rebooting consumerism and a Keynesian boom.

Helicopter money was first mooted by the prophet of supply side, the Nobel-winning economist Milton Friedman in his 1969 paper "The Optimum Quantity of Money." "Suppose one day a helicopter flies over this community and drops an additional $1,000 in bills from the sky, which is, of course, hastily collected by members of the community. Let us suppose further that everyone is convinced that this is a unique event which will never be repeated." Friedman also believed money could be given directly to business rather than go through banks in order to maximize the "potency" of money, especially at a moment when banks are caught in a liquidity trap.

Ben Bernanke revived the idea of helicopter money in November 2002 in a speech about heeding the lessons of deflation in Japan. "Keynes once semi-seriously proposed, as an anti-deflationary measure, that the government fill bottles with currency and bury them in mine shafts to be dug up by the public . . . essentially equivalent to Milton Friedman's famous helicopter drop of money."

QE happened but the radical version, dropping money in people's accounts, was vetoed. Raghuram Rajan of the Reserve Bank of India said people would not spend the money. They'd hold on to it. Claudio Borio of the Bank for International Settlements said there was "no such thing as a free lunch" and helicopter money was legally problematic, blurring the lines between fiscal and monetary policy. Bundesbank president Jens Weidmann argued that it "would tear gaping holes in central bank balance sheets."

Parachuting money to families had been endorsed by economists across the political spectrum from neoliberal thinkers such as Deirdre McCloskey to Keynesians like Kaletsky, Eric Lonergan and Simon Wren-Lewis. But it was opposed by the big guns of the monetary mechanisms in the United States and in Europe. In a letter to parachute money advocate and member of the European Parliament José Fernandes, the European Central Bank explained that "legal complexities could still arise if the scheme could be seen as the ECB financing an obligation of the public sector vis à vis third parties, as this would also violate the prohibition of monetary financing." The use of direct payments as a substitute for welfare payments was also vetoed. There was, however, a politically expedient solution: more debt, which—David Graeber argues—was the plan all along.[11]

"Our indebtedness, our addiction and entrapment by debt, fueled London and New York as finance centers in the wake of the crash. It was at the heart of the recovery of finance, and our debt was the engine. So what you see after the crash are some fairly intentional government policies which are designed to guarantee most people are in debt."

Citigroup's 2006 report was a prophetic document. No one outside that boardroom on the forty-ninth floor of Citigroup knew it was coming, but the deals it enabled were going to change the lives of millions of people walking the streets below.

Why the Middle Class Matters

One of the research papers mentioned in the footnotes of the Citigroup report was by a then unknown postgraduate student at the London School of Economics named Thomas Piketty, who was writing a dissertation on inequality—the dissertation that ten years later became *Capital in the Twenty-First Century*.

I asked Piketty, now one of the world's most celebrated economists, about the importance of the middle class.

"The middle class is very important for the economy because they have been the means by which it's been possible to develop mass consumption and mass investment in construction," Piketty says. The opportunity to become middle class in the 1950s and 1960s was what drove greater equality and distributed wealth evenly throughout society, reaching a high watermark in 1976, when the Office of National Statistics declared society most equal. Between 1945 and 1978, wealth was more evenly distributed throughout society than at any other time in history. It was a thirty-year aberration of equality sandwiched between two periods of huge inequality: the 1930s and now.

"The middle class has begun to shrink in the last twenty years," Piketty says. "And this is a major threat to democracies if it continues shrinking in the coming decades."

The middle class has historically had the means to own private property. Broad aspiration toward home ownership began in earnest in the 1930s, was interrupted by World War II, but then vastly expanded in the 1950s, as a huge building program enabled millions of people to buy their own homes for the first time. It was the dream my immigrant grandfather followed as he moved out of the poverty of Kentish Town to the clean air and neatly trimmed hedges of suburbia.

Yet since 1996, that dream has dissolved, as fiscally responsible home ownership has become an increasingly remote possibility for many Americans. Widening inequality has coincided with the stagnation of wages and the consequent end of access by the young to the property ladder. If my grandparents aged twenty-five were looking to buy now, they would be stuck in the slums, lucky to even cobble a monthly rent together.

"Are we going to continue in the direction of a shrinking middle class?" Piketty asks. "It's difficult to know how far this will go. What we know for sure is that in recent years, what we've observed in Britain and other countries is that the wealth of the top wealth holders—billionaires—is rising much faster than average wealth and much faster than the size of the economy. You can see that if this continues for several decades more, the share going to the middle class will decline." In years to come, renting—not ownership—will become the norm. In 2013, rents rose significantly more rapidly than salaries.[12]

And this will be make it virtually impossible to reverse inequality, because the middle class (and those aspiring to become middle class) will have lost their primary means of wealth accumulation. The hourglass will be structurally entrenched.

"How unequal will we become?" Piketty asks. "On these trends, it looks pretty frightening." But if you disenfranchise the middle class, you are also dealing with a highly combustible force. A contented middle class does nothing, but if they are either scared for their future security or growing greedy on a rising economic tide, they will drive revolution.

In 1917 Russia, an impatient and newly emboldened bourgeoisie drove the provisional government that replaced the tsar, which in turn was overthrown by the Bolsheviks. In Paris 1968, middle-class intellectuals and organized labor nearly toppled President Charles de Gaulle (but famously didn't). In both cases, a disgruntled if ambivalent middle class was at the heart of the mobilization.

Nick Hanauer lives in Seattle and was one of the first investors in Amazon. He is now worth $6 billion, and sees the hollowing of the middle class in the new hourglass model of society as a threat to capitalism. "Capitalism, the greatest economic system ever created, does need some inequality, just like plants do need some water to grow. But in precisely the same way that too much water kills plants, too much inequality kills capitalism by drowning the middle class."

Hanauer stands in a modest office with a spectacular view of Puget Sound, watching sailing boats darting across the water. "In the Middle Ages, inequality was not a problem. You grew up expecting the world to be unequal. He's a peasant. He's a king. That's how it works. But when you live in a modern capitalist culture that encourages everyone to have more and to believe you can have it, then equality becomes a much bigger problem. You can't have what other people have and this is the cause of discontent. Capitalism has bred resentment, and the equality of opportunity it promised hasn't happened."[13]

Hanauer has a personal stake. He is worried that when this happens, the massed ranks at the bottom of the hourglass will be coming for him. "Are the pitchforks coming? Maybe not tomorrow, but for sure they will come. You show me a highly unequal society and I will show you either a revolution or a one-party state."

GLOBALIZATION
How Asia Rewrote the Rules

THE DEAL: Chinese President Xi Jinping signs the One Belt
One Road (OBOR) agreement with sixty-eight countries,
including the United States.

AIM: To invest an estimated $1 trillion in giant
infrastructure projects across the world—from the
building of road systems and ports to railways and power
stations

WHERE: Beijing

WHEN: May 13, 2017

Playing with my Hot Wheels car set as a kid, I was struck by
something odd.

To a child growing up in the late 1970s and early 1980s, Hot
Wheels was the epitome of cool American culture. The cars
spoke of Evel Knievel jumping gorges on his stars-and-stripes
rocket bike; the go-fast flames on the Mustangs and Dodge
muscle cars were pure *Dukes of Hazzard*. Yet if you turned
the car over, it was stamped not with "Made in the USA," but
"Made in China."

So how did China become the world's workshop?

The answer is simple, as Harvard economist Joseph Nye explains: "If we looked at the world in 1800, you'd find that more than half of the world's people lived in Asia and they made more than half the world's product. Now fast forward to 1900: half the world's people—more than half—still live in Asia, but now they're making only a fifth of the world's product.

Now, it seems, Asia has caught up. The Industrial Revolution had made Europe and America the engine of the world economy. But that dominance is widely argued to be ending, with China setting itself the task of once more becoming the dominant economic power broker, as it was three hundred years ago, under the Qing Dynasty. In October 2017, China's leader Xi Jinping set out a new phase of communism that, according to Howard Schell of the Asia Society's Center on US-China Relations, "suggests Socialism with Chinese Characteristics is a viable counter-model to the presumption of western liberal democracy and capitalism . . . not only a clash of civilization and values, but one of political and economic systems."

In the late 1970s and early 1980s, when I was playing with my Hot Wheels toy cars, that resurgence of Asian economic might was just beginning. It was not only Hot Wheels that got made in China. All sorts of other cheap consumer goods that fueled the consumer spending boom of the West had "Made in China"— or Korea or Japan or Singapore—stamped on them too.

Tiny metal toy cars became big real cars as Asia began to dominate the world's automobile market as well. Japanese tech innovation soon turned around the country's onetime reputation for cheap, shoddy radios and TVs into one of reliable, affordable excellence. Toyota and Nissan had meanwhile gone after the market share of General Motors and Chrysler.

China's economy today is bigger than India's, Russia's and Brazil's put together. Though not growing at the phenomenal 10 percent per annum rate it was prior to the financial crash of 2007–2008 (it mitigated the effect of the crash on the rest of the world by mounting a campaign of state-directed spending that created huge debt for itself), China is still growing at 6 percent a year. The country's middle class has grown to 100 million people and in spite of extraordinary pollution levels created by rapid industrialization—as bad as the industrial heartland of nineteenth-century England—life expectancy is seventy-six years, higher than the world average or that of any other developing country.[1]

So should China's born-again might be hailed, or feared? Protectionist guru Peter Navarro fears that the West will inevitably suffer "death by China" as the rest of the world's dependence on China's economic power combined with China's economic expansionism make its hegemony inevitable.

But others aren't so sure. Will China's hegemony necessarily play out badly for the rest of the world? Less than 10 percent of the world's population is fully industrialized. As China industrializes further, it could triple that global figure, sucking in and industrializing a further 20 percent of the planet's population by igniting growth in Asia, Latin America, Africa and even reinvigorating the old industrialized West. "Death by China" could well turn out to be the opposite, "rescue by China."[2] This positive view of China is put down to a plan to create the largest infrastructure program in human history, the global equivalent of Franklin D. Roosevelt's New Deal. A mammoth state-sponsored injection of cash to kick-start economic growth not just in one country but across the planet.

OBOR: The New Silk Road

On May 13, 2017, President Xi Jinping signed a cooperation agreement in Beijing with sixty-eight countries, including a delegation sent by President Trump. China, Xi said, would be offering to invest close to a trillion dollars in infrastructure spanning the globe.

The deal was called simply OBOR—One Belt One Road. If realized, it could make China's global hegemonic ambitions real. The scale was breathtaking: an extraordinary initial $900 billion investment strategy beginning in Asia, encompassing the building of a deep-water port in Gwadar, Pakistan, and a "port city" in Sri Lanka's Colombo; high-speed rail links in East Africa and from southwest China to Singapore; and gas pipelines across the whole of central Asia. OBOR is, as the *Financial Times* reported at the time, "arguably the largest overseas investment drive ever launched by a single country."

OBOR is a conscious remapping of the Silk Road from China through central Asia and the middle East to Europe, and from China to Southeast Asia and East Africa by sea. It was first signaled with an announcement by President Xi Jinping in 2013 as a response to the effect the slowing of growth in Western economies was having on China's own economic well-being. For three decades, China's growth had largely depended on exports, such as my Hot Wheels toy cars. Now, to keep Western consumer spending going, China was going to inject an unprecedented sum of cash into the equation. In 2015, China launched the Asian Infrastructure Investment Bank (AIIB) with the explicit aim of funding OBOR. That same year, it transferred $82 billion to three state-owned banks for OBOR projects.[3]

Beijing then identified the sixty-five countries along the belt and road that could benefit from OBOR. The plan is not geo-specific to China's neighbors. New Zealand, Britain, even the Arctic, are all on the list. Projects such as the building of the Hinkley Point C nuclear power station in the UK with a Chinese-French consortium are viewed in China as OBOR projects.

Tom Hancock of the *Financial Times* described OBOR as a potential Trojan horse for China's global dominance. "As China's foreign policy becomes more assertive, OBOR is a geopolitical gambit . . . drawing comparisons with what Edward Luttwak, the military strategist, has called 'geo-economics'—when the 'logic of conflict' is pursued through 'methods of commerce.'" No need to use tanks when investment will do the job far more effectively.[4]

Yet on May 11, as President Xi Jinping prepared his speech in Beijing to announce OBOR to the world, President Trump made an announcement of his own: a trade deal with China, part of which involved sending a delegation to hear Jinping's speech in two days' time. Trump had, critics said, flip-flopped on China. It was seen by commentators and former supporters of Trump's protectionist rhetoric as a defining moment in his early presidency. The day he became globalist. As Linette Lopez wrote in *Business Insider* on the day of the announcement, "This [deal]," she wrote, "isn't just a love song for globalization, it flies in the face of the 'Buy American, Hire American' ideology Trump has touted. The entire point, after all, is China helping to build infrastructure in other countries. [It] is clear the tough-on-China Trump we met during the 2016 campaign is no longer with us."[5]

But the deal that had killed the "tough-on-China Trump" had already been done a month earlier, on April 6 at Mar-a-

Lago, at the US president's country club in Florida when President Xi Jinping and President Trump met in private.

In the days leading up to the meeting, President Trump had been bullish about confronting China on its imperialist ambitions. He said negotiations would be "very difficult" and he would be driving a hard bargain. But the tone was very different when Xi and Trump walked out together at the conclusion of the meeting. Trump had flip-flopped, announcing they would be working together on a trade deal.

"He is a very good man," Trump said about Xi. "He loves China and he loves the people of China. . . . I really liked him a lot. I think he liked me. We have a great chemistry. I think in the long term, we are going to have a very, very great relationship."[6]

What had happened in those forty-eight hours at Mar-a-Lago? One theory is that Trump was simply made aware of the reality of their relationship. In October 2016, six months earlier, the Chinese Communist Party's senior officials met in secret and raised their hands in unison to declare Xi Jinping China's "core" leader, a position of supreme political unassailability, elevating Xi to the level of a new Mao Zedong.

According to Chinese political analyst Professor Zhang Haibin, "Trump [by contrast] faces a lot of resistance at home with Congress and protests. The two leaders' domestic political situation isn't the same. Xi is "the core" and China is very stable. Trump has yet to establish his authority in the US and is facing a divided society."[7]

China's strategy at Mar-a-Lago was to talk to Trump in terms he would be receptive to—to talk business and offer a straightforward bilateral business deal between China and the United States. And because Trump had talked repeatedly about bilateral deals as his answer to trade across the world, in offering one, China was also offering a deal that could save Trump face back in the United States, should it be argued he was climbing down.

Beyond this bilateral agreement, when OBOR was announced a couple of months later, it too could be justified in Trumpian terms as a series of bilateral agreements between China and sixty-eight separate countries.

The deal also forced an issue within a divided White House by clarifying where the president stood on trade. The disagreement on strategy between anti-globalist advisors like Steve Bannon, who'd been by Trump's side for the election, and the newer pragmatist globalists, like Secretary of State Rex Tillerman and Chief of Staff General John Kelly, remained at the time of Mar-a-Lago unresolved.

Steve Bannon viewed the talks with China, according to Linette Lopez, as "a slap in the face" for the policies Trump had stood for on the campaign trail. Pragmatists like Rex Tillerman, by contrast, stated at the outset of the China talks that "all options were on the table." By siding with the pragmatists at Mar-a-Lago, Trump had struck a blow against the Bannon faction in the White House, preempting Bannon's departure in August. The power within the White House was seen as having shifted toward the globalist-pragmatists. For the moment.

Before Mar-a-Lago, OBOR might have been portrayed by Trump as "geo-economic" imperialism by China. Instead, it had President Trump's tacit blessing. And the ground was set for the OBOR announcement.

The Mar-a-Lago meeting was spun by the United States as a meeting of equals. But China believed it came to the table stronger. An unnamed former EU diplomat was clear that China's plan was (and is) political expansionism. "OBOR is a domestic policy with geo-strategic consequences," he said, regardless of the interpretation put on it by either the United States or China. Infrastructure is what China does best, and doing it effectively abroad will also reap benefits for its domestic economy, the continuing growth of which will in turn stimulate colossal demand for raw materials, energy, imports and capital flow. China argues OBOR is a virtuous circle, benefiting all OBOR's signatories.

China is the largest trading partner for 120 countries. It will be a bigger net importer than the European Union by 2020. As the former chairman of Goldman Sachs, Jim O'Neill, puts it succinctly: "China is the biggest example of growth and poverty reduction in history."[8]

But in July 2017, two months after OBOR's announcement, President Trump flip-flopped back to trade war talk with China. The Mar-a-Lago honeymoon was over and largely because a new dynamic had been thrown into the equation: the renewed military threat from North Korea.

China had refused to give the United States the support the president sought over ramped-up aggression from North Korea, and this had fatally flawed their blossoming trade relationship. "So much for China working with us," Trump tweeted tersely. Orville Schell, director of the Center on US-China Relations at New York's Asia Society, believed this moment reiterated China's upper hand in its relationship with the United States. "Had [Xi] buddied up with Trump and put the screws on North Korea I think [Xi] would have gained . . . [but] I wouldn't say it was a mistake for Xi not to take that offer in exchange for peace on the trade front. I don't think there was real space for a deal."

China, in short, held the stronger cards. OBOR was in place, and moving forward like a trillion-dollar juggernaut regardless of the United States. Any trade war with the United States in the aftermath of a disagreement over North Korea might be unwelcome, and unwanted by both parties, but it was not the main show for China. Pivoting into the position of chief global broker for a new Silk Road was, and the plan remained on track.

Gold, China and Globalization

How did China become the preeminent broker of global commerce? The roots lie over seventy years ago, in leafy New Hampshire. On July 1, 1944, a deal was struck by the most powerful postwar economies on earth—the forty-four allied nations—at the United Nations Monetary and Financial Conference at Mount Washington Hotel, overlooking the sleepy town of Bretton Woods. The aim of the Bretton Woods agreement was simple: to establish rules for creating monetary control and stability for postwar capitalism to avoid a repeat of the dire economic conditions that led to World War II. National currencies would be tied to a fixed exchange, pegged to gold and the US dollar, and a bank of last resort called the International Monetary Fund (IMF) would provide nations with bridging loans on imbalances of payment. Bretton Woods sought to ensure that rules and institutions would govern the flow of global finance, allowing for regulated free trade across

the globe within firm parameters. In exchange for being po-
liced, nations would have access to a system that enabled them
to trade equitably.

There is considerable disagreement among economists about
the long-term effectiveness of Bretton Woods. Keynesians and
those on the Democratic Left tend to look at the twenty-seven
years it was in operation—between 1944 and 1971—as a
golden age of capitalist stability, with the US dollar as the pillar
of that stability. Because the dollar had been pegged to gold at
Bretton Woods, it became the default world currency.

This was both a blessing and a curse. Economic commentators both positive and negative of Bretton Woods generally
concur that because the United States contributed the most
funds to both the IMF and the World Bank, originally set up
"to facilitate the investment of capital for productive purposes"
of the defeated war nations (Germany, Japan and Italy), to its
broken Western European allies (Britain and France) as well as
developing the developing world (South America, Asia, Africa)
this meant the US could run a trade deficit without having
to devalue its currency. This worked temporarily but couldn't
sustain long term.

Advocates of Bretton Woods maintain that after the war,
Bretton Woods established firm rules by which to conduct in-
ternational trade, leading to a prolonged and unprecedented
period of stability and prosperity. In 2014, Paul Volcker, one
of the world's most influential economists who'd served as
Chairman of The Federal Reserve under presidents Carter and
Reagan, made a speech on the twenty-first May anniversary of
the annual meeting of the Bretton Woods Committee at the
World Bank HQ in Washington. "What about a new Bretton
Woods?" he asked. Volcker said it wasn't mere "nostalgia" but

the need for a guarded return to a "more orderly, rule-based world of financial stability . . . by now I think we can agree that the absence of an official, rules-based cooperatively managed monetary system has not been a great success."[9]

Yet critics say that the stability and prosperity attributed to Bretton Woods was a mirage. Matt Johnston, an economic commentator formerly of the World Economic Forum,[10] argued in *Forbes* in 2015 that "there were signs of instability throughout the era and perhaps not enough has been made of the relative difficulty in trying to maintain the system. Rather than seeing Bretton Woods as a period characterized by stability," he concluded, "it's more accurate to consider it being a transitional stage that ushered in a new monetary order."

How did it work and why did it end? The US bank-rolling of the recovery of post war capitalism had a sting in its tail. By the late 1950s, the defeated powers of Germany and Japan were in remarkable turnaround and serious trade competitors to the United States. Dollars had been printed to rebuild the very economies that now posed a renewed threat, through trade. The expansionary monetary policy required to do this had the knock-on effect of creating a balance of payments deficit in the States.

This strain on the US economy in turn meant Bretton Woods began to creak under the strain. On the surface, the world economy appeared to be flourishing but beneath something else was going on. By the late 1950s, says Johnston, "dollar claims on gold [exceeded] the actual supply of gold, [and] there were concerns that the official gold parity of $35 an ounce now overvalued the dollar."

An extraordinary situation began to arise in which the newly emboldened trade competitors to the US—Britain, France and

Germany—began to see arbitrage opportunities in this stretching of the system to potential breaking point: making a fast buck. The dollar pegged to gold was coming under extreme strain.

For the next decade, a game of cat and mouse ensued: European countries didn't want to revalue their currencies as the United States may have wished them to, so losing the trading advantage cheaper exports gave them, but neither could these countries nor the US afford to let the Bretton Woods system break. There appeared to be no alternative to what capitalism had, and sterling efforts were made on a coordinated international basis to keep the dollar pegged to gold afloat.

These included the creation in 1961 of a "Gold Pool" in which even gold from Apartheid South Africa and the Communist Soviet Union was thrown into the reserve in a desperate attempt to keep pace with demand for dollars (it collapsed in 1969). A new type of currency—a supplementary reserve issued by the IMF and called SDR (Special Drawing Rights) was also mooted, and dropped.

The entire global economy teetered precariously like a giant inverted pyramid, bearing down on a single point. The weight of all global currencies was bearing down on the dollar, which in turn was bearing down on gold. On the cusp of the 1970s, with the US in the inescapable position of having to run a massive trade deficit, and with US foreign liabilities some four times the amount of US gold reserves, there just wasn't enough gold in the vault. Pressure increased to inject some give for currencies trapped in a hamstrung global system: one that gave no option to adjust value ("float") free of the dollar, since they were tied to it.

A run on US gold reserves looked inevitable. On August

15, 1971, President Nixon called time, unilaterally terminating convertibility of the dollar to gold. The G10 countries met at the Smithsonian Institute in Washington in December 1971 to sign the Smithsonian Agreement to formally establish that exchange rates would henceforth float without the reserve backing of either gold (or silver). Nixon called the Smithsonian Agreement to end fixed exchange rates "the most significant monetary agreement in world history."[11]

Bretton Woods had officially collapsed, and Nixon was right—it was a sea-change in the way the world would work. Exchange rates were now officially "floating" and governments would no longer determine currency price. Markets would. But the collapse of Bretton Woods was even more significant for paving the way for the deregulated business culture we have today. What Paul Volcker might call the end of "rules." From now on, currency prices would be set by commercial trades on Forex, the largest and fastest moving currency trading market in the world.

Open twenty-four hours a day, five days a week, Forex is not a physical space but a global currency exchange through which New York, London, Tokyo, Zurich, Frankfurt, Singapore, Sydney and Paris all continuously trade currencies and thus perpetually recalibrate their value.

At the Smithsonian Agreement signing in December 1971, capitalism changed to the system we have today. The keys were handed over from men with clipboards in Washington and Geneva, who'd been prescribing what nations could and could not do for nearly three decades, to traders across the world, scrutinizing the markets twenty-four hours a day.

Regardless of what view one might have for the reasons for the postwar economic stability of the international system, or the wisdom of adopting the dollar as a fixed exchange pegged to gold, there is little doubt Bretton Woods had been instrumental in rebuilding the postwar world. It had allowed US trade surpluses to be recycled by countries with trade deficits, which enabled the United States to continue sending money to rebuild Germany, Japan and Korea.[12] By 1971, however, the world was rather different from the one in which Bretton Woods had been first devised.

Yanis Varoufakis, the economist and former Greek minister of finance, believes Nixon's desire to come off the gold standard was not the primary reason for the collapse of Bretton Woods. "Bretton Woods worked until the US stopped running trade surpluses," he says, which was effectively by the end of the 1960s. After 1971, the system simply couldn't continue because the United States lost its surpluses with little hope (bar a blip in 1968–1969 when there was a surplus) returning in the long run. "Then America started recycling everyone else's surpluses. It was operating like a vacuum cleaner, sucking in the net surplus wealth and net profits into Wall Street to close the loop."

In spite of the continuous pressure exerted on the entire system by international demand for dollars, Bretton Woods had done its job, supporters such as Varoufakis argue, in maintaining stability and preventing a return to the economic crises of the 1930s. But it had also stymied the free flow of capital by maintaining restrictive barriers on trade and currency exchange, and thus holding back globalization. By 1971, business, not government, was perceived as the engine for future prosperity—through free trade, not government control.

In the 1980s and 1990s deregulation on Wall Street, freeing banks to trade more freely, symbolized by the eventual repeal of the Glass-Steagall Act in 1999, allowed business to begin taking advantage of floating exchange rates and make globalization happen. According to economist Dani Rodrik, by the late 1990s, "an intellectual framework became established . . . by the World Bank and the WTO [World Trade Organization], whereby globalization was seen as the way countries would grow." If countries opened themselves up to big corporations (by providing attractive employment laws and low corporate tax rates), then they would get payback in the shape of jobs, investment and the chance to attract more business.

This was a not unreasonable assumption to make; indeed, supply-side economic orthodoxy endorsed this view. But there was a problem, according to Rodrik. "That narrative failed to see that countries that did well under globalization did so on their own terms. They maintained strong infrastructure and investment in combination with taking advantage of globalization. So we only got half the story."[13]

While big economies like those of the United States and Britain acted, Rodik argues, like developing countries desperate to attract global corporations by offering tax cuts and the most attractive cheap labor conditions, yet were inevitably undercut by South America and South East Asia, countries like Germany and Sweden maintained a strong commitment to infrastructure spending, higher levels of corporation tax and state-heavy expenditure on health, retraining and benefits for working parents. In spite of these seemingly antibusiness measures, these countries managed to still attract global corporations looking for higher-paid skilled workers in new technologies and maintained respectable growth rates as a result.

But China, Rodrik says, went one step further when it came to globalization, behaving as one giant highly secretive corporation. It protected its own interests while playing hardball on the global stage as ruthlessly as any globalized corporation. "When you look at how China achieved this feat," says Rodrik, "it controlled capital flows, subsidized industries, it required investors to use local content, violated trade agreements, violated property rights. It maintained wide state ownership, largely to protect employment. [China] benefited from all the other countries following the rules of hyperglobalization."[14]

While Western nations went for an authentic free market vision of globalization, China cunningly had its cake and ate it too—protecting its own citizens from the tough economic realities that swept across industrial America and Europe but behaving beyond China as if it were the most ruthlessly competitive company on earth. China held on to pre–Bretton Woods assumptions about investing in infrastructure and subsidizing industry while simultaneously joining in the post–Bretton Woods free market free-for-all. Jim Yong Kim of the World Bank sums it up neatly: "Globalization worked marvelously for Korea, China, and for most of East Asia, but not in Iowa—who voted Trump."

Does Democracy Impede Growth?

In recent years, China has been especially keen to buy up businesses is the United States. Foreign ownership has increased steadily over the last two decades, and the Chinese appetite is growing across a bewilderingly varied array of industries.

In 2013, processed-meat conglomerate Smithfield Foods was bought by Shuanghui International for $7.1 billion. Professor Minxin Pei at Claremont McKenna College called the deal "a masterstroke to expand its ability to supply a fast-growing market with premium-brand pork at higher prices. . . . Shuanghui might [also] use Smithfield as a channel to sell its products in the US."

According to *Fortune,* in just one year—2016—Chinese investors bought the following:

- Starwood Hotels, incorporating the W Hotels chain, bought by Anbang Insurance in a deal worth $14.3 billion
- Ingram Micro, a tech company and number sixty-two on the list of Fortune 500 companies, bought by Tianjin Tianhai Investment for $6.3 billion
- General Electric Appliances, selling toasters and dishwashers, bought by Qingdao Haier for $5.4 billion[15]

Dalian Wanda bought film company Legendary Entertainment Group, which made *Jurassic Park* and *Pacific Rim,* for $3.5 billion (to go with AMC, America's largest cinema chain, which it bought in 2012 for $2.6 billion).

And this only skims the surface of Chinese investments in the States in a single year. China is now one of the biggest investors in American real estate. One might imagine an Amazon or Google being given tax breaks or a land grant to invest in the United States but in Thomasville, Alabama, in 2014, land was given for free as part of an "economic development project" to attract Chinese copper tubing conglomerate Golden Dragon, luring it to the American South.

The 2013 Smithfield Foods deal with Shuanghui was followed by ChemChina's $43 billion bid for agrichemical giant Syngenta. These deals marked continuing Chinese encroachment on America's agricultural industry. The Smithfield deal was accompanied with the reversal of a 1999 law by Nebraska's governor Pete Ricketts preventing meat packers from owning livestock for more than five days prior to slaughter in order to make the deal more attractive to Chinese agribusiness looking to vertically integrate and turn American pork into a huge contract farming concern: owned by Chinese business based in the States, exported to China.

But the repeal was interpreted by local journalist Tove Danovitch[16] as an attempt by local politicians to woo the Chinese and reboot the local economy, not as a crude Chinese takeover. "Most other Mid-Western states long ago repealed their own packer bans and have seen pork production climb as Nebraska's slipped. Nebraska was the last holdout . . . and Nebraska's legislators [were] courting China as an important trading partner. China is in dire need of both food and farms. More than 40% of China's existing arable land has been degraded by pollution. As a result, China is investing in the best agricultural technology and best farmland—regardless of where it lies—to keep its people fed. The United States, with six times more arable land per capita, is the perfect contract farmer."

When one begins to understand who really owns what in any country, and what the complexity of the relationship is, talk of a trade war starts to sound a little imbecilic. Trade war with whom? With yourself?

Some may yearn for the "stability" of a world under Bretton Woods. That world was never as truly stable as one might imagine, but there is little doubting the new world of globalized trade is significantly volatile too. Even Yanis Varoufakis, a self-proclaimed "leftist," is realistic about the options when it comes to redesigning stability back into the system. "What we don't need is what we did between the mid-1970s and 2008, allowing Wall Street bankers to financialize, creating torrents of speculation on the stream of capital flows. We need a new Bretton Woods: a new managed capitalism just like we had between 1944 and 1970."[17]

"Of course," Varoufakis continues, "this is a new paradigm. We're not going to have fixed exchange rates, or a dominant power like the US, so we better learn how to cooperate at the political level in order to create economic equilibrium that is capable of averting the rise of nationalism."

One of the primary drivers for a rise of political nationalism is job insecurity from the perceived influx of cheaper immigrant labor, and perhaps in this respect, the West could learn from what China does when redundancies happen. In 2016, when 2 million Chinese steelworkers were laid off due to overcapacity, Minister for Human Resources Yin Weimin announced that "adequate measures" were in place. The government would simply retrain them as entrepreneurs. A policy decision was made to boost income in the aftermath of the layoffs rather than cut it, and maintain rising wages as well as improve the condition of migrant workers. The slogan for this mammoth program was telling of China's approach to reinvestment in the workforce and thus the economy as a whole: "Do not leave a single individual behind."[18]

As economist Yasheng Huang notes in his book *Capitalism with Chinese Characteristics*, it is China's authoritarianism and lack of democracy that make such a sweeping transition possible. Huang argues that in the 1980s, entrepreneurial rural China was the engine of capitalist growth for the economy. But in the 1990s, the urban elite that coalesced around the Communist Party began to reverse many of the rural experiments in capitalist enterprise. In the United States, this may have resulted in a protracted standoff between the powerful farming lobby and the political establishment in Washington, resulting in a compromise. But because this was a command economy, the Communist Party simply did it.

The party even used the promise of capitalist opportunities to the growing urban wealthy to reinforce an anti-democratic agenda across China and quell desires for greater democracy. The party offered prosperity to a growing middle class and achieved growth without a need to make political concessions.

Huang points out that China was not the only populous nation to go through huge economic change in the 1980s and 1990s; so too did India, and India's commitment to secular democracy didn't waver as rapid economic growth was achieved. Huang says the "democracy hinders rapid industrialization" thesis does not hold true for all countries.

One consequence of China's command economy has been to put dynamic coordinated policy—like OBOR—into action. Jim Yong Kim of the World Bank compares what China did with mass redundancies with what happened in the West. "When NAFTA [the North American Free Trade Agreement of 1994] and the great trade agreements were made, there was [always] a plan to retrain people with programs as jobs were lost." These programs were known as Trade Adjustment Assistance (TAA) and have existed in one form or another since 1974. They are designed by the federal government to minimize the adverse effects of globalization by paying for job training and compensating workers who have lost jobs to offshoring. TAA has been the subject of controversy as to its effectiveness. A study by Kara Reynolds and John Palatucci of the American University in 2006 concluded that "the TAA program is of dubious value to displaced workers."

Those who took up TAA retraining—2.2 million of the 4.8 million the Department of Labor estimated were displaced by foreign trade—still took a pay cut of roughly 30 percent. Workers who didn't retrain also saw their income fall, but only by 9 percent. Robert Z. Lawrence, former economic advisor to President Bill Clinton, concedes that the effectiveness of TAA depends on how you measure it. "If you view it as a compensation scheme, I would say it's reasonably effective as compensation."[19] Not, one notes, as a means to retrain.

Unsurprisingly, given the criticism TAA has received, budget cuts to a scheme costing the government on average between $500 million and $750 million a year were inevitable. In 1997, the Economic Policy Institute issued a study estimating that only 10 percent of American workers who lost their jobs due to plants being moved to Mexico following NAFTA ratification in 1994 actually received retraining assistance. Though President Clinton attempted to expand the scheme with an $800 million injection, criticism from academic reports and economic think tanks in the context of a worsening economic climate axed the plan.

In February 2017, a Reuters review of US Labor Department records revealed that President Trump, who "vowed to stop US manufacturing from disappearing overseas, is seeking job creation advice from at least six companies that are laying off thousands of workers as they shift production abroad."[20] Caterpillar Inc., United Technologies, Dana Inc., 3M Co, Timken and General Electric were moving US jobs to Mexico, China, India and across the world, whilst simultaneously sitting on the White House's Manufacturing Jobs Initiative advisory council.

The companies could legitimately be said to be squaring the circle because the offshoring picture is complex: new jobs are created in US factories at the very moment other jobs move abroad. The degree to which American workers believe this was tested in 2016, when candidate Donald Trump stood on a protectionist ticket, promising to Make America Great Again, and won.

Jim Yong Kim says the United States has paid the price less for offshoring than for sinking funds into the wrong kind of retraining, such as TAA—one that focuses on creating more replaceable jobs rather than looking to make the jobs of the future. "Silicon Valley complains there's not enough skilled people for jobs, while in Iowa there are people who need jobs but don't have the right skills because they weren't retrained."

In Asia, retraining is not an add-on but core to business strategy. "In China and South Korea, there's a paranoia about being ready for the next wave. They've perfected the semiconductor business, of going faster and faster, but now they're going 'what's next?' and there is a paranoia among parents about preparing children for what happens next. That didn't happen in Iowa."[21]

20,000 Elon Musks

GWC is a Sino-Japanese tech company with ambitions that make the Silicon Valley tech giants look modest. GWC is basically a giant entrepreneur-training operation with offices in Beijing, Tokyo and in Mountain View, California, where Google is based. GWC is industrializing the idea of entrepreneurship with the aim of producing 20,000 Elon Musks.[22]

In 2013, GWC hosted a pitching session in Beijing for budding mobile executives, developers, investors and entrepreneurs at its annual Global Mobile Internet Conference (GMIC). The aim was fulfilled: 20,000 hopefuls turned up and began frantically pitching ideas.[23]

The "G-Summit"—short for the GMIC—is a global competition to find innovations backed with $1 million. GWC functions like a large-scale venture-capital firm. In 2016, winners from Bangalore, São Paulo and Taipei were given the green light to develop ideas with multiplatform potential across the planet.

Silicon Valley is alert to the threat. "The Valley needs to think more globally," says Facebook vice president Vaughan Smith. "With its focus on Asia, GMIC is among the few tech conferences that's focused on important trends happening outside the US."

In 2015, Apple's CEO Tim Cook signed up for a social media site: Weibo, China's answer to Twitter. This was not because Apple's boss wanted to post cuddly pictures of pandas. Since both Twitter and Facebook are banned in China, joining Weibo was a rare opportunity for Apple to reach millions of Chinese people through the portal of Cook's verified account.

Apple is one of the few Western tech giants that is also entrenched in the Chinese market. The Chinese have their own equivalents to Google, Facebook, Uber and Amazon.

Baidu is similar to Google, providing an array of services, from maps and cloud storage to payment systems, food delivery, health-care ventures, driverless cars and research into AI. Alibaba is China's leading digital payment platform, the largest e-retailer on earth. Tencent is China's Facebook, with WeChat—a clever combination of WhatsApp, Facebook, Apple Pay and Google News—reaching more than 700 million subscribers.

JD.com is China's Amazon but, as Jason Hiner of tech innovation website ZDNet points out, "It's actually racing ahead of Amazon." JD.com has addressed Chinese consumers' concern about mass-produced fake goods by authenticating deliveries of global brands and is now offering same-day deliveries to 600 million customers (next-day delivery to the whole of China), working on drones to remote areas.

Didi is China's Uber, with a $1 billion investment from Apple. And Didi even has some additional features in comparison to Uber itself, like the "Didi Bus," a driver service that will pick you and your car up if you have had too much to drink. Didi is also using big data and machine learning to attempt to solve China's huge traffic congestion and pollution problems in cities by moving cars off the streets at peak hours.[24]

These companies—like the Silicon Valley Big Five—are fiercely ambitious. But they also have a systemic business advantage over their American and Western counterparts because they have an inextricable, almost umbilical link with government. In South Korea, this relationship is epitomized by the "chaebol": huge family-controlled companies such as Hyundai and Samsung with direct access and influence over the government. In 1988, Chung Mong-Joon, president of Hyundai Heavy Industries, successfully ran for South Korea's National Assembly. This relationship is sometimes referred to as "corporate governance," in which brand and national identities and interests are perceived as one and the same.

The chaebol system has recently come under attack, however, as an institutionalized form of corruption. In August 2017, South Korean president Moon Jae-in dispensed with the traditional custom of pardoning chaebol family members charged with bribing government officials by allowing heir apparent to the Samsung empire Jay Y. Lee to be convicted and given a prison sentence. In the past, chaebol family heads could escape imprisonment by making a donation to charity, as Hyundai chairman Chung Mong-Koo, convicted of embezzlement, did in 2007, giving away $1 billion and gaining a pardon from President Lee Myung-bak.

Clamping down on chaebol corruption is a sign that the overly close relationship between government and the big family-run companies is coming to an end. But only as these companies seek to move beyond Asia to become global competitors rivaling Google, Amazon and Facebook.

In 2016, Walter Price, a San Francisco–based fund manager at Allianz Global Investors, noted a tipping point being reached with the Asian tech competitors to Silicon Valley. Four companies in particular—Samsung, the phone and electronics giant; internet provider Tencent; online retailer Alibaba and electronics company Taiwan Semiconductor—were all being tipped by investors in the West to grow faster over the next ten years than their US equivalents. Tencent had seen its share price rise by 5,000 percent in less than a decade. In 2016, it became the most valuable company in Asia. "The companies in China," Price said, "are basically shaping up as the global rivals to the US-centered internet rivals."[25]

So how will "Stat" (Samsung, Tencent, Alibaba and Taiwan Semiconductor) match up against "Fang" (Facebook, Amazon, Netflix and Google)? James Yardley, a senior research analyst at comparative investment specialists Chelsea Financial Services, believes Stat has the edge on its Western counterparts. "Some of these companies have really good technology, in some cases better than Western technology," he says. Even Stat's Asian competitors are barking at its heels.

Huawei and Xiaomi make mobile devices and are looking to break into the market that Samsung and Apple have dominated. Xiaomi hired Google's Android chief Hugo Barra to realize their ambitions, not just in Asia but across the globe.

But the key to Stat's advantage over Western companies, Yardley says, is its launch-off point. "[Investors see] they have more growth potential—they have emerging middle classes in Asia to sell to, whereas Western markets are more mature." Plus they can double down on this bigger market potential. "Adoption of technology in Asia is much faster than in Western nations, giving better prospects for growth too." Not only is the market bigger, meaning they can potentially grow bigger, but the quicker rate of technology take-up means they'll be selling more product to more people twice as fast.

This would not matter to the Western Fang companies if the two markets were compartmentalized and separate, but they're not.

Once upon a time, Silicon Valley could comfort itself with the thought that Silicon Valley was where innovation happened and its Asian equivalents were simply facsimiles. But the fact that the Stat companies have a better long-term growth trajectory means they have ambitions to leapfrog their Western competitors not just in scale but innovation too. The desire of their innovation-hungry consumer base will make it a necessity. Whether they can do this as effectively as Apple and Facebook once did is the trillion-dollar question. Time will tell.

Could the Western tech companies survive this coming storm of competition from the East by making their brands as aspirational in Asia as say Gucci and Bentley are in China, so insulating themselves from eventual eclipse? The problem with technology is that it is not a conspicuously consumed object of desire like a handbag or a luxury car. In 2016, *Business Insider* noted an interesting development in sales of smartphones in China—the Apple iPhone was in decline, dropping 9 percent, while sales of Asian smartphone equivalents from Huawei, Oppo and BBK were all sharply up. A Chinese super-rich consumer may own a Gucci handbag but they're more than happy to take a Huawei phone out of it.

Does the secret to Asian reascendency lie simply with economics and scale? These companies think as big and ambitiously as any great American company, but not simply because they want to beat their competitors and reward shareholders but because of a fundamental philosophical predisposition.

The Rice Field and the Hunter

In 1999, psychologists Kaiping Peng of Berkeley and Richard Nisbett of the University of Michigan ran a fascinating experiment into the difference between Western and Eastern ways of approaching problems.[26]

They gave Chinese and American college students a range of scenarios describing conflicts between people and asked for advice on how best to resolve them. Seventy-two percent of the Chinese students gave compromise-oriented responses, taking into account the arguments on both sides. Seventy-four percent of American students found fault on one side or the other, and advised adopting the "correct" side's viewpoint.[27]

The Peng-Nisbett "contradiction" experiment tested a two-thousand-year-old philosophical schism. Many Western conceptions of the truth date back to the principle of *principium tertii exclusi*—"the law of the excluded middle" as defined by Aristotle in *Ethics*: "There cannot be an intermediate between contradictories. But of one subject we must either affirm or deny any one predicate."[28]

A Western answer to a problem is often resolved by two people debating. One is exclusively right and the other is exclusively wrong, and the exclusively right "answer" prevails. The Chinese, by contrast, follow the "doctrine of the mean." In a debate, both parties will be partly right and partly wrong in their argument. The truth will lie somewhere in the middle.[29] Confucian scholars Li-Jun Ji, Albert Lee and Tieyuan Guo argue that the "doctrine of the mean" comes directly from Confucius and is thus widely considered the highest ideal of Confucianism.

"Chinese are encouraged to argue for both sides in a debate or to assign equal responsibilities in a dispute. This presents an interesting contrast with the law of the excluded middle in Western philosophies, according to which one ought to eliminate ambiguity or inconsistency by selecting one and only one of the conflicting ideas. Unlike the Chinese tradition, it assumes no merit in the middle ground."[30] The middle ground does not mean wishy-washy consensus, but a pooling of knowledge in the service of the communal good.

When it comes to business this puts Western companies at a disadvantage. It means they're not just competing with companies with a greater potential customer base, who will adopt technology at a faster rate, but with companies whose employees are more likely to have a philosophical commitment to the

communal good of the company. Not because they seek promotion over their colleagues, or want a pay raise but because
it's embedded in the national character.

Nisbett ascribes this fundamental difference between East
and West to landscape:[31] "The ecology of China, consisting as
it does primarily of relatively fertile plains, low mountains and
navigable rivers, favored agriculture. . . . Agricultural peoples
need to get along with one another. This is particularly true
for rice farming, characteristic of southern China and Japan,
which requires people to cultivate the land in concert with one
another."

The rice field became not merely a place for collaboration,
but a metaphor for the nation: people are like grains of rice,
both supremely significant and insignificant. In a company, the
devotion of an employee—from the mail clerk to the CEO—is
total and genuine. Employees contribute to the annual profit
of the company as once they would have contributed to the
overall harvest.

By contrast, Western individualism grew out of personal
struggle. On the barren terrain of the Greek islands two thousand years before the birth of Christ, survival depended on
a solitary hunter outwitting the hunted animal. When this
translated to the Greek *polis* of Plato and Aristotle, the cut and
thrust of the hunt became the cut and thrust of debate: the
dialectic, the basis for Western philosophy and a cult of the
individual that sent us down a route of enlightenment, individualism, property and democratic rights for the next two mil-
lennia, for better or for worse. In business, it translated into
the ruthless determination of the individual to win, and win
at any cost.

In America, individualism and the pioneering spirit grew

directly from conquering the sheer scale of the American land-scape, with the mammoth challenges this landscape threw at anyone who tried to conquer it. A big country with big chal-lenges requires ambitious thinking, the pioneering spirit that is echoed in the hero portrait of a successful CEO as he or she poses for the cover of *Fortune*.

The question—when we face a choice between whether the Western or Asian approach to business will win out—is whether we even face this binary choice. What we have seen over the last forty years in the West is the incremental eclipse of government by business. Ambitious business ideas for the future, such as artificial intelligence, the reinvention of the transport system or colonization of space come from Google, Amazon and SpaceX, not the White House, Downing Street or the Élysée Palace.

Compare this with Asia. When OBOR was announced, it was not China's answer to Steve Jobs—Ma Huateng of Ten-cent or Alibaba's Jack Ma—who stood before the world to an-nounce the biggest infrastructure program in history. It was a politician—China's Xi Jinping. As Newman M. K. Lam, professor of government and public administration at the Uni-versity of Macau, explains, business growth in Asia is seen as dependent on the lead of government, with full cooperation be-tween government and business essential for that rapid growth to be managed at a steady controllable pace.

In spite, Lam says, of the superficial differences between a communist command economy like China's and smaller cap-italist economies like Singapore and Taiwan, both share this commitment to managed growth through "corporate gover-nance." Capitalist or communist, business and government alike treat the nation as a giant company to be properly managed. Whether "employees" (citizens) get to vote as shareholders or not does not detract from the fact that they work for the benefit of their nation/company.

Both China and its capitalist neighbors face the same challenge: managing rapid economic growth over a short period, and this rapid growth creates both huge opportunities for the private sector as well as inevitable flash points with government. The contract made by both business and government, Lam says, is that growth must be firmly managed by government.

Lam uses what happened in Macau in the 2010s as a microcosm of what happens across Asia. "In Macau, rapid economic growth led to escalating property prices, a problem that could not be solved with timid policy." The Macau government adopted a strategy used previously in South Korea, Taiwan and Indonesia when faced with the same problem of escalating prices in rapidly urbanizing areas. A quid pro quo agreement was made with property developers that rent or property price increases would be staggered and explicitly managed by government. "Only government had the mechanisms to control the pace of development," Lam says, and everyone understood this.

In the West, we see such interventionism by government as interference in the free market, but in Asia, this is normal practice. Lam cites Hong Kong and Taiwan as two of the most interventionist free market economies in the world, and the aim of intervention is to create stable, managed growth as opposed to unmanaged rapid growth that ultimately runs into the ground.

OBOR is in essence the ultimate exercise in corporate governance—the biggest government management scheme in history. Its success will depend not just on whether China can afford it but on whether the West will buy into its philosophy—the greatest entrepreneurial opportunity ever presented to business with autocratic politicians dictating terms. The very definition of a blessing and a curse.

10

ROBOTS
The Human Swap

THE DEAL: The Fukoku Mutual Life Insurance Company of Japan signs a deal with IBM to bring artificial intelligence software Watson into the first workplace on earth.

AIM: To use AI to make health insurance decisions for millions of holders, speed up claims, and in the process, make 127 employees at Fukoku redundant. The first people on the planet to lose their jobs to AI

WHERE: Tokyo, Japan

WHEN: March 2017

"I propose to consider the question: can machines think?"

So opens Alan Turing's most famous paper, "Computing Machinery and Intelligence," written in 1950.[1] Turing had been integral to winning World War II by deciphering the Enigma code of German U-boats. After the war, he used what he had learned from code breaking to take on what he considered to be the biggest challenge facing humanity.

To break the Enigma code, Turing had used unimaginably complex sequences of numbers. These, thought Turing, now offered a glimpse into the future consciousness of machines. Could a computer develop to such a point that it could successfully mimic a human? "Are there imaginable digital computers," he wondered, "which would do well in 'the imitation game'?"[2]

Turing created a test: a human talks to a number of other humans behind a screen. But one of the humans is not human at all—it is a computer pretending to be human. If the questioner cannot tell which respondent is the computer, then the computer has successfully presented itself as human, and passed the "Turing test." Turing surmised that computers would pass his test in "about fifty years."

It took sixty-two. In 2012, Vladimir Veselov at the University of Reading in England created a software program that successfully mimicked a thirteen-year-old Ukrainian boy called "Eugene Goostman."[3] Veselov's reasons for this adopted persona were cunning: "Our main idea was that Eugene can claim that he knows anything, but his age also makes it perfectly reasonable that he doesn't know everything."

Computers trying to pass the Turing test in the past had fallen at the first hurdle by failing to even understand the questions asked by humans. But increasingly complex machines since 2010 have been able to develop strategies for fooling humans: they change the subject, ask questions of the judges, and even simulate moods and typos in text exchanges, all strategies to make themselves look more human.

As a result, the bar for the Turing test has been raised from Turing's original iteration—one computer fooling one human just once—to today's iteration: a computer fooling at least one out of three human judges after a number of conversations with each judge lasting up to two hours.

This is a transcript of one such conversation between Eugene and a human in 2012:

Judge: What music do you like?

Eugene: I like Eminem—because he doesn't have a thing to do with polite-correctness.

Judge: OMG I love Eminem, he's my favorite artist!

Eugene: I wonder what Eminem's nick mean. I associate it only with a word "enema." But he is a cool guy, I like his "The Real Slim Shady."

Judge: I know what his nickname means, his real name is Marshall Mathers. From the initials M&M phynetically [sic] sounding like Eminem.

Eugene: Eminem is a famous crapper. No, raper . . . ripper . . . Yeah, I like his "Stan" and "The Real Slim Shady."

Judge: I like "Hailie's Song."

Eugene: Interesting tastes. I like science fiction books, by the way.

How anyone could seriously be fooled by Eugene is hard to imagine. But Eugene, in spite of "his" idiosyncratic answers, successfully fooled one judge.[4] And in passing the Turing test, Eugene also made apparent that the test might be missing the point about robots.

Artificial intelligence is not just about simulating humans to variously convincing degrees; the implications run much deeper, to the potential to "augment" everyday life into a wholly new experience. In 2017, I visited Uber's headquarters in San Francisco to meet one of its head designers, Didier Hilhorst, to see what this augmented reality might look like.

Uber has the potential, Didier says, to immerse itself fully in a digital representation of a city. At the moment, Uber primarily only provides cabs, with a little car you can follow on screen en route. But the data Uber is amassing allow the algorithms to begin predicting user's needs and make suggestions: Would you like to go to a favorite restaurant, take your child to day care or go to your girlfriend's place? How about doing something you have never done before? The next step is a sophisticated representation of you in a virtual environment: a figure walking through the city. Do you want a coffee? It can be ready in the coffee shop as you approach. "The job is to make the Uber experience as seamless as breathing," says Didier. "The potential for augmenting reality and making that our version of singularity is very exciting."

This total Uber experience will mean the avatar of you will be three steps ahead of the real you: shopping, buying tickets for the cinema, or dealing with problems such as a traffic jam before you have to. Whatever you do now on your phone will have been "gamified"—turned into a game-like experience.

This is not us versus robots, but a future enmeshed together in which the boundaries of where they end and we begin are blurred. Didier sees this robot future not as a Jetsons world of tin-can machines doing things for us, but digital technology and human life as a seamless whole: a singularity.

This augmented reality in our eye will be supplemented by in-body technology—blood-cleaning microcomputers, thermostatic control of heart rate, blood pressure and stress levels. This is not a world of giant striding machines, but microscopic tech hacks of human life.

Uber has watched as Amazon and Apple have developed mass-market automated assistants, Alexa and Siri, respectively. A soothing voice can now book a restaurant, turn on the lights, coach you through your morning workout, or play your favorite song. Alexa has seemingly limitless potential to revolutionize commerce and Siri the potential to revolutionize our most ubiquitous technological device, so the question must be asked of Uber: what can it—a company known for cabs and food—achieve in this already fast-moving market of ever-improving digital assistants?

Uber, and indeed Apple, have grander ambitions than an Alexa or Siri. They are both racing to bring augmented reality to life for the consumer. Uber and Apple are developing AR not merely as an assistant but as a parallel reality of shopping, maps, games, news and GPS-specific information, supplementing our peripheral vision through discreet, wearable technology. Their plan is to enmesh predictive purchasing (a coffee ordered from your favorite coffee shop as you approach), even gaming à la Pokémon GO, and social media into every step we take throughout the day.

Neither Google nor Uber want to repeat the failure of Google Glass—a premature attempt to get AR off the ground that didn't exactly catch fire with the public. Even though the talk now in Silicon Valley is of a post-smartphone future, it's questionable whether we all want to have a thousand things going on in our digital contact lenses as we walk down the street, even if it were possible. Both Uber's Didier Hilhorst and Apple's Tim Cook acknowledge that they don't want to rush in and make the Google Glass mistake again. But both clearly see huge potential or they wouldn't be trying to conquer the AR market.

So what happens in the interim as we wait for this long-awaited AR breakthrough, or beyond that, singularity, to happen? I asked Didier what the main problem with the implementation of driverless cars has been, and he gave me a surprising answer.

Uber has already extensively road-tested driverless fleets with paying passengers in San Francisco, Pittsburgh and Tempe, Arizona. And what it found was that it was not the new technology that was the problem, but when human error and new technology collided. In other words, the old human infrastructure of a higgledy-piggledy city clashing with the new technology of driverless cars inevitably creates a period of transitional mess.

For technology to truly revolutionize our lives, it requires an entire reboot of the infrastructure: a clean slate from which to start again. But this opportunity rarely happens: only after natural disaster or a war. In New Orleans, the school system was entirely rebuilt in the wake of Hurricane Katrina but for most cities, most of the time, new technology has to fit around old infrastructure. This, Didier says, is why technology takes longer than we anticipate to become realized in our everyday lives. The transition can be a long one.

I, for One, Welcome Our New Computer Overlords

As the thirteen-year-old "Eugene Goostman" was being built in Reading, another computer was being prepared for a very different challenge.

In January 2011, Ken Jennings and Brad Rutter, two former champions of the TV quiz show *Jeopardy!*, sat down before a TV audience of 20 million to face their toughest opponent yet: IBM computer Watson.[5]

In 1998, an IBM supercomputer called Deep Blue had destroyed the world chess champion Garry Kasparov over six frantically fought matches. Deep Blue's emphatic victory was hailed as a kind of Turing test being passed, but it was not.

Chess is a game with distinct rules and finite (if multiple) options for any one move. It is merely a test of computing power and complexity, not true artificial intelligence. But *Jeopardy!* is another matter entirely.

In 2004, IBM executive Charles Lickel was in a steakhouse near Poughkeepsie, New York, eating dinner when he noticed something strange: the restaurant was emptying out, even though it wasn't yet eight o'clock. People were rushing out to the bar to watch TV. On it was America's longest-running quiz show, *Jeopardy!* The diners were hooked on a phenomenon gripping America: the latest installment of the amazing winning streak of Ken Jennings, which would eventually reach seventy-four games.[6]

In that moment, Lickel had an idea. Days later in a brainstorming session at IBM, in which executives were being asked to come up with IBM's next "grand challenge," Lickel suggested they take on Ken Jennings in the ultimate *Jeopardy!* showdown. Man versus robot.

It wasn't immediately clear to outsiders why a huge company like IBM wanted to pour resources into what was in effect a quixotic project, but to IBM staffers it was natural: they saw such quixotic projects as core to the business. Thomas J. Watson, who led the company from 1914 to 1952, had a one-word motto that summed up IBM's business strategy for continual innovation: "THINK." Tackling board games was frequently part of this innovation, a way to both hone the company's technical methods and generate publicity for the more lucrative pieces of their business. In 1956, IBM programmer Arthur L. Samuel was encouraged by his superiors, led by Thomas Watson's son and successor, Thomas Watson Jr., to work on a project that would put IBM at the forefront of developing the first model for artificial intelligence. At IBM's Poughkeepsie laboratory, Samuel programmed an IBM7070, the follow-on to the 650 (the world's first mass-produced computer) to not just play checkers but to "learn" from the experience, using its computing power to work out an optimal game plan, after crunching the numerous mathematical permutations as it played. So when Lickel sought a new, more demanding challenge for IBM's programmers in 2004, he was following a long IBM tradition, and a tried-and-trusted formula for business success.

Dave Ferrucci, a fiercely smart programmer, was assigned to the *Jeopardy!* project. I met Ferrucci in New York, where he is now working with the world's largest hedge fund, Bridgewater, to use artificial intelligence to hire and fire a staff that handles $160 billion worth of assets.

"In terms of complexity," Ferrucci says, "*Jeopardy!* was a huge step up from playing the world chess champion."

The randomness of *Jeopardy!*'s questions—from obscure 1980s pop culture to seventeenth-century philosophy and quirky, counterintuitive and problematically human phrasing—made it a far more difficult challenge for a computer. Compared to *Jeopardy!*, a game of chess was child's play,[7] because *Jeopardy!* was outside the computer's comfort zone.

IBM had no idea what it was up against. To begin with, Watson was uploaded with a Wikipedia's worth of information. But searching through this database using algorithms for an answer took Watson hours, not seconds.

"We initially made progress very quickly, but then it slowed and that was frustrating. We played an early game and it was terrible. Watson was destroyed and we just thought this was impossible."

Asked what "no" is in German, Watson answered, "What is 'fuck'?" (The answer was "What is '*nein*'?").[8] Even when Watson got the answer right, it could take hours.

"I was called in by the bosses at IBM and told, Get this right, Dave. This whole thing rests on you."

So Ferrucci brought in an entirely new team of programmers simply to deal with the idea of what a question was to a computer, and another to deal with the speed at which this information could be processed. The breakthrough for Watson was in 2007, when the computer could suddenly take advantage of spectacular new advances being made in the ability of a machine to harvest big data and use the complex algorithms of machine learning. According to Ferrucci, these developments meant it no longer needed to worry about the semantics of a question or the formulation of a clue; all it needed to do was use the hundreds of bots, or programs, Ferrucci and his team had designed to scrutinize a different aspect of a clue and produce possible responses.

The genius of Ferrucci and his team was to get Watson to treat each question like a military target in battle, a missile locking on to a set of coordinates. The job of the bots was to find the coordinates of the question and dispatch the right answer. Each variable of the answer would be weighed up by the bots, racing through encyclopedias, websites, reference books and its own database of millions of previous answers. Watson assigned algorithms to evaluate candidate answers using semantic context, proximity and divergence from previous questions, and even to identify tricks that might be embedded in the way the question was phrased.

Slowly, incrementally, Watson speeded up. At the beginning, Ferrucci and his team could set Watson a task, go to lunch, and still find the lights flickering when they returned, with no answer in sight. But by 2009, Ferrucci believed they were ready.

Five years after starting the project, IBM finally began testing Watson against former *Jeopardy!* contestants as a dry run for the Jennings showdown. Watson still had glitches. Responses could be unpredictable and wildly inaccurate. Questioned about the main characters in Dickens's novel *Oliver Twist*, Watson said, "The Pet Shop Boys."

But luckily for Dave, and Watson's other programmers, the difference between machines and humans is that once machines are given exactly the right tools for a task, they can make improvements rather dramatically. Watson was learning on the job, a lesson the human contestants of *Jeopardy!* were about to find out the hard way.

On February 14, 2011, Watson was ready for its big day on TV. A large computer sat in the studio between two humans. Watson was, Dave says, "about the size of a restaurant fridge." It was the most complex machine ever programmed.

A blue, convex robot eye stared out impassively and HAL-like from the middle of a blank screen as the two humans fidgeted on their podiums. Watson was facing off with the all-time *Jeopardy!* champion, Ken Jennings, and another *Jeopardy!* super-brain, champion of champions, Brad Rutter.

Dave sat in the audience with the IBM bosses. He was so nervous, his fingernails dug into his legs. "I knew we going to win, though." How come? "We had worked so hard, we knew it. Watson was ready. It was going to be a walkover."

It wasn't, at least not at first. Initially, the contest appeared pretty even. But then Watson suddenly kicked into gear. It began beating Jennings and Rutter to every answer; the same solemn unblinking eye staring out over the audience as it delivered correct response after correct response.

The glitches were gone. Jennings and Rutter looked at each other in bewilderment. Watson's supremacy over its human rivals was breathtaking. "There were still times it could have gone the humans' way," Dave says, "because with *Jeopardy!* there's always a chance you can come back. And that came into my head."

By the final question, these were the positions: Brad Rutter had amassed $21,600. Ken Jennings: $24,000. Watson had $77,147. When the very last answer was given, "William Wilkinson's 'an account of the principalities of Wallachia and Moldavia' inspired this author's most famous novel," to which they had to supply the correct question, all three correctly said—"Who is Bram Stoker?" But it didn't matter. Watson had crushed its rivals.

Watson's victory was greeted with stilted applause from the audience. Humans were applauding their own defeat. Ken Jennings smiled wryly and wrote a message on his answer card, which he showed to the millions of people watching at home: "I, for one, welcome our new computer overlords."

Their Weak Spot: Making a Bed

On April 5, 2014, two of the world's foremost AI experts, Professors Erik Brynjolfsson and Andrew McAfee of MIT, authors of *The Second Machine Age,* held a meeting in New York with a roomful of the world's top programmers. On the agenda were the implications of Watson's victory.[9]

Brynjolfsson and McAfee showed a graph with two lines of blue dots. One line marked the cognitive advancement of human *Jeopardy!* players; and the other showed the progress of Watson from the moment IBM began work in 2004 to the day Watson trounced Jennings and Rutter in 2011.

The human advance of dots went moderately upward. A straight ramp of steady improvement. But Watson's advance of blue dots was astonishing: initially tentative; then moderate; then suddenly steep. An incline that turned into a ski slope when mapped on a graph. From 2008 on, the dots rose exponentially, like a skyscraper. Watson had gone from terrible to genius in just seven years, and its rate of learning in the last twelve months had accelerated at a speed never seen before.

This meant, Brynjolfsson and McAfee said, that once robots get to a baseline of learning, they can very quickly learn to do what we do. First conquering simple manual tasks, then moving on to more complex managerial skills, which means they have the potential to oversee human work.

"Think of the world of work," Brynjolfsson said, "as divided between 'power systems' and 'control systems.'" The power systems are people, forklifts, planes and trucks; they move things. The control systems are plant managers, business plans and engineering diagrams; they decide where things move.

In the nineteenth century, the first industrial revolution automated engines and factories and created a machine age that potentially threatened the entire usefulness of humans. The power systems were disrupted and reshaped. But after a period of dislocation we adapted, taking over the control systems by becoming engineers and managers. But this second machine age could be quite different. Now machines might not only reshape the power systems, but the control systems too.

"We are beginning to automate a lot more cognitive tasks, a lot more of the control systems that determine what to use that power for," they say in their book. "In many cases today artificially intelligent machines can make better decisions than humans."[10]

The Deal

In March 2017, thirty-four employees at the Fukoku Mutual Life Insurance Company in Tokyo became the first humans made redundant by Watson: the first employees anywhere in the world to be openly replaced by artificial intelligence.[11] The Watson software had been bought by Fukoku to automate health insurance across the whole of Japan. The IBM computer that had won *Jeopardy!* would now be making important medical decisions for a country of 127 million people.

The software that Dave Ferrucci developed to answer nuanced, complex questions has business applications in a seemingly infinite number of commercial environments. IBM puts it very simply in its sales pitch to potential customers: "Watson can understand all forms of data, interact naturally with people, and learn and reason, at scale." IBM has now sold Watson in forty-five countries working in over twenty diverse industries—everything from design solutions and management consultancy to health and medical care management.

Fukoku calculates it will save 140 million yen (£1 million) a year in wages by cutting these thirty-four jobs. But by laying off thousands of people in similarly well-paid, middle-management jobs, they could save a fortune.

IBM says that Watson possesses "cognitive technology that

can think like a human enabling it to analyze and interpret all data, including unstructured text, images, audio and video." Fukoku uses it to read tens of thousands of medical certificates, working out length of hospital stay and appropriate surgical procedures before calculating payouts.

In southwestern Japan, Henn-na Hotel is staffed entirely by robots. There is a multilingual dinosaur at reception and a hairless doll concierge with blinking geisha eyes that answers any queries about breakfast. A robot trolley takes your bags to the room: face recognition is used as your key. A drone delivers room service. Japanese hotels are generally quite expensive, but the Henn-na costs only 9,000 yen ($80) a night.

Yet when it comes to making your bed, humans are not redundant. The robots can't do it. No matter how hard the hotel owner, Hideo Sawada, tried, he could not get robot maids to successfully fold down and tuck under a sheet, pulling it tight to the degree that humans desire.

Beds, it turns out, are surprisingly complex in AI terms. They vary in size and shape; they are positioned differently in different hotels, with surrounding furniture making access difficult. They require moving and repositioning. Making a bed is a multidisciplined affair that requires both delicate skills and spatial awareness as well as manual strength, and it stumps robots. The only human employees of Henn-na Hotel are Hideo Sawada and the maids, who have the requisite and exclusively human skills of turning down a bed, skills the robots cannot master, at least not yet.

Robots are also used extensively in nursing homes across Japan. "Carebots" are a fraction of the cost of humans to employ, and appear to offer a way out of the coming global care crisis.

Three models will cover the basic needs of a nursing home

resident in the near future: "Resyone" is a robotic hybrid device with no humanoid characteristics that transforms from a bed to a wheelchair. "Robobear" is more overtly humanoid in appearance and is a lifter. The developers believe a semi-human-looking lifting device is comforting and reassuring to clients, as it feels nurturing, like a giant mechanical hand. The Riken robot lab is working on a fully human-looking nurse, capable of complex bedside care combined with factory robot strength, for moving "multiple persons." Riken may well be able to one day craft a robot that can make a bed too.

In Japan, robots are also being used to decommission the three reactors in Fukushima, which went into meltdown in 2011, the worst nuclear disaster since Chernobyl. Japan is fully embracing its robot destiny.

Companies across the world are also racing to produce the first fully functioning sex robot. The sex industry has always been quick to take up new technology. Pornography pioneered the switch from film to videotape in the 1980s, and streaming on the internet in the 2000s. Now four companies—Realbotix and BodAI in the United States, Z-Onedoll and Doll Sweet in China—are all looking to launch synthetic sex robots with AI that are "fully responsive."

With integrated virtual reality and added warmth to the skin and genitalia through heat pads, the most expensive of these silicon companions retail for tens of thousands of dollars.

Who Loses Out?

In 2013, a research paper by Carl Frey and Michael Osborne at Oxford University gave a stark prediction of where Watson would shortly take the human race. By 2030, they said, half of all jobs could be automated.[12]

Previous crystal-ball gazing about automated work was beginning to look irrelevant. It had quickly becoming apparent that obsolescence could strike a whole range of professions: doctors, lawyers, accountants, supermarket staff, cab drivers, care workers, journalists, even tech analysts assessing the future of robots. In May 2017, an AI algorithm developed by the Illinois Institute of Technology was better at predicting the outcome of high court cases than high court judges were, correctly predicting 72 percent of verdicts (human judges could predict 66 percent).

MIT's Brynjolfsson and McAfee, working with colleagues Daron Acemoglu and David Autor, summed up the potential outcome of the robot revolution in simple but stark terms. All human jobs, they said, could be summarized as falling into four basic categories: manual routine, manual nonroutine, cognitive routine and cognitive nonroutine (creative).

The highest-paid jobs are clustered in cognitive nonroutine or creative: managing a hedge fund, litigating a bankruptcy or creating a piece of art. Manual, routine jobs tend to be the lowest paid: emptying bedpans, waiting on tables at a restaurant, cleaning hotel rooms. Factory floor and payroll or accounting jobs tend to fall in between. Of these four boxes—four boxes that categorize all human jobs—robots could potentially do three and a half. Many traditional middle-class jobs are most vulnerable to AI: clerical, administrative and any number-crunching such as accounting.

Predictions by AI experts of the extent to and speed at which automation happens vary hugely. AI expert Martin Ford says the big problem with this crystal-ball gazing is not making predictions about robots but a failure to analyze what humans do in the first place. We assume our job is safe because it is "complex," when often it is not. People tend to conflate the complexity of being human with the specificity of their job, which does not require human complexity. As Ford puts it, "A computer doesn't need to replicate the entire spectrum of your intellectual capability in order to displace you from your job: it only needs to do the specific things you are paid to do."[13]

Governments jumped when they read the reports written by experts like Ford, Brynjolfsson and McAfee coming out of Oxford and MIT. President Obama was sufficiently panicked to commission a White House report published in 2016: "Artificial Intelligence, Automation and the Economy." "In recent years," it concluded, "machines have surpassed humans in the performance of certain tasks related to intelligence. It is expected that machines will continue [rapidly] to reach and exceed human performance on more and more tasks . . . aggressive policy action will be needed to help Americans who are disadvantaged by these changes."[14]

Governments across the world began commissioning their own reports and all came to the same conclusion: action was needed. If machines make everyone redundant, how will people earn a living, and what will they do all day? It was not just Turing who had prophesized this future. In the 1930s, John Maynard Keynes had painted the utopian and dystopian alternatives to automation—would we lie in fields sunbathing all day long, or be enslaved?

In recent years, many tech industry leaders have weighed in with potential solutions. Elon Musk has resurrected the idea of a "universal living wage": an amount of money we are all paid to exist. Our job will be simply to be human and spend money in shops (something robots cannot yet do). By spending, we will keep consumerism alive and capitalism afloat, so the job is a serious one.

An addendum to this perspective comes from Bill Gates, who advocates taxing robots on their labor. By charging companies on the savings made from cutting humans, a universal living wage could be funded and continue to pay for the state: roads, hospitals, armies and social safety nets.

Daron Acemoglu and Pascual Restrepo at MIT, two of the AI experts the US government has been reading assiduously, began to view this coexistence less as an inevitable, anxiety-inducing fait accompli than an arms race to tool up and be smartest. A race humans need to win.[15]

The Robot Schools

EdTech or "educational technology" seeks to capture and monetize global education. Underpinning this momentous deal is a particular proposition: teaching, as we now conceive of it, is an inherently unpredictable practice delivered by a human, with all the quirks and inconsistences a human brings to the job. Computers, on the other hand, do not have prejudices. By using computers, EdTech's advocates say, children are able to "personalize" their own software teaching program and learn what they are interested in.

The inspiration for the EdTech revolution was an experiment carried out by educational guru Sugata Mitra of Newcastle University in England. In 1999, a computer appeared overnight in an empty ATM spot in New Delhi. No one knew how it got there. Street kids began to gather around and after a few minutes, they had figured out how to turn it on. Within a day, these same kids—some of whom did not go to school and were illiterate—were solving complex mathematical problems by asking the internet, which they had worked out for themselves how to use.

Mitra did not hold back. Describing the children's achievements on BBC Radio 4, Mitra said they could solve questions of moral philosophy and physics, and they had worked out these answers with ease, because they had not been discouraged by a teacher; no one had told them that the questions were hard to solve.[16] What the kids did not know was that they were part of an experiment. Mitra wanted to test how technology would be used by children in the absence of teachers, and found that it freed the kids to learn quickly themselves. When all the world's knowledge is available at a swipe, teachers are not merely redundant, he argued, they actively hinder the child's learning.

Word of Mitra's experiment spread through Silicon Valley, where he became an influential figure, arguing that teaching and schools themselves were a colonial Western construct. The Indian school system, designed originally to provide an army of obedient workers to service the British colonial machine, had cemented inequality. Technology, he argued, offered opportunity to the world's poor. But Mitra had his critics. He wove, according to educationalist Neil Selwyn, "a seductive story that masked insidious hyper-individualistic Silicon Valley thinking, at complete odds with genuine learning. Global standardization under the smokescreen of freeing the child."

The Mitra torch was picked up by two Stanford academics, John Chubb and Terry Moe, authors of two books proposing a free-market revolution in education: *Politics, Markets and America's Schools*[17] and *Liberating Learning*.[18] "The world,"

Chubb and Moe said, "is in the early stages of a historic transformation in how students learn, teachers teach, and schools and school systems are organized." From Chubb and Moe's viewpoint, teachers are "vested interests" that block change or progress by protecting their own jobs at the expense of the needs of children. Educational technology, they argue, can be used to liberate children from these vested interests.

The Tech Trojan Horse

I met Terry Moe at Stanford University in a huge, circular, wood-paneled room where, for over two hundred years, presidents, philanthropists and now tech billionaires have come to address professors and alumni about their grand plans for the future.

Terry was not what I expected: a wiry man with a skeptical twinkle in his eye. He told me excitedly how he was now working on a book about New Orleans after Hurricane Katrina. Because the city's entire infrastructure was wiped out, the "vested interests" of the teacher unions were washed away too, allowing the education system to be built again from the ground up. The results, he said, had been "remarkable."

I asked him why he felt teachers were a negative rather than a positive when it came to education.

"I'm painted as this neoliberal market guy, I'm not. Teachers have a role to play, I'm not saying they don't, but the vested interest of teacher unions is not in the interest of children."

Change, Moe argues, is coming whether we like it or not, and thus, he advocates, teachers should work to incorporate new implements into their teaching methods rather than fighting them.

In *Liberating Learning*, Chubb and Moe have a plan for how technology can be used to "seep" into the classroom, drip by drip—first through iPads, then rolling out personalized teaching to every single child. Chubb and Moe's strategy for using technology as a Trojan horse to break the unions could work not only in education, but across the public sector: in health, social care, all forms of public service.

To see what Terry Moe's school of the future might look like, I visited the Flextech lab in San Diego, one of the most advanced examples of so-called blended learning using technology in the world. The school was quite extraordinary. The executive principal, Sean, showed me around an open-plan class with about seventy pupils. They all work with laptops or desktop computers. There is only one teacher for the entire room, whom pupils consult if they have a problem.

Each pupil I met was pursuing their own interest, which had become their personalized learning plan: Stephanie, who was sixteen, wanted to be a marine biologist. Brendan was interested in astrophysics and was watching an advanced astronomy lecture online. He made notes on the side of the screen and stopped the lecture if he wanted to go back.

Sean was evangelical about Flextech. But it was not the straightforward transplant that Moe envisions one day. Sean said the school had undergone "several iterations using technology. We began with a far more technology-based model and found it was too much, it didn't work. The teacher needed to come back in the classroom to guide learning and so now we have what we describe as 'blended learning.'"

I asked the teacher, Steve, what it was like overseeing seventy pupils. "Sometimes, it's a bit like being one of those checkout supervisors at a supermarket waiting for something to go wrong with a bar code. But for the children, it's a huge improvement. They are genuinely self-motivated and learn at their own speed, rather than having that dictated by a teacher at the front."

Flextech has a waiting list of over a thousand pupils and is undoubtedly a very successful school. It is now talking to the designers of Google Maps to create a "Google Maps for learning."

But it is also in a prosperous part of San Diego—would it work in a poor neighborhood in Detroit? Terry Moe says technology is inherently more democratic and open to poorer pupils because it smooths out inequalities. A classroom divided between poor pupils and richer ones who might dominate a class setting by being more assertive is no longer a problem, because each pupil determines their own learning.

Sean also sees a paradox at the heart of their success at Flextech. "We are using technology in a blended learning setting to create focus, where technology has defocused kids through phones and video games. We have never seen children more defocused and demotivated than now, and our job is to reverse that."

Sean thinks children are robots before, not after, they come into his classroom. They have already been trained for repetitive work by the repetitive-task patterns of social media and gaming. He believes technology in the classroom can be used to deprogram and focus kids: as a Trojan horse for good, not bad.

The Car Wash Paradox

The automation revolution has been widely seen as an unalloyed negative for human employment, but is this inevitable?

Perhaps a lesson can be learned from what economic forecasters like Paul Mason are calling the "car wash paradox." In 1959, a Detroit businessman named Dan Hanna created the first automated car wash. Big fluffy wraparound brushes passed over a car as it moved conveyor-belt-like through the cleaning process: sprayed with water and detergent, then blow-dried with huge heaters.

By the 2000s, Hanna Car Wash Systems International was the world's biggest automated car wash company, with 30,000 car washes in 90 countries washing 650 million vehicles a year. But since 2010, something unexpected has happened. Automated car washes in big cities like London and New York have begun to shut down and be replaced with humans.

Small gangs of poorly paid "manual routine" workers appear at various sites, frantically cleaning cars with sponges and cloths. The reasons for the demise of the automated car wash were clear. The real estate many automated car washes were built on had become more valuable when redeveloped for luxury rentable property than when used as a car wash. As a result, the machines have been made redundant and replaced with humans.

These new human car washes aren't on prime real estate but often on the edge of town, in disused parking lots and old gas stations. The demand for cleaning cars is as great as it was when Dan Hanna went into business in the late 1950s, but humans have proved more economic in delivering the service than machines.

These pop-up car wash sites can appear and disappear again in days. Humans are adaptable to this constant relocation. Neither do they require moving, hefty maintenance or constant servicing. Humans don't break down, they can wash a car in half the time and do a consistently better job because they fear losing their job; and here's the key thing: they cost less.

The automated car wash was not the inevitable story of robot takeover that was predicted in the 1950s, as it is again now. Instead it became a potential prelude to a new world not of total human redundancy but instead, of full yet low-paid mobile employment, with Watson in the control center, an unblinking blue eye monitoring which is the most efficient human car wash in town.

EPILOGUE
Now: The New World

THE DEAL: Facebook and the OECD/World Bank jointly propose the "Future of Business Research Initiative" in 2016.

AIM: To identify and promote the SME (small- to medium-sized business) rather than global corporations as the primary driver of twenty-first century prosperity

WHERE: Across the world

WHEN: Now

Camden, New Jersey, appears on the surface to be a casualty of America's onetime industrial boom. Its once-great factories producing machine goods and textiles lie derelict. Avenues of once-prosperous housing are boarded and chained up with the same municipal stamp on the door telling drug dealers this is a "monitored property." Gardens are piled high with refrigerators, TVs, sewing machines, tires. I have to swerve my car to avoid a sofa sitting proudly in the middle of the road. Buicks and Cadillacs, once driven by businessmen, now stand tireless on bricks in alleyways with curtains across the windshield, makeshift accommodations.

Camden may initially seem to some outsiders, myself included, like something out of a postapocalyptic movie, but as I spent more time there, I found that this couldn't be further from the truth. Because behind the sensationalist facade of violence and urban decay, Camden has an essentially optimistic message for the whole of America, a message with business at its heart. For Camden is the town with the fastest growing number of start-up companies anywhere in the United States.

Adam is a Texan with a broad smile and a wry, sardonic manner. In the 2000s, he moved to Camden with plans to start a handmade screen-printing press. In 2014, he took over Camden Printworks, a local business that had fallen on hard times. It is now one of the most successful screen-printing businesses anywhere in the United States, with a reputation for detailed, high-quality work produced for clients across the globe. Adam took over an old car body repair shop to house the revitalized printing business, and now employs thirty people, with plans to expand into the derelict backyard due to a two-year backlog of orders.

Joe is one of the locals who works for Adam. A giant of a man—literally twice my size—Joe turns out sixty or seventy T-shirts a day for everyone from local pizzerias and colleges to record labels, skate-wear shops and boutique fashion brands across the globe. "People like the handmade quality, people even come in to see how we do it. We've spotted a gap in the market and it's booming."

Joe grew up in Camden when it was a thriving and prosperous town. "People would come to the waterfront on Sunday afternoons and dress up and promenade. This was a place people dreamed about moving to!" he says, laughing.

A huge shipyard and countless factories, including Campbell's Soup, the New York Shipbuilding Corporation and RCA Victor Company provided employment for tens of thousands. Then globalization happened.

In 1950, Camden had 43,267 manufacturing jobs. By 1982,

that had fallen to just 10,200. Deindustrialization in turn accelerated depopulation, across the bridge to Philadelphia and elsewhere. In 1950, Camden had 124,555 residents. By 1980, that number had fallen drastically to just 84,910. And the people who'd gone were the professionals and those who ran small- and medium-sized local businesses.

In a bid to attract money back to the city in the 1980s, as business was in full flight out of town, Camden's Mayor Randy Primas campaigned to have antisocial business ventures unattractive to other areas opened in Camden instead. In 1985, the Riverfront State Prison was opened, followed by a waste-water sewage facility, given the go-ahead in 1989.

But something else was also going on. In 1984, a private real estate company called Cooper's Ferry was started by a group of local businesspeople worried by the perception that their city was being handed over to businesses that would only worsen the city's reputation and chances of renewed prosperity. Cooper's Ferry's strategy for Camden was to hold on to the existing businesses that had built Camden in the first place by partnering them with other struggling businesses in the area, so pooling expertise and resources. They read "community" as "business community," using business to hold the wider community together.

Yet Cooper's Ferry initially struggled to keep Camden afloat, largely because the reputation of Camden as a failing city became a downward spiral. The incineration plant, despite protests from environmentalists and locals concerned about pollution, eventually opened in 1991, offering much-needed employment. In 1992, General Electric made an agreement with the state of New Jersey to keep its existing business in Camden rather than leave. In return, the state agreed to build a hi-tech facility on the site of the old Campbell Soup factory. The project ran into difficulties and finally ended up being owned by Lockheed Martin, but proved to be an important step in the business rehabilitation of the city.

In 2001, Camden's business leaders and community leaders came together to create the Greater Camden Partnership (GCP), which sought a strategic development plan for the city. It targeted the worst affected parts of the city with a "clean-up" campaign. It then made these cleaned-up downtown areas favorable to new businesses by offering low rents and subsidies with the aim of fostering a new culture of entrepreneurism in a distinct, specially prepared area.

In 2011, Cooper's Ferry and GCP formally merged to become the Cooper's Ferry Partnership. And in 2014, it identified Camden Printworks, under Adam's new leadership, as a business it could invest in.

Since 2014, Camden has been seized on by hundreds of entrepreneurs who have flocked there to start businesses. Part of the reason is the low rents and close access to major metropolitan areas (such as Philadelphia across the river), but the other reason is that the city has managed to rebrand itself as a center for EdTech and medtech. As part of the Cooper's Ferry drive to revitalize the city in the 2000s, Cooper University Hospital and the Cooper Medical School of Rowan University became centers of EdTech and medtech excellence, in the hope this would attract satellite start-ups.

The business upswing for Camden had an unexpected boon. In 2014, car manufacturer Subaru announced it would be relocating its American base to Camden with a new 250,000-square-foot headquarters costing $118 million, and creating 500 new jobs for local people. Just as the downward spiral for

Camden became a self-fulfilling prophecy in the 1980s, so too did the upswing after 2014 in the wake of the Subaru deal, sucking new start-ups into Camden.

Down the road from Adam's printing press is a digital tech company start-up, a shoe business and a whiskey distillery run by two twenty-three-year-olds from New York. Like Camden Printworks, they have orders from across the world. These businesses support each other with regular social get-togethers and by creating a deep sense of community within Camden. They put on regular events encouraging local kids to get involved or start their own business, food and music nights showcasing local restaurants, artists and new businesses. As one of their satisfied customers puts it on Facebook: "Great people. Great product. A truly compassionate and caring business devoted to making excellent work and supporting the community."

And this entrepreneurial spirit has reached other parts of Camden's economy as well. In 2013, Paymon Rouhanifard, a one-time financial analyst on Wall Street, was appointed to turn around Camden's schools. In 2016, they began to see an upswing in attendance. Poverty, he says, impedes everything they try to achieve, but the schools are now beginning to show signs of being in turnaround and, most important, kids are showing up in the morning.

Camden's crime figures are down as well. Joe, who works for Adam at Camden Printworks, says that the example business is showing at street level is key. "If I was not working [here] I would one hundred percent be selling drugs, and after a couple of years of that probably dead.

"A kid can earn two hundred bucks a day on the street and what could I earn on minimum wage—fifty? Sixty? What are you going to choose when that legitimately earned money can't feed a family? Those kids selling drugs are putting their lives at risk, but they're smart. They know how to turn cocaine into crack. That makes them chemists. They need to put those skills to something legal. They're also the sharpest businesspeople on this street because they've survived and grown their business. That skill needs to be channeled properly."

Camden's new business outliers reminded me of what Tom Peters, the man who remade the workplace with his vision of self-determined work back in the late 1970s, told me when we met in Boston. "Whoever you are, however safe you think your job is, and well insulated your future looks, forget it. It's over."

Employees working for big unwieldy corporations that struggle to adapt to the new fast-moving business world may find their jobs at risk. But salvation is at hand, in the shape of the SME: the small- and medium-sized enterprise, businesses that employ fewer than 250 people.

SMEs: The Future

In April 2017, Ciaran Quilty, Facebook's Regional Director of SME for EMEA, declared that "SME's are the undisputed engine of economic growth [so] it's in all our interests for these businesses to succeed."

In 2016, Facebook and the OECD and World Bank launched a unique research initiative into the future of the SME. The FoBS (Future of Business Study) analyzed 140,000 SMEs in thirty-three countries in an attempt to understand the forces underlying the dynamics of the global economy, seen from the perspective of the small business.

What the FoBS found was surprising and counterintuitive.

In 2016, the IMF announced a global slowdown, a stuttering Chinese economy, geopolitical instability in the wake of the election of Donald Trump and business uncertainty in Europe following Brexit. But for small- to medium-sized enterprises, things were looking good. Sixty-six percent of SMEs across the world said they felt "optimistic" about not just their own business's performance but the economy as a whole.

And these businesses are not an add-on to capitalism. SMEs account for over 95 percent of firms and up to 70 percent of all employment. As larger firms downsize and outsource, the weight and dependency of the Western industrialized economy on SMEs is increasing. According to the OECD, up to 60 percent of new SMEs in the last five years are involved in either "innovative" product or employ dynamic and unorthodox business structures. They are "disruptive" and risk-taking not through choice but because they need to be. Over half of SMEs go bust within five years but 80 percent of those involved go on to start new SMEs.

And this approach to business gets results. The 5 percent fastest growing companies on earth are dominated by SMEs in the technology sector, and with a job creation rate that exceeds larger corporations. High-growth small firms spend less on R&D than these big companies but innovate in literally everything else they do and often, because the nature of their business is innovation; they do not see a distinction between what the company does and the need to innovate. It's simply, to use an overused business cliché, part of their DNA. Interestingly, R&D is now viewed by bigger companies as an extraneous cost. Tim Cook of Apple has said that companies like his can learn from the low-cost R&D approach taken by digital start-ups and SMEs, who will spend less time working on many ideas rather than a long time working on one. Especially as ideas are now out of date so quickly.

One less-commented-upon effect of the technological revolution is the dramatic effect it has had on the proliferation of SMEs. Of course, technology connects businesses with customers across the world and means being in a low-rent location in Camden, New Jersey, is no disadvantage when compared to being in a high-rent location in Brooklyn. Globalization has been good for the digital SME. Seventy-five percent use online tools to attract new customers. But technology has also dramatically reduced start-up costs, as well as advertising costs. This has been perhaps the most dramatic effect on the rise of the small business. You literally need a phone and something to sell, and you're in business. As Facebook's Ciaran Quilty observed, "Today, small businesses are finding that all they need is a mobile phone and a few dollars budget to experiment with."

The FoBS also found that women rather than men were the most enthusiastic users of digital tools when it came to running a small business. And women in some of the most patriarchal and repressive cultures across the world are the ones with some of the fastest-growing businesses. This, they concluded, is a global trend, and means that SMEs may come to define business in the second third of the twenty-first century, just as the Silicon Valley start-ups that became tech giants did in the last twenty years.

If you walk down any street anywhere in the world, what do you see? You see people who have an idea. They have taken that stupid, crazy notion to run a shop selling coffee, cleaning services, haircuts or screen-printed clothing, and turned it into a reality. After five years, that business has either gone under or thrived. The people have either made a go of it or they have moved on to another stupid, crazy idea that has either thrived or gone bust.

To look at a main street is to see human endeavor and capitalism at its purest. The main street is a rolling conveyor belt of human beings forever striving, each with their own individual epiphany made real through business. This is the one thing that remains beyond the ambit of their control: the primal, human engine of the mind, pumping out ideas. We as humans cannot help it; we see an opportunity and go for it.

SMEs are the future because they tap into and most closely embody this instinct. They are to some extent a chance to reset capitalism. And places like Camden could be in pole position to take advantage fastest.

This is the twenty-first-century twist of fate. The cities that built a deep, complex infrastructure for the first industrial revolution and then extracted further power and resources for themselves in the late twentieth century by allowing places like Camden to fall prey to globalization are now going to get their comeuppance.

Once London and Paris and Nairobi and Shanghai and New York could suck the life from the hinterland around them, but there was a price to pay: they saddled themselves with an unwieldy infrastructure. They believed themselves indispensable and all-powerful. But then the twenty-first century happened.

The tech revolution offers a new paradigm. The very places where the infrastructure was either wiped out or never happened—rural Malawi, rural Wales, the Rust Belt of the American Midwest, the Australian outback—suddenly have the advantage. In one technological jump, they can leapfrog the twentieth-century mega-cities held back by cumbersome twentieth-century infrastructure and complacent twentieth-century thinking.

One word will enable a company, an individual, a city, to survive this coming revolution: adaptability. The obstacles preventing adaptation are not simply physical, but mental. The enemy is not robots or the tech companies, immigrants or the Chinese, it is complacency and the sense that you either do not need to change because you are safe from change or cannot change because you don't know how.

To anyone saddled by this thinking, Camden is not the past, it is the future, and with a lesson for all of us. Here, as elsewhere across the globe, the deals made are not the deals of the twentieth century, those made between the CEOs of huge multinationals intent on reshaping the existing market or getting the consumer to think about product in a different way. These new deals are the deals of the twenty-first century, deals made by two people no one has yet heard of. Or between an inventor and thousands of small investors. Entrepreneurs with a business idea that falls outside the categorizations of this book, because it hasn't been invented yet, who took the initiative to start their business in a place no one would dream of starting a business, and will in twenty years' time be hailed as the Steve Jobs or Mark Zuckerberg of their generation. The future—in short—starts small.

ACKNOWLEDGMENTS

I want to thank everyone who took the time and effort to be interviewed. Nick and everyone at Harper. Robert, Kate and everyone at UA. Rupert at Hodder. Jonathan at Curtis Brown NY. Everyone I worked with on the films at the BBC, including Tom, Fiona, Mike, Charlotte, Janis, Kim, Patrick, Adam, Don, Martin, Gian and Clive. Everyone at Pulse, including Will, Stu, Ed, Tom, Annabel, Izzy, Emma, Claire, Marisa and Thomas. Everyone who shot, researched and edited the many series including Johan, Andy, Ariel, Adam, Jay, Brendan, Tim, Petra, David and Alex. Everyone at *The Guardian* and *The Observer,* including Malik, Tim and my old friend Ian. Melanie and Rachel at Oxfam. Jo, Gudren, Holly and everyone I worked with at Fresh One. Roy, who was instrumental in getting me to write a book, and has been a ceaseless advocate and loyal friend. David Glover and Helen, Lucy C for all the empathy, advice and support over so many years, Vic for understanding exactly how hard it is to write a book. Tamasin at Spinwatch. Gerard, Janet and Fenton. Everyone who worked with me on the Channel 4 films. Hannah who was there from start to finish, and without whom I couldn't do any of this. My parents Alina and Peter, and my brother Andreas for all their love and encouragement.

NOTES

Chapter 1: The Upgrade: Engineering Dissatisfaction

1. I visited Livermore fire station in 2014. For the full history, its website is "Home of the World's Longest Burning Light Bulb": www.centennialbulb.org.
2. "Death of the Seven Year Itch: Average Relationship Is Now Just 2 Years 9 Months," *Daily Mail*, February 4, 2014.
3. *The Light Bulb Conspiracy*.
4. *The Men Who Made Us Spend*, Episode 1, BBC2, September 2014.
5. Ibid.
6. Glenn Adamson, *Industrial Strength Design: How Brook Stevens Shaped Your World* (Boston: MIT Press, 2003).
7. Alfred P. Sloan Jr., *My Years with General Motors* (New York: Bantam Doubleday Dell, originally published 1964, reprinted 1998).
8. *The Men Who Made Us Spend*, Episode 1.
9. Ibid., Episode 3.
10. Dr. Susan Weinscheuk, "Shopping, Dopamine, and Anticipation," *Psychology Today*, October 22, 2015.
11. Steve Jobs—iPhone Introduction, January 9, 2007, YouTube.com.
12. Mark Harris, "Documents Confirm Apple Is Building Self-driving Car," *Guardian*, August 14, 2015.
13. Christina Rogers, Mike Ramsey, Daisuke Wakabayashi, "Apple Hires Auto Industry Veterans," *Wall Street Journal*, July 20, 2015.

Chapter 2: Food: Owning Fat and Thin

1. Greg Critser, *Fat Land: How Americans Became the Fattest People in the World* (Boston: Houghton Mifflin Harcourt, 2003).
2. John Yudkin, *Pure, White and Deadly* (New York: Viking, 1986).
3. Professor Philip James: http://www.iaso.org/about-iaso/iasomanagement/experts/wptjames/.
4. "Pharmaceutical Innovation: Revolutionizing Human Health" ed. by Ralph Landau, Basil Achilladelis and Alexander Scriabine. Chemical Heritage Foundation, December 1999.
5. Gianluca Castelnuovo, Giada Pietrabissa and Enrico Molinari, *Cognitive Behavioural Therapy to Aid Weight Loss in Obese Patients: Current Perspectives*. Dove Medical Press Ltd., 2017.

Chapter 3: Drugs: The Medication of Modern Life

1. Centers for Disease Control and Prevention (CDC), Therapeutic Drug Use, US overview, January 19, 2017.
2. "The Hispanic Paradox," *Lancet*, May 16, 2015.

3. For a full account of Gadsden's interview and its ramifications: Ray Moynihan and Alan Cassels, *Selling Sickness: How the World's Biggest Pharmaceutical Companies Are Turning Us All into Patients* (Vancouver: Douglas & McIntyre, 2006).

4. Moynihan and Cassels, *Selling Sickness.*

5. R. D. Laing, *The Divided Self: An Existential Study in Sanity and Madness* (London: Harmondsworth Penguin, 1960).

6. Philip K. Dick, *A Scanner Darkly (London:* Granada, 1978).

7. "Is the FDA Being Compromised by Pharma Payments?" John La Mattina, *Forbes,* August 7, 2013.

8. Peter Rost, *The Whistle Blower: Confessions of a Healthcare Hitman* (Berkeley, CA: Soft Skull Press, 2006).

9. John LaMattina, "Is the FDA Being Compromised by Pharma Payments?" *Forbes,* August 7, 2013.

10. Ibid.

11. "Direct-to-Consumer Advertising under Fire," *Bulletin of the World Health Organization,* vol. 87, no. 8, August 2009.

12. WHO, "DTC under Fire," August 2009.

13. Ibid.

14. Parry, "The Art of Branding a Condition."

15. David T. Wong, Frank P. Bymaster, Eric A. Engleman, "Prozac (fluoxetine, lilly 110140), the First Selective Serotonin Uptake Inhibitor and an Antidepressant Drug: Twenty Years Since Its First Publication," *Life Sciences,* vol. 57, issue 5, June 23, 1995.

16. Ibid.

17. David Rosenhan, "On Being Sane in Insane Places," *Science,* January 19, 1973.

18. Robert Spitzer obituary, *New York Times,* December 26, 2015.

19. Allen Frances, *Saving Normal: An Insider's Revolt Against Out-of-Control Psychiatric Diagnosis, DSM 5, Big Pharma, and the Medicalization of Ordinary Life* (New York: William Morrow, 2014).

20. Ibid.

21. Moynihan, Cooke, Doust, Bero, Hill, Glasziou, "Expanding Disease Definitions in Guidelines and Expert Panel Ties to Industry: A Cross-sectional Study of Common Conditions in the US," *PLOS Medicine,* February 7, 2013.

22. Erin White, "'Behind the Boomer Coalition: A Heart Message from Pfizer," *Wall Street Journal,* March 10, 2004.

23. Garth S. Jowett and Victoria J. O'Donnell, *Propaganda and Persuasion* (Sage, 2011).

Chapter 4: Cash: Killing Physical Money to Monetize the Internet

1. UK Payment Methods 2016 report, Payments Council, May 20, 2016: www.paymentsuk.org.uk/industry-information/annual-statistical-publications.

2. "Brother, Can You Spare a Contactless Payment? Homeless Go Hi-Tech," *IBTimes,* March 1, 2017.

3. Bill Maurer, *How Would You Like to Pay? How Technology Is Changing the Future of Money* (Durham, NC: Duke University Press, 2015).

4. "Paypal Co-Founders Met in Terman at a Seminar," Thiel and Levchin discussing their first meeting at https://ecorner.stanford.edu.

5. Ibid.

6. Ashlee Vance, *Elon Musk: Tesla, Space X and the Quest for a Fantastic Future*, (New York: Ecco, 2015).

7. MIT *Spectrum*, Winter 1999.

8. "Credit Card Debt: Average US Household Owes $16,000," *Time*, December 20, 2016.

9. For a full account of how debt window-dresses the figures on growth, see interview with Matt Whittaker, Resolution Foundation, in my series *The Super-Rich and Us*, BBC, 2015.

10. Interview with Benjamin Barber in *The Men Who Made Us Spend*, Episode 3, BBC, 2014.

11. "Customer Data: Designing for Transparency and Trust," *Harvard Business Review*, May 2015.

12. Steve Jobs introduces the App Store—iPhone Software Roadmap Event, 2008.

13. Nathaniel Popper, "Banks Did It Apple's Way in Payments by Mobile," *New York Times*, September 11, 2014.

14. Maurer, *How Would You Like to Pay?*

15. "How Big Is the Black Market?" Freakanomics.com, June 25, 2012.

16. "The Defence Advanced Research Projects Agency (DARPA) Awards $1.8 Million Contract to Research Block Chain for Military Security," *Quartz*.

17. "Man Tries to Rob Cashless Swedish Bank," https://www.thelocal.se /20130422/47484, April 22, 2013.

Chapter 5: Work: From What We Do to Who We Are

1. "A Tech Free Bedroom for a Peaceful Sleep," May 3, 2015: https://www .silentnight.co.uk/sleep-matters/sleep-news/2015/march/a-tech-free-bedroom-for-a-peaceful-sleep/.

2. "Most Work Emails Are Opened within 6 Seconds," *Business Insider*, Eames Yates, March 28, 2017.

3. Daniel Nelson, ed., *A Mental Revolution: Scientific Management since Taylor* (Columbus, OH: Ohio State University Press, 1992).

4. Matthew Stewart, *The Management Myth: Why the Experts Keep Getting It Wrong* (New York: W.W. Norton, 2009).

5. Frederick Winslow Taylor, *The Principles of Scientific Management* (New York: Harper and Brothers, 1911).

6. "Guru: Frederick Winslow Taylor," *The Economist*, February 6, 2009.

7. Joseph Raynus, *Improving Business Process Performance*, Auerbach Publications, 2011.

8. Richard Sennett, *The Culture of the New Capitalism* (New Haven: Yale University Press, 2007), is a superb overview of the development of the ideas underpinning corporate belief systems.

9. John Hayes, *The Theory and Practice of Change Management* (New York: Palgrave MacMillan, 2014).

10. Tom Peters and Robert Waterman, *In Search of Excellence: Lessons from America's Best-Run Companies* (New York: Warner, 1984).
11. Tom Peters, "Tom Peters's True Confessions," *Fast Company*, November 30, 2001.
12. Ibid.
13. Duff McDonald, *The Firm: The Story of McKinsey and Its Secret Influence on American Business* (New York: Simon & Schuster, 2014).
14. "Inside McKinsey," *Financial Times*, November 25, 2011.
15. Ed Michaels, Helen Handfield-Jones and Beth Axelrod, *The War for Talent* (Harvard Business Press, 2001).
16. Enron Annual Report 2000, http://picker.uchicago.edu/Enron/EnronAnnualReport2000.pdf.
17. "The Firm that Built the House of Enron," *The Observer*, March 23, 2002.
18. Ben Chu, "McKinsey: How Does It Always Get Away with It?" *Independent*, February 7, 2014.
19. My interview with John Bennett in *Who's Spending Britain's Billions?* BBC2, October 2016.
20. "Owning a McDonald's Franchise: Purchase Cost V Annual Profit," Jonathan Ping, October 19, 2015, MyMoneyBlog.com.
21. "Uber CEO Caught On Video Arguing with Driver About Fares," Bloomberg, March 2017.
22. Hannah Summers, "Balearic Islands caps number of beds available for tourists," *Guardian*, August 9, 2017.
23. Hailey Branson-Potts, "Santa Monica convicts its first Airbnb host under tough home-sharing laws," *Los Angeles Times,* July 13, 2016.
24. Nicholas Cecil, "MPs Demand Crackdown on Illegal Lets in London as Airbnb Trend Sparks 'free-for-all," *Evening Standard*, March 21, 2017.
25. "The Box That Changed the World," BBC4, 2010.
26. Marc Levinson, *The Box: How the Shipping Container Made the World Smaller and the World Economy Bigger* (Princeton, NJ: Princeton University Press, 2008), tells the whole incredible story in forensic detail.
27. My interview with Steve Howard in *The Men Who Made Us Spend*, Episode 1, BBC2, September 2014.

Chapter 6: Risk: How Chaos Was Harnessed by Wall Street

1. Interview with Robert Dall in *The Super-Rich and Us*, BBC, 2015.
2. John Lanchester, *Whoops!: Why Everyone Owes Everyone and No One Can Pay* (Penguin, 2010).
3. *Der Speigel*, February 8, 2010; "Greek Debt Crisis: How Goldman Sachs Helped Greece to Mask Its True Debt," *Independent*, July 10, 2010, on the plan to sue Goldman Sachs for massaging Greece's accounts; and BBC News, February 20, 2012, with an account on the history.
4. Michael Sandel, *What Money Can't Buy: The Moral Limits of Markets* (New York: Macmillan, 2012), for the context of viaticals and the "death futures" market.
5. "Lest We Forget: Why We Had a Financial Crisis" *Forbes*, November 22, 2011.

6. US District Court notes: Southern District of Florida. Case no. 04-60573–CIV–Moreno/Simonton.
7. Philip Inman, "Drive Carefully—I Can See a Credit Car Crash Up Ahead," *Guardian*, May 8, 2017.
8. Ibid.
9. "The Slap That Sparked a Revolution," *The Observer*, May 14, 2011.
10. There are many accounts of Bouazizi's death, but the most detailed are in "The Real Mohamed Bouazizi," *Foreign Policy*, December 16, 2011, which pieces events together one year on, and "How a Man Setting Fire to Himself Sparked an Uprising in Tunisia," *Guardian*, December 28, 2010, for a report on the immediate aftermath.
11. This specific quote has been widely repeated in reports of Bouazizi's death. In the myth-making of the Arab Spring that followed his suicide, Bouazizi was alleged to have also threatened the officials with setting himself alight. No one except the officials present will ever know the truth.
12. *Guardian*, June 2, 2011.
13. Greg Critser, *Fat Land* (Boston: Houghton Mifflin, 2004), is superb on the back story of the power wielded by the farming lobby and corn producers in 1970s American politics.
14. Professor Jane Harrigan's inaugural lecture at SOAS, 28 April 2011: "Did Food Prices Plant the Seeds of the Arab Spring?" puts the rise in wheat prices in the wider context of the fragile food system of North Africa.
15. Professor Rami Zurayk, "Use Your Loaf: Why Food Prices Were Crucial in the Arab Spring," *Guardian*, July 16, 2011.
16. William Pesek, "Why China's Bailout Could Reach $10 Trillion," Barrons .com, July 6, 2016.
17. Sophia Murphy, David Burch, Jennifer Clapp, "Cereal Secrets," Oxfam Research Reports, August 2012.
18. "Chinese Banks Disguise Risky Loans as 'Investments,'" *Financial Times*, April 29, 2016.
19. "China: The Power Behind the $700 Billion Bailout," *Wall Street Journal*, December 10, 2008.
20. William Pesek, Barrons.com, July 6, 2016.
21. *Financial Times*, April 29, 2016.

Chapter 7: Tax: Why Everywhere Wants to Be the Cayman Islands

1. Richard Stott, *Daily Mirror* archive.
2. For a full account of Rossminster: Nigel Tutt, *The Tax Raiders: The Rossminster Affair*, Financial Training Publications, 1985.
3. *The Super-Rich and Us*, BBC, 2014: Ex-tax inspector Richard Brooks gives a detailed account of Rossminster's business practices.
4. Roger L. Martin, "A Brief History of America's Attitude toward Taxes," *Harvard Business Review*, September 16, 2014.
5. "Laffer Curve: Napkin Doodle Launched Supply-Side Economics," Bloomberg, December 4, 2014.

6. Jan Fichtner, *The Anatomy of the Cayman Islands Offshore Financial Center: Anglo-America, Japan, and the Role of Hedge Funds* (Amsterdam Institute for Social Science Research, University of Amsterdam, 2016).
7. Nicholas Shaxson, *Treasure Islands: Tax Havens and the Men Who Stole the World* (London: Bodley Head, 2011), gives a full account of George Bolton and the key role of the Eurodollar in the offshore story.
8. Ibid.
9. Alan Markoff, "The Cayman Islands: From Obscurity to Offshore Giant," *Cayman Financial Review*, April 17, 2009.
10. Ibid.
11. Ibid.
12. Ibid.
13. Financial Secrecy Index 2015: Cayman Islands No.5, www.taxjustice.net.
14. Fichtner, *Anatomy of the Cayman Islands Offshore Financial Center*.

Chapter 8: Wealth: The Business of Inequality

1. Melanie Kramers, "Eight People Own Same Wealth as Half the World," Oxfam pre-Davos report, January 16, 2017.
2. "Never Mind the Gap: Why We Shouldn't Worry About Inequality," Institute of Economic Affairs, May 23, 2016.
3. Miguel Niño-Zarazúa, Laurence Roope, Finn Tarp, "Income Inequality in a Globalizing World," VoxEU, September 20, 2016.
4. "Revisiting Plutonomy: The Rich Are Getting Richer,'" Citigroup Equity Strategy, March 5, 2006.
5. Richard Baldwin, *The Great Convergence* (Cambridge, MA: Harvard Press, 2016).
6. Angela Monaghan, "US Wealth Inequality," *Guardian*, November 13, 2014.
7. "Monitoring Poverty and Social Exclusion," Joseph Rowntree Foundation and New Policy Institute, 2015.
8. Paul Marshall, "Central Banks Have Made the Rich Richer," *Financial Times*, September 22, 2015.
9. David Graeber interviewed in *The Super-Rich and Us*, BBC, 2015.
10. Simon Jenkins, "We Should Cash-Bomb the People Not Banks," *Guardian*, November 26, 2014.
11. David Graeber, *Debt: The First 5,000 Years* (New York: Melville House Publishing, 2013), for the historical context to the ideas outlined by Graeber in *The Super Rich and Us*, BBC, 2015.
12. Zoe Williams, "Housing: Are We Reaching a Tipping Point?" *Guardian*, March 29, 2015.
13. Nick Hanauer interviewed in *The Super-Rich and Us*, BBC, 2015.

Chapter 9: Globalization: How Asia Rewrote the Rules

1. Jim O'Neill, "The New World: Fixing Globalisation," BBC Radio 4, January 6, 2017.

2. Peter Navarro, *Death by China: Confronting the Dragon—A Global Call to Action*, (Upper Saddle River, NJ: Pearson FT Press, 2011).
3. Charlie Campbell, "China Says It's Building the New Silk Road. Here Are Five Things to Know ahead of a Key Summit," *Time*, May 12, 2017.
4. Tom Hancock, "China Encircles the World with One Belt, One Road Strategy," *Financial Times*, May 3, 2017.
5. "Trump sends delegation to One Belt One Road forum," *Business Insider*, May 13, 2017.
6. "Donald Trump's Romance with China's Xi has Cooled, 'Ass-kicking' Could Lie Ahead," *Guardian*, July 6, 2017.
7. "Xi Jinping Holds All the Cards ahead of Mar-a-Lago Meeting with Trump," *Guardian*, April 5, 2017.
8. O'Neill, "The New World."
9. Ralph Benko, "The Global Importance of Paul Volcker's Call for a "New Bretton Woods," *Forbes*, June 16, 2014.
10. *Forbes* Investopedia, December 22, 2015.
11. Ibid.
12. Paul Mason, *PostCapitalism: A Guide to Our Future* (London: Allen Lane, 2015).
13. Dani Rodrik interviewed for "The New World," January 6, 2017. For more on the roots of globalization: Dani Rodrik, *The Globalization Paradox* (Oxford: Oxford University Press, 2012).
14. Ibid.
15. Stephen Gandel, "The Biggest American Companies Now Owned by the Chinese," *Fortune*, March 25, 2016.
16. takepart.com, February 22, 2016.
17. O'Neill, "The New World."
18. Ibid.
19. "Sizing Up the Trade Adjustment Assistance Program," http://www.cnbc.com, June 26, 2015.
20. Andy Sullivan, "Trump to Seek Jobs Advice from Firms That Offshore U.S. Work," *Reuters*, February 22, 2017.
21. Ibid.
22. "History—GWC—to Be the World's Most Influential Mobile Innovation Platform," GWC's official website at en.gwc.net.
23. Ibid.
24. Jason Hiner, "Chinese Companies That Will Shape the Future of the Tech Industry: My Week in Beijing," ZDnet.com, May 22, 2016.
25. "Forget Google and Amazon, and Invest in these Tech-Giants," *Daily Telegraph*, October 30, 2016.
26. Kaiping Peng and Richard E. Nisbett, "Culture, Dialectics and Reasoning about Contradiction," *American Psychologist*, September 1999.
27. Drake Baer, "The Fascinating Cultural Reasons Why Westerners and East Asians Have Polar Opposite Understandings of Truth," *Business Insider*, May 21, 2015.

28. Aristotle, *Ethics* (Oxford: Oxford University Press, World Classics, 2009).
29. Baer, "The Fascinating Cultural Reasons Why Westerners and East Asians Have Polar Opposite Understandings of Truth."
30. Michael Harris Bond, ed., *The Oxford Handbook of Chinese Psychology* (Oxford: Oxford University Press, 2015).
31. Richard E. Nisbett, *The Geography of Thought: How Asians and Westerners Think Differently and Why* (New York: Free Press, 2004).

Chapter 10: Robots: The Human Swap
1. Alan Turing, "Computer Machinery and Intelligence," University of Manchester, 1950; and Jack Copeland, *The Essential Turing: The Ideas That Gave Birth to the Computer Age* (Oxford: Oxford University Press, 2004).
2. Ibid.
3. "Computer AI Passes Turing Test in 'World First,'" BBC News, June 9, 2014.
4. "Eugene the Turing Test-Beating 'Human Computer' in His Own Words," *Guardian*, June 9, 2014.
5. John Markoff, "Computer Wins on *Jeopardy!*: Trivial, It's Not," *New York Times*, February 16, 2011.
6. Stephen Baker, *Final Jeopardy: Man vs. Machine and the Quest to Know Everything* (Boston: Houghton Mifflin, 2011).
7. Ibid.
8. Elizabeth Kolbert, "Our Automated Future," *New Yorker*, December 19, 2016.
9. Ibid.
10. Erik Brynjolfsson and Andrew McAfee, *The Second Machine Age: Work, Progress and Prosperity in a Time of Brilliant Technologies* (New York: WW Norton & Company, 2014).
11. "Japanese Insurance Firm Replaces 34 Staff with AI," BBC News, January 5, 2017.
12. Carl Benedikt Frey and Michael A. Osborne, "The Future of Employment: How Susceptible Are Jobs to Computerisation?" Oxford Martin School, University of Oxford, September 17, 2013.
13. Martin Ford, *The Rise of the Robots: Technology and the Threat of Mass Unemployment* (London: Oneworld Publications, 2016).
14. "Artificial Intelligence, Automation and the Economy," Executive Office of the President of the United States, Washington, DC, December 20, 2016.
15. Daron Acemoglu and Pascual Restrepo, "The Race between Machine and Man: Implications of Technology for Growth, Factor Shares and Employment," MIT, 2016.
16. Sugata Mitra, "The Hole in the Wall Project and the Power of Self-Organized Learning," Edutopia, February 3, 2012.
17. John Chubb and Terry Moe, *Politics, Markets and America's Schools* (New York: Perseus, 1990).
18. John Chubb and Terry Moe, *Liberating Learning: Technology, Politics and the Future of American Education* (San Francisco: Jossey-Bass, 2009).

INDEX

RAROC, 157
"securitization," 154–155, 161–162, 163
"shorting," 157
stock options, 155–157
subprime mortgages, 165–167
viaticals, 163–165
risk adjusted return on capital. *See*
RAROC
"risk and reward contract," 141
"Risky Drugs: Why the FDA Cannot
Be Trusted" (Light), 59
Ritalin, 76, 76–77
Robobear (robotic hybrid device), 265
robots. *See also* automation; artificial
intelligence
in education, 268–269
for Fukushima nuclear disaster
clean-up, 265
as hotel staff in Japan, 264
mass-market automated assistants,
254–255
as nursing home "carebots," 264, 265
sex robots, 265
Roche, 61
Rodrik, Dani, 233–234
Rogoff, Kenneth, 109
Roope, Laurence, 204–205
Roosevelt, Franklin D., 221
Roosevelt, Theodore, 120
Rosenhan, David, 71, 72
Rossminster, 183–184
Rost, Peter, 58, 79
Rouhanifard, Paymon, 279
Rumsfeld, Donald, 135, 186, 195
Rutter, Brad, 256, 260

Sabshin, Melvin, 72
Saez, Emmanuel, 209
Samba, Richard, 30–33
Samsung, 242, 243, 244
Samuel, Arthur L., 257, 258
Sanford, Charles, 157
Sarafem, 70
Sark (island), 180
Sarkozy, Nicolas, 174
Sawada, Hideo, 264
Schell, Howard, 220

Schell, Orville, 226
schizophrenia, 71–72, 73
Scholes, Myron, 155–157, 177
Schur, Sylvia, 26
Schwarz, Jean-Marc, 38, 39
scientific management, 118–120
Sclafani, Anthony, 38
Scour (music site), 145
Sea-Land Service Inc., 151
Seamless, 99
The Second Machine Age (Brynjolfsson
& McAfee), 261
"securitization," 154–155, 161–162,
163
security, block chain, 110–111,
113–114
Selby, Jack, 93, 95
selective serotonin reuptake inhibitors
(SSRIs), 68–69
selling, endorphin rush, 15–17
Seneca, on, 117
sequential binge approach, 46
7S Framework, 123, 129, 132
sex robots, 265
shadow banking, 176–177
"shadow" economy, 109–110
sharing economy, 149
Shatford, Scott, 148
Shelby Electrical Co., 7–10
shipping, containerization, 151
shopping, endorphin rush of, 15–17
"shopping addiction," 17
"shorting," 157, 171–175
Shuanghui International, 234–235
Siemens, 116, 129–131
Silicon Valley, competition from Asian
companies, 243–245
Simvastatin, 49, 50
Sinclair, Upton, 55
Singapore, 248
Singh, Narendra, 206
Siri (automated assistant), 254–255
Skilling, Jeffrey, 137, 138
sleep, digital devices and, 117
Slim, Carlos, 202
SlimFast, 24, 28–30
Sloan, Alfred P., Jr., 12–13, 15